大学英语立体化网络化系列教材·拓展课程教材

澳大利亚历史与文化影视教程
Australian History and Culture Through Classical Films

张 华 编著
［澳］Greg McCarthy 审阅

北京大学出版社
PEKING UNIVERSITY PRESS

图书在版编目(CIP)数据

澳大利亚历史与文化影视教程/张华编著. —北京： 北京大学出版社，2018.9
（大学英语立体化网络化系列教材·拓展课程教材）
ISBN 978-7-301-29328-7

Ⅰ.①澳…　Ⅱ.①张…　Ⅲ.①英语—阅读教学—高等学校—教材②电影评论—澳大利亚
Ⅳ.①H319.4：J

中国版本图书馆 CIP 数据核字（2018）第 036893 号

书　　　名	澳大利亚历史与文化影视教程 AODALIYA LISHI YU WENHUA YINGSHI JIAOCHENG
著作责任者	张华　编著
责任编辑	黄瑞明
标准书号	ISBN 978-7-301-29328-7
出版发行	北京大学出版社
地　　　址	北京市海淀区成府路 205 号　100871
网　　　址	http://www.pup.cn
电子信箱	zpup@pup.pku.edu.cn
电　　　话	邮购部 62752015　发行部 62750672　编辑部 62754382
印　刷　者	北京溢漾印刷有限公司
经　销　者	新华书店
	787 毫米 × 1092 毫米　16 开本　10.25 印张　300 千字 2018 年 9 月第 1 版　2018 年 9 月第 1 次印刷
定　　　价	35.00 元

未经许可，不得以任何方式复制或抄袭本书之部分或全部内容。
版权所有，侵权必究
举报电话：010-62752024　电子信箱：fd@pup.pku.edu.cn
图书如有印装质量问题，请与出版部联系，电话：010-62756370

本书由北京大学澳大利亚研究中心提供出版资助,特此鸣谢!
The publication of this textbook is sponsored by Australian Studies Center at Peking University

作为社会历史与文化叙事的经典电影(代序)

刘树森

自21世纪初以来,我国高等院校的英语教学呈现出具有重要意义的两个显著特征,在一定程度上体现了高等教育在改革开放不断深化与民族复兴的历史进程中所形成的一些新的本质特征。首先,学习英语的学生人数持续增加,不断刷新我国高等教育历史上学习英语人数的峰值,使得我国成为世界各国高等院校学习英语学生人数最多的国家,掌握与使用英语的能力已经成为高等院校培养新世纪人才的一项重要指标。其次,英语教学的内容与形式不断丰富和多元化,不再将英语教学仅仅限定在传统二语习得的语言范畴,也不再仅仅将英美文学作为英语教学高级阶段的核心学习内容。因此,在教学内容中陆续纳入英语与其所依存的诸多国别的社会历史与文化,包括一些高校陆续为非外语专业的学生开设与英语国家相关的本科生课程与研究生课程,例如有关澳大利亚、加拿大和新西兰等国家的历史、社会文化乃至文学等方面的英语课程,或者相关国别与区域研究的英语课程,扭转了我国高校英语教学长期以来仅仅以英美文学与英美两国的历史、文化与文学为主要教学内容的局面。上述英语教学内容的变化不仅体现了在全球化的背景下多元文化价值观越来越得到认同与尊重,而且也有助于促进人类不同语言、文化与文明在彼此交流与融合的过程中增进了解与认识,取长补短,共同发展与繁荣。

按照国家教育部公布的统计数据,截止到2017年5月31日,我国高等学校共计2914所[1],与2015年统计的2852所高等学校相比[2],两年之内增加了62所。就我国现有高等学校的数量以及高等学校增加的数量与速度而言,当今世界上任何国家都难以与之相比。因此,我国高等学校在校学生的人数也一直保持逐年递增的态势,截止到2015年底,全国各种形式高等教育在学人数为3647万人,其中包括普通、成人本专科在校生3261.2万人,在学硕士研究生与博士研究生共计191.1万人[3]。人数如此庞大的高校学生群体足以等同于甚至超过世界上许多国家一个国家的人口总和,而对于这些不同教育层次、形式与专业的学生而言,英语作为必修课程,开设与教学的难度之大不难想象,包括需要考虑培养方案、师资条件、教学目的、课程的内容、层次、类型、课时设置,以及教学方法与课程测验与考试等诸多方面的内容,加之教学更改与创新,以便不断提高教学质量,满足人才培养目标以及学生的不同学习需求。

---

[1] 参见国家教育部《全国高等学校名单》中的相关信息(http://www.moe.gov.cn/srcsite/A03/moe_634/201706/t20170614_306900.html)。

[2] 参见国家教育部《中国教育概况:2015年全国教育事业发展情况》(http://www.moe.gov.cn/jyb_sjzl/s5990/201612/t20161219_292432.html)。

[3] 同上。

在上述背景之下,近十余年来,北京大学陆续开设了一系列讲授与中国密切相关的国家的国情文化与文学的外语课程,包括分别为本科生与研究生开设的课程,其中向全校学生开放的课程一般采用英语为授课语言,诸如为非英语专业本科生开设的英语课程"澳大利亚概况",这些课程都取得了较为理想的教学效果。"澳大利亚概况"这门课程使用的教材《澳大利亚社会与文化》,由张华副教授编写,2015年由北京大学出版社出版发行;教材的研究与写作工作得到了澳大利亚外交部下属澳中理事会(Australia-China Council)的研究课题立项与资助。此外,北京大学与澳大利亚外交部、澳中理事会及其下属在华澳大利亚研究基金会(Foundation for Australian Studies in China)合作,在北京大学设立北京大学必和必拓澳大利亚研究讲席教授项目,旨在推进澳大利亚研究的发展,加强北京大学与澳大利亚大学与教育机构的合作与交流,并协助国内其他高校的澳大利亚研究中心促进澳大利亚研究的发展,包括为分布在全国各地高校的三十余个澳大利亚研究中心提供学术指导与支持。

在北京大学必和必拓澳大利亚研究讲席教授项目启动之际,2011年4月7日,时任澳大利亚总理茱莉亚·吉拉德访华期间,在北京出席并见证了北京大学必和必拓澳大利亚研究讲席教授项目谅解备忘录的签字仪式,显示澳大利亚联邦政府对这一项目的高度关注与支持。作为这一高端学术合作项目的首位讲席教授,著名历史学家、澳大利亚人文科学院院士暨澳大利亚社会科学院院士、澳大利亚迪肯大学大卫·沃克(David Walker)教授2013年2月至2016年1月在北京大学澳大利亚研究中心担任全职教授。在此期间,沃克教授每学年为北京大学英语语言文学专业的高年级学生开设澳大利亚研究专题课程,并讲授面向全校本科生的英语国别文化课程"澳大利亚通史",全面介绍自从1788年英国殖民者踏足澳大利亚之后的历史、社会发展与变迁,以及澳大利亚的民族性等人文特征。沃克教授所开设的上述澳大利亚研究课程成为校园中知名度很高的英语国别与国情课程,为在现有课程体系中推广澳大利亚研究,以及为在本科生阶段培养未来从事澳大利亚研究的人才做出了重要贡献。沃克教授在北京大学工作三年届满之后,著名的政治学专家、西澳大学格雷戈里·麦卡锡(Gregory McCarthy)教授自2016年2月开始在北京大学澳大利亚研究中心任职,接替大卫·沃克教授,担任北京大学必和必拓澳大利亚研究讲席教授。麦卡锡教授继续在北京大学开设上述两门澳大利亚研究课程,同样致力于培养未来从事有关澳大利亚研究的人才,推进北京大学与国内相关大学的澳大利亚研究。

张华副教授是北京大学澳大利亚研究中心的主要成员,长期以来为推广澳大利亚研究做出了重要贡献,其中包括开设有关澳大利亚社会历史及其文化的英语课程。作为英语国家国情文化与文学系列课程之一,张华副教授2016年开始讲授"澳大利亚历史与文化影视专题"课程,并在授课内容与教学方法等方面进行了具有新意的探索,在此基础上编写了该课程的教材《澳大利亚历史与文化影视教程》。这部教材的内容具有两个显著特点,二者相辅相成,相得益彰。首先,教材聚焦有关澳大利亚国情与民族文化本质的核心内容,按照国家与民族的认同感以及多元文化价值观组成两个专题板块,以重要的历史事件为基点,分层次逐步阐述与探讨上述两个方面内容。其次,以上述两个专题的内容为主题,选择了五部公认为经典之作的澳大利亚故事片,拍摄的时间从20世纪80年代到21世纪初叶,以此作为展现澳大利亚社会与文化以及澳大利亚人个性特征的叙事,分别从不同侧面刻画不同历史语境中的澳大利亚民族个性的建构与多元文化价值观的塑造,具有不同寻常的艺术魅力与感人至深的主题内涵。

作为精心选择的经典视觉叙事文本,这部教材收入的五部影片包括《加里波利》(*Gallipoli*,1981)、《舞国英雄》(*Strictly Ballroom*,1992)、《寻找阿里布兰迪》(*Looking for Alibrandi*,2000)、《防兔篱笆》(*Rabbit-Proof Fence*,2002)与《苦战科科达》(*Kokoda*,2006)。《加里波利》以第一次世界大战期间发生在土耳其加里波利半岛的加里波利战役为背景,主要刻画了阿奇里和法兰两个土生土长的澳大利亚青年在参战前后的成长经历。他们家境平凡,年轻气盛,但不谙世事,玩世不恭,因此在家乡历尽坎坷;应征入伍之后,他们前往前线作战时仍对战争的残酷与军事纪律所知甚少,时常擅自行动,多次做出阴差阳错的事情,最后阿奇里甚至付出了生命的代价。在影片的背景中,作为一个1901年刚刚独立的年轻国家,澳大利亚也在战争中经历了磨练与成长,犹如阿奇里和法兰所经历的事情促使他们对民族身份与自身的个性具有了成熟的认识。《舞国英雄》改编自导演巴兹·鲁赫曼(Baz Luhrmann,1963—)根据个人经历创作的同名短篇小说,以现当代澳大利亚的多元文化交融为背景,描写了一对来自不同文化背景的舞者如何历尽艰辛,刻苦努力,在舞蹈事业与爱情两个方面获得成功,显示了拥有不同文化背景的人们之间互相包容与融合的价值与意义。因为父母均为艺术家,男主人公斯科特自幼酷爱舞蹈,他的理想是能够创作出独具艺术个性的舞蹈,参加泛太平洋舞蹈大赛并获得冠军。在斯科特遇到困难、陷入事业低谷时,与其素昧平生的西班牙裔舞蹈学员弗兰自告奋勇与他合作。他们共同创作舞蹈,克服了各种困难与歧视,成功将西班牙斗牛舞的节拍等元素融入他们创作的舞蹈作品,最终在比赛中荣获了桂冠。与上述两部作品一样,《寻找阿里布兰迪》也是塑造青少年成长的主题,故事情节是基于作家真实的个人经历。这部影片改编自女小说家梅莉娜·马尔凯塔(Melina Marchetta,1965—)1993年出版的同名小说,背景是20世纪90年代的悉尼等城市,女主人公乔茜是一位17岁的高中生,出身于一个普通的意大利移民家庭,在一所天主教私立学校就读,因为文化与性格差异时常受到歧视和排挤。当得知自己是私生女之后,她发现凡是与她有关的事情似乎都是事与愿违,包括她暗恋的一位男生自杀,她希望毕业后能够考取大学的法律专业,也得不到母亲的支持。然而乔茜没有放弃,始终坚持自己的梦想与追求,也逐渐自觉地改善了自己与所在环境的关系。最后,乔茜从未见过面的父亲也回归家中,与家人团聚,全家人逐渐得以互相认同与接纳。

作为为数不多以描写澳大利亚原住民的生活与命运为主题的经典影片,《防兔篱笆》是一部深刻反思历史、探讨澳大利亚多元文化复杂现实的史诗般的作品,改编自女小说家多丽丝·皮尔金顿(Doris Pilkington,1937—2014)的小说《沿着防兔篱笆》(*Follow the Rabbit-Proof Fence*,1996),以20世纪初叶澳大利亚政府歧视原住民并强行实施"白澳政策"的历史悲剧为背景。从1910年开始,在所谓改善原住民儿童生活的名义下,约上万名白人与原住民生育的混血儿童被政府强行从其原住民家庭带走,遣送至专门设立的教养营地,接受白人文化的教育。这些儿童被阻断了与其原住民亲属的联系,严禁使用土著语,以便能够成长为英裔澳大利亚人,史称"被偷走的一代"。影片描写了20世纪30年代生活在西澳的莫莉、黛西与格雷茜等三名10岁左右的混血原住民姊妹被警察粗暴地掠走,强行送至1500英里之外的营地,接受白人文化的教育。她们不屈不挠,顽强反抗,设法逃离,最后莫莉与黛西沿着沙漠中漫长的防兔篱笆步行跋涉1500英里,终于返回家园,与父母团聚,但格雷茜却在途中被抓获,遣送回教养营地。

《苦战科科达》与《加里波利》一样,描写战争题材,以二战期间1942年发生在新几内亚岛抵抗日本侵略军的战斗为背景,刻画了澳大利亚军人誓死抗击法西斯与保卫祖国的英勇气概。澳大利亚军队的一个小分队在科科达地区巡逻时,不幸被日军围困在丛林中,与大部队断绝了联系。因为日军连续三天狂轰滥炸,他们伤亡严重,食物断绝,加上疟疾等疾患的折磨,危在旦夕。然而当他们得知前方要塞即将沦陷,仍毫不犹豫地前去支援。作为该影片一个独特的叙事特征,画面中几乎没有出现日军人员的形象,而是以镜头所描写的日军惨无人道的狂轰滥炸及袭击与澳大利亚军人的殊死抗击形成鲜明的对照,凸显了澳大利亚军队的正义与勇敢,以及战争的残酷及其对人性的摧残。

这部教材的另外一个特征,是在导读与注释等方面具体而详细地说明了五部澳大利亚经典影片与在英语世界占主导地位的好莱坞影片的不同之处,阐释了澳大利亚独特的电影艺术特征,深入浅出地讲解每部影片的历史背景、内容题材、主题内容、叙事特征,以及人物刻画的风格等诸多方面的特点。此外,与好莱坞以虚构为特征的商业艺术影片不同,入选这部教材的经典影片大多是基于真实历史事件与个人经历,无论是影片中叙述的故事与塑造的人物形象,还是影片中展示的自然环境与社会背景,例如澳大利亚所特有的沙漠、丛林、海洋、野生动物以及澳大利亚英语,都具有感人至深的真实性,适合于用作教材,有助于学生更为直观与深刻地感知澳大利亚国情、社会历史与风土人情。

总之,与传统的纸质版教科书不同,用于教学的经典影片是特殊的叙事文本,其中不仅包括人物塑造、故事、背景、对话、情感、表达叙事方式等文字文本拥有的叙事元素,以讲故事的方式叙事,还包括使用背景音乐、人物声音、面部表情、肢体语言、多元化的叙事结构与蒙太奇等等影视艺术形式所特有的叙事元素。因此,如果说传统的纸质版教科书是以诉诸客观叙述与理性分析见长,后者则以形象思维和感性认知为主,在此基础上启发受教育者在观看影片的过程中自然而然地萌生感同身受的感知效果,进而通过同步的思维分析将感性认知与理性判断有机地融合在一起,容易对研习对象产生浓厚的认知兴趣。

期待《澳大利亚历史与文化影视教程》的出版能够有助于拓展澳大利亚研究的教学工作,丰富教学内容,以脍炙人口的经典影片激发学习兴趣,便于学习者更为直接和深刻地了解与认知澳大利亚的国情、社会与历史文化以及民族个性等方面的内容。

前　言

《澳大利亚历史与文化影视教程》是北京大学非英语专业本科生英语必修课"澳大利亚历史与文化影视专题"课的教材。"澳大利亚历史与文化影视专题"课属于语言与文化类型的英语课程，是澳大利亚研究在北京大学本科生课程体系中的延伸和拓展。自2016年开课以来，学生通过澳大利亚电影这个独特的窗口，在提高语言能力同时，深层次地了解澳大利亚多元的社会文化形态，拓宽文化视野并在此基础上建构对多元文化的认同和理解，为学生日后从事跨学科研究积累知识与经验。认识这样一个国家，也是构建21世纪青年学生跨学科知识框架中不可缺少的一部分。课程以观看七部电影来解读历史和多元文化两个主题。

一、国家民族认同感和多元文化价值观的历史建构

首先课堂电影讲述的是澳大利亚历史故事。澳大利亚是个独特的国家。澳大利亚联邦成立于1901年，迄今仅有100多年。从1788年英国人进入澳大利亚算起，澳大利亚的历史也仅有200多年，所以它是个年轻的国家。从历史角度看，原住民早在六万多年以前就在这里繁衍，世代相传，澳大利亚又是一个古老的国家。澳大利亚历史的独特性决定了它文化的特殊性。

其次，课堂电影展示澳大利亚多元文化部分。澳大利亚文化包括以盎格鲁—凯尔特血统的白种人为主体的白人文化，第二次世界大战以后的移民文化和澳大利亚最早定居者的原住民文化。今天澳大利亚移民或移民后裔分别来自世界上200多个国家和地区，为构建澳大利亚这个世界上多种语言和多种文化共存的多元文化国家，共同做出了贡献。澳大利亚文化也成为世界上文化差异最多的国家之一。课堂上展示的多元文化电影讲述了澳大利亚在过去一二百年里，各种不同文化相互依存、相互包容，形成今天繁荣稳定的多元社会文化形态的经历。

（一）关于国家民族认同感的历史建构

在"澳大利亚历史与文化影视专题"课上放映两部历史影片。一部是《加里波利》(*Gallipoli*)（1981），叙述了澳大利亚作为一个新建立国家参加第一次世界大战的痛苦经历；另一部是《苦战科科达》(*Kokoda*)（2006），涉及澳大利亚参与第二次世界大战获得主场胜利的过程。两部影片展示了澳大利亚国家诞生与成长和民族意识觉醒的历史进程。澳大利亚原属英联邦，1901年宣布独立，成为澳大利亚联邦。然而，澳大利亚人并未随着国家独立而自然产生国家意识和民族认同感，依然对英国王室效忠。1914年第一次世界大战期间，澳大利亚追随原宗主国英国奔赴加里波利半岛参战，但遭到惨败，六万条年轻的生命埋葬在遥远的加里波利半岛。为他人火中取栗的惨痛教训让澳大利亚人开始反思：我们为谁而战？我们为什么要参战？一战前，澳大利亚人被问到是哪国人时，他们会回答："我是新南威尔士人。""我

是维多利亚人。"很少有人回答:"我是澳大利亚人。"一战后,澳大利亚人同样被问到此问题时,他们都会回答:"我是澳大利亚人。"澳大利亚于1901年独立,第一次世界大战开始于1914年。十几年的时间过去了,澳大利亚人心目中没有树立起国家的概念。可以说,加里波利战役的失败唤醒了澳大利亚人的国家认同感和民族主义意识。随后澳大利亚遭受了1929—1933年世界经济危机,失业率剧增,国民经济崩溃。一个又一个灾难让澳大利亚人看清现实:这块危难的土地才是自己的国家,澳大利亚人不应该是英国的附属品,并由此产生了一种独特的民族存在感。爱国主义变成澳大利亚那个时代视阈下的主旋律。富有强烈历史感的澳大利亚著名导演彼得·威尔(Peter Weir)完成拍摄小成本制作的影片《加里波利》(*Gallipoli*)。电影于1981年在全澳放映,反响空前。彼得·威尔将人性光辉描写得相当淋漓尽致,撼动人心,本片荣获澳大利亚电影奖最佳影片、导演、剧本、男主角、男配角、摄影、录音、剪辑八项大奖。这部影片以现实主义的视角,揭开这个年轻国家"醒来的历史",以反省的态度,重新审视、反思澳大利亚早期历史,发出了"什么是我们澳大利亚人的澳大利亚"的追问和思考。加里波利战役成为澳大利亚人的历史记忆。

第二部历史影片《苦战科科达》(*Kokoda*)(2006),源自一个真实的二战故事。导演阿里斯特·格里尔森(Alister Grierson)以现实主义风格将澳大利亚军队进行的科科达战役还原于现实。科科达小径位于巴布亚新几内亚山区。1942年第二次世界大战期间,作为太平洋战争整体战略的一部分,澳军在这里与日军展开了一场殊死的战斗。如果科科达失守,日军便可以通过这条小径入侵澳大利亚本土。领土的神圣不可侵犯成为民族国家认同感的基质。澳大利亚军队怀着保卫祖国的信念,在极端艰苦的情况下,击败日军,打破日军进攻澳本土的企图。科科达战役是澳大利亚人为了保卫家园和效忠祖国的胜利,是为"我为澳大利亚而战"观念的胜利。限于制作成本,影片没有宏大的战争镜头,因陋就简,反而烘托、成就了《苦战科科达》的独特气质,险僻难行的山道、昏暗压抑的丛林、神出鬼没的日军,无不透出战争带来的窒息感。作为澳军在二战中的光荣战绩之一,科科达战役是澳大利亚人心中的骄傲,深化了国家认同感,升华了澳大利亚人的民族自豪感。科科达战役的胜利,凸显出澳大利亚士兵对国家的忠诚。从一战加里波利战役的失败,到二战科科达战役的胜利,是澳大利亚人的国家和民族认同感从萌发、形成到强化的心理过程。彼得·威尔和阿里斯特·格里尔森两位导演通过影片对自己民族历史进行了描述,对国家形象完成了塑造,并借助历史表达,诠释了在战争语境中国家认同感的提升。

反观现实,值得一提的是,在好莱坞历史大手笔、大制作横行天下之时,澳大利亚战争影片受到学生的青睐并唤起他们心中的共鸣。两次大战是澳大利亚人对自己民族和国家认同感从产生到不断强化的关键历史节点,展示加里波利战役和科科达战役的两部澳大利亚影片通过对历史的回顾与反思,让学生们看清一个国家诞生、成长的脉络,以及民族存在感和自豪感获得的过程。加里波利战役后表现出的民族认同感集聚了澳大利亚人的民族向心力,而科科达战役后国家认同感增加了澳大利亚人国家的凝聚力。

今天的澳大利亚是南半球经济最发达的国家和全球第12大经济体。经济高度发达没有让澳大利亚电影人忘记他们的历史,他们通过再现澳大利亚历史上某一独特片段,唤起国人对自己历史的关注。澳大利亚电影人对历史纵深认识引起学生们的共鸣:"我们以前没听说过加里波利半岛,不知道那里还曾有过这么感人的故事,让人难以忘怀。"通过澳大利亚历史影片再现,学生们见识了一个民族自我认同的完整过程,完成了对这个年轻国家民族形象和历史认同的构建和理解。

历史建构主义倡导学生是建构知识的主体,是意义的主动建构者。电影意义只有通过观看电影而习得,任何关于电影的诠释都是对历史的解读。"澳大利亚历史与文化影视专题"课上放映的历史题材影片为学生了解澳大利亚民族精神和国家性格提供了平台,开拓了历史影片的教育维度和向度,加强了学生国别研究的思考能力。

(二)关于多元文化价值观的建构

"澳大利亚历史与文化影视专题"课上展示反映澳大利亚本土不同文化冲突、碰触、摩擦、融合的影片,虽然这些影片对文化的阐述不尽相同,但都反映了澳大利亚从30年代由盎格鲁—凯尔特人为主的单一白人文化,到上世纪六七十年代由于移民涌入对单一文化的冲击、磨合,最后逐步过渡成为一个多元文化,形成民族、种族、文化,乃至于文明、宗教多样性的一种新型社会形态。澳大利亚多元文化的发展反映了一个世纪的文化变迁。

澳大利亚诞生时,国家由盎格鲁—凯尔特人主导,政治上实施同化政策,即"漂白"政策,试图通过此政策把土著族裔肤色"漂白",以确定未来的澳大利亚文化、文明、政治、经济、社会发展由英格兰裔白人主导,也就是全英式的发展道路。《防兔篱笆》(*Rabbit-Proof Fence*)(2002)描述的正是这个政策实施中间阶段历史。澳大利亚当时约有十万名原住民儿童,只是因为他们的肤色比来自欧洲的白人更黑,就被政府以合法的、公开的形式,从他们的家人身边强行带走,被政府安置到白人集中营驯化。所有孩子只能说英语,接受基督化教育,导致他们忘记自己的母语和文化。从白人集中营出来后,他们被安置到白人家做佣人。白人可以合法地与他们生下孩子。根据当时流行的优生学理论,一代一代土著族裔肤色会"漂白"为近似白色,以实现澳大利亚成为英格兰裔纯白人的单一基督教文化国家。这些孩子称为"被偷走的一代"(the Stolen Generations)。三个被抓进集中营的姐妹最后穿越1500英里(这段距离相当于今天从北京走到福建),逃回自己的家园(除去有一个孩子中途受骗又被抓回集中营)。《防兔篱笆》刻画了"白色"的澳大利亚拥有一段最黑暗的历史,即政府同化政策对土著族裔强制性的人性践踏。这部影片中"漂白"政策最后以失败告终。

第二次世界大战结束后,大量外来劳工,特别是希腊人和意大利人等非英格兰裔率先涌入,紧随其后是南欧、东南欧的白人。澳大利亚梦想建立"纯白色"的同化政策面临挑战,因为白澳政策优先考虑的是纯粹的英格兰裔白人,或者说盎格鲁—凯尔特人。60年代后,由于美国在越南战争、法国在印度支那战争在东南亚引发的大规模人道主义危机,作为西方盟国之一的澳大利亚需要接纳大量来自越南、柬埔寨、老挝等地的战争难民。有色族裔移民涌入,导致白澳政策的终结,使得澳大利亚进而转化为一个文化多元、宗教多样、国民组成多样性的国家,尽管这是一种被动的发展过程,可过去一百年文化的发展却见证了澳大利亚文化变迁的历程,多元文化并不是澳大利亚发明的,但确实是目前澳大利亚的独特文化形态,也是澳大利亚文化从单一的"白色"发展到200多个国家和地区的不同民族文化组合。

澳大利亚位于南太平洋,是世界上最大的岛屿,是一个漂移出去的板块,是一个与其他大洲相隔的空间。独有的空间地理位置造成了澳大利亚独特的历史,推动了澳大利亚政治、社会、历史、文化多元化发展。当作为一个巨大岛屿的漂移性开始削弱时,澳大利亚受到资本的流动、移民的流动、不同文化流动的巨大冲击,使得澳大利亚本土拍摄的电影始终保持着一种开放性，一种面向社会现实的敞开性，一个在影片收束的时候仍然打开着的社会关注视点。澳大利亚民族的形成和民族认同感的相应产生往往离不开它地理环境、历史境遇、社会土壤的特质，其中历史和文化是塑造民族的重要因素。从多元文化的冲突走到多元文化的融合和认同，新一代移民在多种文化磨合中寻找到自己作为一个澳大利亚人的家园，这种多元文化认同感的建构，也折射出每个新移民最现实的心声。

电影《寻找阿里布兰迪》(Looking for Alibrandi)(2000)讲述了从意大利西西里移民的中学女生乔茜·阿里布兰迪，由于学习优异拿到奖学金就读于私立女校的故事。她出身于工人家庭，与单身母亲和外祖母生活，她不喜欢意大利移民身份。在学校里，她渴望认同，渴望被关注，却又融不进周围上流社会同学中。在家里，她不得不面对由于不知道她生父阿里布兰迪是谁而整天唠唠叨叨的外祖母。边缘身份以及跨文化的经历让她陷入苦恼。一个偶然的线索让乔茜明白，在她出生前，她的生父阿里布兰迪离开了她们母女。生父最终找到乔茜·阿里布兰迪，他们关系和解了，同时外祖母原谅了乔茜的生父。在这个过程中，乔茜认识了自我，即她就是爸爸妈妈的女儿，是外祖母的外孙女，移民的后代。乔茜在"寻找生父阿里布兰迪"的过程里，认识了真实的自我：挣扎、求索、抗争、自我和解。电影"寻找"隐含着新一代移民对自我归属感和认同感的渴望：我到底是谁？我来这里该做什么？这部影片主题"寻找"反映澳大利亚新移民扎根新大陆后所面临的困顿和思考。在多元文化碰触的社会现实面前，对自我的认定与重塑的渴望是移民内心的诉求和精神的写照。

《舞国英雄》(Strictly Ballroom)(1992)讲述了移民来到澳大利亚这块新大陆与不同文化融合，最后找到认同感并获得成功的故事。《舞国英雄》是著名导演巴兹·鲁赫曼(Baz Luhrmann)的处女作，也被称为巴兹·鲁赫曼"红幕三部曲"(Red Curtain Trilogy)的第一部。影片讲述了青年舞蹈家斯科特不满传统舞蹈比赛的评判规则，梦想创新，却屡遭批评。在他最痛苦时候，从小热爱舞蹈的西班牙移民女孩弗兰自愿做斯科特的舞伴，并将西班牙的斗牛舞曲融入他的舞蹈创作中，随后他们的舞步配合默契，舞技突飞猛进。观众开始不接受他们的激情自创，但是他们一如既往地汲取不同舞蹈的精华，大胆创新，突破成规。在"泛太平洋舞蹈大赛"上，两人以华丽的表演惊艳四座，大放异彩的独创引起观众共鸣。这部歌舞片打破了单一舞种和僵化的评舞标准一统天下的局面，将传统舞蹈融入不同类型舞蹈元素中，让舞蹈种类更加多元、丰富。电影中主人公斯科特和弗兰的故事正是在舞蹈领域中多元融合最后获得认可的例子。

这些文化影片会使学生感到澳大利亚今天不再是孤独的岛屿，也不再是以白澳文化政策为主导的国家。二战后各国移民的涌入，使得它成为建立在200多个不同民族、文化、宗教基础上的独特融合，并由此共同创造出一种新的生活方式。这种方式让移民在新的世界里找到"我是澳大利亚人"的归属感和荣誉感，正像《舞国英雄》里西班牙移民女孩弗兰，同时像《寻找阿里布兰迪》中从意大利西西里来的女孩乔茜一样，并没有放弃"我是从哪里来的"身份认同。对新一代移民来说，每个人都在寻找自己心中的"阿里布兰迪"。有的同学看完这两部影片后，在课程BBS讨论区写到：澳大利亚为移民多重身份提供了相互对话的空间，是个有迹可循的地方。14级哲学系从孟晗同学写到：愿有一天，我们能够不再因为彼此的身上的标签而误解、伤害；愿有一天，这个世界能够包容颜色不一样的你们、我们、他们；愿有一天，每一个人都能够不再为偏见所囚禁，每一个人都能够自由地去追求自己的愿望和幸福。学生的观影感受说明了他们对澳大利亚多元文化的理解。

电影是文化的载体，也是文化的产物。电影形式是一个国家和民族历史和文化最直观、最生动、最深刻的反映。今天中国的很多大学生是在汉语和汉民族文化环境中长大，缺少对多元文化理解的经验，因此了解澳大利亚多元文化的发展过程是个体悟我们自己思维视野有限性的过程，从而唤起学生真诚地学习他人文化的激情。"对不同文化的理解以及能够包容文化间的差异是基于'人'的内在素质。具有这种素质的人能够敏锐地意识到差异的可能性以及不同价值观念的相对性，从本群体中心主义中超脱出来，用多元视角来看世界，看自己，看与其他人、其他群体的关系，从而能够适应不同的文化环境"（高一虹，2008：59－63）。澳大利亚多元文化的建构过程就是这样一个典型范例。学生们从电影课中获得的经验也是他们人生经验的一部分。

二、《澳大利亚历史与文化影视教程》

2016 年 12 月北京大学出版社通过了此课程教材的出版计划。2017 年 5 月，教材的出版得到了北京大学澳大利亚研究中心研究基金的支持。《澳大利亚历史与文化影视教程》分为历史和文化两个部分。历史部分共两个章节，由三部电影以及陆克文讲演视频构成。多元文化部分共分三个章节，由四部电影组成。每个章节里的电影分别配有电影背景、电影内容、电影情节、电影主题、电影导演、电影主要演员的细致解释和分析。每个章节后附有相关内容的阅读文章。电影以及阅读文章均附有详细单词表、正误判断题、名词解释和论述题；六篇阅读文章含有术语注释。所有练习都附有明确的答案。正误判断题目中的错误答案分别给予正确的分析和说明。

本教程具有以下几个特点。第一，教程弥补了澳大利亚电影教材在中国市场的空缺。在中国涉及澳大利亚研究的教材不少，但影视研究领域的教材却不多见。今天澳大利亚电影已经跻身于全球电影产业最具影响力的国家之一。澳大利亚本土电影不仅获得奥斯卡多项大奖和颇多国际荣誉，而且在本土和国外的票房成绩很好，引起世界的关注。澳大利亚电影工业近三十年突飞猛进，需要我们提供文本教材跟进并记录这一视觉文化发展的进程。第二，《澳大利亚历史与文化影视教程》是以电影为蓝本的语言教材。电影语言不仅是影像符号，更是理解语言传达意义的视觉源泉。教材配置大量语言练习，读者观影后，能够通过练习以及练习答案检验自己对电影的理解，从而提升语言水平和理解能力。第三，教程中的七部电影在本书出版前曾在"澳大利亚历史与文化影视专题"课上使用过四次并受到学生的好评。因此，将受学生欢迎的影片编成教材可以惠及更为广泛的读者群。六篇选文均得到选文作者以及出版商的认可，其中北京大学必和必拓澳大利亚研究讲席教授 Greg McCarthy 主动为本教材撰写两篇影评文章。

在《澳大利亚历史与文化影视教程》编写过程中，得到专家学者宝贵支持和大力相助。北京大学澳大利亚研究中心主任刘树森教授亲自作序。Greg McCarthy 教授通览全书，提出宝贵建议。此外，北京大学元培学院 12 级戴锴和经济学院 15 级王陈薇同学参加教程的资料收集工作，特别是元培学院戴锴同学选课时正值大四上学期。教程完成之后，他从一个学生角度通读全书，提出了建议。教程成书之时，他已经是清华大学公共管理学院研二的学生了，由此见证了课程的成长和教程的诞生。北京大学出版社黄瑞明老师非常重视澳大利亚研究在北京大学本科生课程建设中的发展，对教材的选题、体例以及最后的审校工作都付出极大的心血，在此一一表示最诚挚的感谢。

  北京大学澳大利亚研究中心自 1996 年成立至今，澳大利亚研究课程在北大的开设从未间断，这一点秉承了中心的宗旨，即在全校范围内为本科生设置澳大利亚研究课程。笔者对澳大利亚课程的研究始于 2007 年，先后开设"澳大利亚概况""澳大利亚社会与文化""澳大利亚历史与文化影视专题"课程。2009 年 9 月"澳大利亚概况"课获得北京大学第二届网络课程大赛三等奖。2009 年年底，课程改名为"澳大利亚社会与文化"，并申请到澳中理事会（Australia-China Council）2009—2010 年度研究基金，用以编写《澳大利亚社会与文化》（*Introducing Australian Society and Culture*）教科书。该教材于 2011 年由北京大学出版社出版，同年 11 月"澳大利亚社会与文化"课程获得第十一届全国多媒体课件大赛一等奖。2017 年 11 月基于澳大利亚课堂多媒体研究的论文《交互模式引领文化教学创新——以"澳大利亚社会与文化"课为例》荣获由北京大学教务部和教师教学发展中心联合举办的北京大学第七届多媒体课件和网络课程大赛论文征集二等奖。在向学生介绍澳大利亚文化的同时，北京大学电影协会与选课同学共同举办了三次北京大学澳大利亚电影周活动，在菁菁校园里为年轻学子呈现了澳大利亚本土历史纵向发展和移民文化的横向交融。在从事澳大利亚研究教学的同时，笔者还发表了澳大利亚历史与文化研究论文十多篇。课程教学和研究奠定了《澳大利亚历史与文化影视教程》出版的基础，最终呈现给广大读者。

编者
2017 年 5 月 14 日

CONTENTS

Part One Australian History

Chapter 1 The Aboriginal History 3
  1.1 Background 3
    1.1.1 The Aboriginal History 3
    1.1.2 The Aboriginal Cultures and Religion 4
  1.2 The film *Rabbit-Proof Fence* 5
    1.2.1 Director Phillip Noyce 5
    1.2.2 Main Characters 6
    1.2.3 Plot 6
    1.2.4 Theme Analysis 6
  1.3 Kevin Rudd's National Apology 9
    1.3.1 Kevin Michael Rudd 9
    1.3.2 A National Apology to Australia's Indigenous Peoples 10
  1.4 Reading Passage: Australian Cinema and Settler-Colonial Imagination: *Rabbit-Proof Fence* 19

Chapter 2 Australian National History 28
  2.1 Background 28
  2.2 The Film *Gallipoli* 29
    2.2.1 Director Peter Weir 30
    2.2.2 Main Characters 30
    2.2.3 Plot 31
    2.2.4 Theme Analysis 31
  2.3 The Film *Kokoda* 34
    2.3.1 Director Alister Grierson 35
    2.3.2 Main Characters 36
    2.3.3 Plot 36
    2.3.4 Theme Analysis 37

2.4　Reading Passage: War and National Survival 39

Part Two　Australian Multiculturalism

Chapter 1　Cultural Clash 54
1.1　Background 54
1.2　The Film *Crocodile Dundee* 55
　1.2.1　Director Peter Faiman 55
　1.2.2　Main Characters 56
　1.2.3　Plot 56
　1.2.4　Theme Analysis 56
1.3　Reading Passage: Cultural Attitudes and Aussie Communicative Style 60

Chapter 2　Cultural Recognition 65
2.1　Background 66
2.2　The Film *Looking for Alibrandi* 67
　2.2.1　Director Kate Woods 68
　2.2.2　Main Characters 68
　2.2.3　Plot 68
　2.2.4　Theme Analysis 69
2.3　The Film *Strictly Ballroom* 71
　2.3.1　Director Baz Luhrmann 72
　2.3.2　Main Characters 72
　2.3.3　Plot 72
　2.3.4　Theme Analysis 73
2.4　Reading Passage: Is Australia a Multicultural Nation? 76

Chapter 3　Multicultural Oneness 87
3.1　Background 87
3.2　The Film *The Castle* 88
　3.2.1　Director Rob Sitch 89
　3.2.2　Main Characters 89
　3.2.3　Plot 89
　3.2.4　Theme Analysis 89

3.3　Reading Passage 1: Creative Nation: Approaching Australian Cinema
　　　　and Cultural Studies ………………………………………………… 92
　　　Reading Passage 2: Governing Australian Diversity: Multiculturalism
　　　　and Its Values …………………………………………………………… 104
Keys to Exercises ……………………………………………………………… 123
References ……………………………………………………………………… 142

Part One
Australian History

The name "Australia" is derived from "terra australis incognita" in Latin, meaning an "unknown land of the south," which dates back to Roman times. In 1814, the name "Australia" was popularised by the British navigator Matthew Flinders, the first person known to have circumnavigated Australia, in his work *A Voyage to Terra Australis*. After 1824, the country should be known officially as "Australia."

It is the smallest continent and one of the world's oldest landmasses. Australia is located in Oceania, lying between the Indian and Pacific oceans, southeast of Asia. Its population is composed of the Aboriginal people, the white and immigrants from some 200 countries of all over the world.

It is estimated that Australia has been populated for 60,000 years. Before the arrival of European settlers, the native people, called Aboriginal and Torres Strait Islander peoples, inhabited most areas of the continent. From the historical point of view, Australia is an old country. However, Australia's European history is relatively short. The first European settlement was established by Great Britain on 26 January 1788. Australia is a country with a 200-year history. The commonwealth of Australia, as a self-governing member of the Commonwealth of Nations, was established in 1901. Therefore, we can say Australia is a young country. The real history and civilization of Australia started from the Aboriginal people. There is no doubt that they were the original inhabitants of a previously silent continent.

Chapter 1
The Aboriginal History

Indigenous Australians, generally speaking, refer to the Aboriginal and Torres Strait Islander peoples. According to prehistorians, Australia's Aborigines were believed to come to Australia by small raft or canoe, crossing the straits between the continent and some islands in Indonesia and New Guinea, that is, South East Asia, during a glacial period (Broome, 1982: 9—10).

1.1　Background

The word "Aboriginal" was used in Australia to describe its Indigenous peoples as early as 1789. It soon became the common name to refer to all Indigenous Australians.

1.1.1　The Aboriginal History

The first Aborigines came from Southeast Asia. The earliest stone tools, lost or discarded by the first Australians conform to a certain type known to many archaeologists as the "core tool and scraper tradition." Some artefacts of similar type and antiquity have been excavated in the Philippines, in many places in the eastern Indonesian islands. The skin of Black Australians is dark chocolate brown to black in color. Head hair may be straight, wavy or curly, but seldom "woolly" as Black Africans (Murray and Helen, 1996: 1—5). Aboriginal and Torres Strait Islander peoples inhabited most areas of the Australian continent. Aboriginal people possessed some unifying links. Aboriginal society was semi-nomadic, and they had their hunter-gatherer lifestyle. The mode of life and material cultures varied greatly from region to region. Their complex social systems and highly developed traditions reflect a deep connection with the land.

At the time of first European contact before 1788, the Aboriginal population was around 750,000 (Shapiro, 1979: 51—69). British settlement in Australia began with the arrival of the First Fleet in Botany Bay in 1788. The colonization brought two main consequences to Aboriginal people. One is a pandemic of Old World disease, for example, smallpox which leads to a fifty percent population decrease. The other is the appropriation of land and water resources. Indigenous people lost the right to take up the land.

In the late 1880s, whites executed the so-called "pacification by force" which resulted in massive depopulation of Aborigines. By the 1940s, most Indigenous people were assimilated into rural and urban Australian society as low-paid laborers with limited rights. From 1880 to 1970, the Aboriginal children were removed from their mothers by Federal and State Government agencies and church missions. These children were called "The Stolen Generations" (Blainey, 1976: 34—54).

The Aboriginal struggle for the right to possess land took almost two centuries. In 1992, the High Court of Australia enacted land-rights legislation and recognized Aboriginal property and native title rights of land (Barwick, 1979: 102). That is the victory of the well-known Mabo Case, which declared the previous legal concept of *terra nullius* to be invalid. On 14 July 1995, the Australian Aborigines have their own flag which was designed as a protest flag for the past land rights movements of Indigenous Australians.

1.1.2 The Aboriginal Cultures and Religion

Indigenous cultures are diverse and form a vital part of Australia's national identity. At the time of European settlement, an estimated 250 languages were spoken by the Indigenous people of Australia, including about 700 dialects (Murray, 1996: 148—159). Tribal membership was based on birth in the tribal territory, speaking the same dialect and holding the same religious ideas. Indigenous people value language as a key element of their identity and spiritual grounding (Horton, 1994: 167). Language is their power, their foundation, their root and everything that holds them together and gives Aboriginal people strength.

Besides the rich languages, the various Indigenous Australian communities developed unique musical instruments and folk styles. Clapping sticks are probably the more popular musical instrument, especially because they help maintain rhythm for songs. The didgeridoo, which was specific to certain regions, is now widely thought to be a stereotypical instrument of Aboriginal people. Australia has a tradition of Aboriginal art which is thousands of years old, the best-known forms being rock art and bark painting. These paintings were usually created in earthy colors, from paint made from ochre. Such ochres were also used to paint their bodies for ceremonial purposes (Rolls, 2011: 89). Traditionally, Aboriginal people have painted stories from their Dreamtime.

The Dreamtime was their own religious tradition. Its core revolves around the land. In the eyes of Aboriginal people, the earth not only gave life but also was life. The essence of this religious belief was the oneness of the land and all that move upon it. It was a view of the world in which humans and the natural species were all part of the same ongoing life force. In the Dreamtime when the great ancestors had roamed the earth, they were human, animal and bird at the same time: all natural things were in a unity (Broome, 1982: 16—19). The lives of the Aborigines were shaped by their Dreamtime stories which were an explanation of how the world came to be, how human beings were created and how the Creator intended for humans to function within the cosmos. Indigenous Australians have a complex oral tradition and spiritual values based upon reverence for the land and a belief in the Dreamtime.

1.2 The Film *Rabbit-Proof Fence*

The name of the film is *Rabbit-Proof Fence*, actually there is no rabbit in the movie. Rabbits were introduced by Europeans in 1788. As a biological invasion in Australian continent, they grew quickly and caused a rabbit population explosion. The government constructed three nationwide rabbit proof fences to keep them out of Western Australian pastoral areas.

In 1996, Doris Pilkington Garimara published her book *Follow the Rabbit-Proof Fence*. In 2002, the film *Rabbit-Proof Fence* was adapted by Phillip Noyce based on this book. Both the book and the film told a story of the Aboriginal girls as part of "the Stolen Generations" in the 1930s. They were caught by whites from their community Jigalong and taken to the Moore River Native Settlement to receive a Christian education. Finally, two of them followed the rabbit-proof fence to walk back to their Aboriginal family.

In the 19th and 20th century, theories on cultural hybridity, polygenism, Darwinism, and eugenics prevailed in Europe. British settlers held that Indigenous group belonged to the lower caste and a hybrid race. Aboriginality was a degenerate trait. The feeling of cultural superiority urged them to make the Assimilation Policy to maintain the British racial purity. Aboriginal children of mixed race were taken by force from their mothers and raised in training schools that would prepare them for lives as domestic servants. The children are known as "the Stolen Generations." Under a policy of assimilation which sought to "breed out" or "purify" the Aboriginal color, mixed-race children were absorbed into white society. Whites believed removing Aboriginal children away from their family is a good way to eliminate the black race and turn them into white. The policy of assimilation drew its rationale from the so-called "White Australian Policy" (Cain, 2004: 297—303).

1.2.1 Director Phillip Noyce

Phillip Noyce is a distinguished Australian film director. He directed 40 films and earned his reputation by winning many film awards. After 1999, Noyce set about adapting the book *Follow the Rabbit-Proof Fence* by Doris Pilkington Garimara. *Follow the Rabbit-Proof Fence*, which is the second book of the trilogy docmenting her family's stories (Brewster, 2007: 143—159), told about the author's mother Molly and two other mixed-race Aboriginal girls, who escaped from the Moore River Native Settlement, north of Perth, Western Australia, to return to their Aboriginal community. These Aboriginal children are representatives of "the Stolen Generations" in the 1930s. They were caught to receive the white education, far away from their parents. Phillip Noyce believes this film to be one of his best films and the one closest to his heart, because it portrays Aborigines in a positive way not seen before in Australia. The film overturned the conventions by celebrating Aboriginal family history as an important component of mainstream Australian history. *Rabbit-Proof Fence* won the Australian Film Institute (AFI) Award for Best Film in 2002.

1.2.2 Main Characters

(1) Molly Craig is a 14-year-old Aboriginal girl. She was captured by whites and escaped from the Moore River Native Settlement.

(2) Daisy Craig Kadibill is an 8-year-old Aboriginal girl and Molly's younger sister. She was captured by the whites and escaped from the Moore River Native Settlement with Molly.

(3) Gracie Fields is a 10-year-old Aboriginal girl, and the cousin of Molly and Daisy. She was captured by whites and recaptured during the way of escaping.

(4) Moodoo is the Aboriginal tracker who serves the whites. When sent to capture the three Aboriginal girls, he chose to give up pursuing them at last.

(5) A. O. Neville is the official Protector of Western Australian Aborigines, and the administrator of the Assimilation Policy in the 1930s.

1.2.3 Plot

Molly, her sister Daisy, and their 10-year-old cousin Gracie live in Jigalong, a Western Australian town, which lies along the northern part of Australia's rabbit-proof fence. The three Aboriginal girls, viewed as "half-castes," were captured by a white authority figure, Neville, as the "Protector of aborigines" and taken to a reeducation camp run by whites in the Moore River Native Settlement, north of Perth. In the camp, Aboriginal children were forced to receive Western training, which made them sick. They ran away from the camp to return to Jigalong, and their Aboriginal families. Neville employed tricks to catch them. Gracie was fooled and recaptured. The other two girls Molly and Daisy finally followed the rabbit-proof fence back to their community.

1.2.4 Theme Analysis

The White Australian Policy from the film *Rabbit-Proof Fence* is more than White racism. As far as the cultural perspective is concerned, it is a monolingual and monocultural policy. The first Europeans landed in Australia with ethnocentric attitudes and cultural superiority. The whites thought that Aborigines were wandering, half-starved, dirty naked savages and did not build houses and develop agriculture. The Aborigines were denigrated as "savages" while the Europeans glorified themselves as "noble pioneers." By 1850, with the spreading theory of "survival of the fittest," the Europeans especially Christians believed the Aborigines were fellow children of God who had unfortunately fallen into paganism and immorality. They held that their coming national greatness rested on their being white, for God is white. With the correct help the Aborigines could also become the equal of Europeans and part of the British race. Therefore, the "keeping the breed pure" policy and the "reeducation of Aboriginal children" policy were enacted. By the early 20th century, White racists fully controlled Aboriginal lives (Broome, 1982: 89—99). A. O. Neville in the film *Rabbit-Proof Fence* is purely a racist and notably chief protector of Aboriginal children in Western Australia.

Around the 1920s, White Christian missions were founded everywhere in Australia for

Aboriginal children who were "stolen" by force from their mothers and Aboriginal land. In these white missions, children must learn to speak English, and were deprived of the right to use their own languages. Gradually, they forgot their mother tongue. The extinction of a language represents the death of a culture. These children, eventually, became a generation of cultural orphans (Cain, 2004: 297—303). The task of A. O. Neville in the film is to educate "the native." In reality his racial Assimilation Policy had little to do with education. Rather it was founded upon belief in the superiority of European "blood" (McCarthy, 2004: 6—17). Neville expressed this concern in 1937 when he asked the rhetorical question "Are we going to have a population of 1,000,000 blacks in the Commonwealth, or are we going to merge them into our white community and eventually forget that there were any Aborigines in Australia?"(Manne, 2002)

In the film *Rabbit-Proof Fence*, Molly, Daisy and Gracie hated English, western foods and Christian songs. With strong self-determinations, they were on the way back to their land and see their mother. In the Aboriginal religion Dreamtime, mam is their home; home is their land; land is their life.

Their strengths not only won the sympathy from the white woman who helped them with food and pointed out the way to the rabbit-proof fence which guided them home, but also made the plan of capturing them designed by A. O. Neville empty.

New Words

aborigine	n.	土著,土著居民,原住民	depot	n.	仓库
			authorize	v.	批准,认可,授权给
guardian	n.	监护人,守护者	rate	n.	价格
ordinary	a.	普通的,平常的	ration	n.	口粮;配给量
application	n.	申请	agitated	a.	激动的

race	n.	种族		fester	v.	化脓,溃烂,恶化
trace	n.	踪迹		terrain	n.	地形,地势,领域
apparent	a.	显然的		tracker	n.	追踪者
infiltration	n.	渗入		probation	n.	试用
stamp	v.	毁掉		dawdling	a.	懒散的
domestic	a.	国内的		inform	v.	通知
labourer	n.	劳动者,劳工		combine	v.	结合
exhausted	a.	疲惫的		notification	n.	通知
prayer	n.	祈祷		impost	n.	税
scrub	v.	擦洗		expense	n.	花费
whip	v.	抽打		filthy	a.	肮脏的
watchwords	n.	口号		promptly	ad.	迅速地
unfathomable	a.	深不可测的,高深莫测的		proceed	v.	继续进行
				recapture	n.	重新逮捕
jeopardise	v.	危及		whereabouts	n.	下落

Exercises

1. **True or false judgments**
   (1) Very early in the film we see the large hawk, Molly's totem. Her mother tells her that it will look after her.
   (2) The black tracker was on the side of the authorities.
   (3) The Aboriginal children in the Moore River Native Settlement were forbidden to speak their native language.
   (4) The three girls ran away from the Moore River Native Settlement without any hesitation.
   (5) Molly took advantage of the rain to cover their tracks, which showed her wisdom.
   (6) At first, the three girls came along a rabbit-proof fence, but it turned out to be a wrong one.
   (7) After the two girls fainted in the desert, the bird appeared. It was the bird that encouraged Molly to go home.
   (8) At the end of the film, the three girls came to Jigalong, their Aboriginal community.

2. **Term interpretations**
   (1) Molly　　　　　　　　　　(2) Gracie
   (3) Mavis　　　　　　　　　　(4) Moodoo
   (5) Mr. Neville　　　　　　　 (6) Jigalong
   (7) the Depot　　　　　　　　(8) the Moore River Native Settlement

3. **Essay questions**
   (1) What impressions did you get of life in the desert Aboriginal community?
   (2) Describe the scene when the children were taken. How was the tension built up?
   (3) What kinds of activities were the children involved in to "civilize" and "Christianize"

them?
(4) Is there any evidence of Mr. Neville's attitudes having changed?
(5) What was the most significant aspect of the final scenes in the film?

1.3　Kevin Rudd's National Apology

Between 1905 and 1970, Indigenous Australian children known as "the Stolen Generations" were forcibly removed from their families as a result of the Assimilation Policy, which was founded on the assumption of black inferiority and white superiority, and which proposed that Indigenous peoples should be allowed to "die out" through a process of natural elimination or should be assimilated into the white society. The story of "the Stolen Generations" is the blackest page of the Australian history.

In November 2007, Kevin Rudd led the Australian Labor Party to a victory. He had committed his party during the campaign to making an apology to the Stolen Generations and he made it the first order of business for the new parliament. On 13 February 2008, Rudd gave a National Apology to Indigenous Australians for "the Stolen Generations." Kevin Rudd acknowledged and took responsibility for past government policies and actions. All Indigenous peoples were mistreated as a consequence of official government policy. Australia as a responsible nation apologizes. The notion of a "stolen generation" struck a deep psychological chord within the nation (McCarthy, 2004: 5).

The apology has become a historic speech and an event in Australia. Kevin Rudd's speech in 2008 marks the beginning of a new perception for the Aboriginal people, and an inclusive definition of Aboriginal identity has been enriched. This apology shapes a new image of Australia in international stage too. We know Australia is a multicultural country, but now, we can describe the country as culturally inclusive and mature.

1.3.1 Kevin Michael Rudd

Australia is a country with a two-party system. One is Australian Labor Party and the other is the National Party of Australia and the Liberal Party of Australia in coalition. Kevin Michael Rudd as the Leader of the Labor Party served as Australia's twenty-sixth prime minister both in 2007 and in 2013.

(https://baike.baidu.com/item/)

Kevin Rudd was born in Queensland in 1957 and grew up on a dairy farm. His father as convict heritage was a farmer and died when he was 11. Due to his unhappy childhood, he joined the Labor Party at 15. Rudd graduated from the Australian National University, majoring in Chinese language and Chinese history. During his two terms as Prime Minister, Rudd adopted policies on domestic and foreign affairs and made contributions to the development of a mature and stable Australia. At the end of 2013, he retired from politics and then went to

Harvard University. Now Kevin Rudd is president of the Asia Society Policy Institute.

1.3.2 A National Apology to Australia's Indigenous Peoples

by Kevin Rudd[①]

The SPEAKER (Hon. Harry Jenkins) took the chair at 9 am and read prayers.

OUR PEOPLE

—APOLOGY TO AUSTRALIA'S INDIGENOUS PEOPLES

Mr RUDD (Griffith—Prime Minister) (9.00 am)—I move: That today we honor the Indigenous peoples of this land, the oldest continuing cultures in human history. We reflect on their past mistreatment. We reflect in particular on the mistreatment of those who were Stolen Generations—this blemished chapter in our nation's history. The time has now come for the nation to turn a new page in Australia's history by righting the wrongs of the past and so moving forward with confidence to the future.

We apologise for the laws and policies of successive parliaments and governments that have inflicted profound grief, suffering and loss on these our fellow Australians.

We apologise especially for the removal of Aboriginal and Torres Strait Islander children from their families, their communities and their country.

For the pain, suffering and hurt of these Stolen Generations, their descendants and for their families left behind, we say sorry.

To the mothers and the fathers, the brothers and the sisters, for the breaking up of families and communities, we say sorry.

And for the indignity and degradation thus inflicted on a proud people and a proud culture, we say sorry.

We the Parliament of Australia respectfully request that this apology be received in the spirit in which it is offered as part of the healing of the nation.

For the future we take heart; resolving that this new page in the history of our great continent can now be written.

We today take this first step by acknowledging the past and laying claim to a future that embraces all Australians.

A future where this Parliament resolves that the injustices of the past must never, never happen again.

A future where we harness the determination of all Australians, Indigenous and non-Indigenous, to close the gap that lies between us in life expectancy, educational achievement and economic opportunity.

A future where we embrace the possibility of new solutions to enduring problems where old approaches have failed. A future based on mutual respect, mutual resolve and mutual responsibility.

A future where all Australians, whatever their origins, are truly equal partners, with equal opportunities and with an equal stake in shaping the next chapter in the history of this

---

① http://www.australia.gov.au/about-australia/our-country/our-people/apology-to-australias-indigenous-peoples.

Chapter 1
The Aboriginal History

great country, Australia.

Mr. Speaker, there comes a time in the history of nations when their peoples must become fully reconciled to their past if they are to go forward with confidence to embrace their future. Our nation, Australia, has reached such a time. That is why the parliament is today here assembled: to deal with this unfinished business of the nation, to remove a great stain from the nation's soul and, in a true spirit of reconciliation, to open a new chapter in the history of this great land, Australia.

Last year I made a commitment to the Australian people that if we formed the next government of the Commonwealth we would in parliament say sorry to the Stolen Generations. Today I honor that commitment. I said we would do so early in the life of the new parliament. Again, today I honor that commitment by doing so at the commencement of this the 42nd parliament of the Commonwealth. Because the time has come, well and truly come, for all peoples of our great country, for all citizens of our great Commonwealth, for all Australians—those who are Indigenous and those who are not—to come together to reconcile and together build a new future for our nation.

Some have asked, "Why apologise?" Let me begin to answer by telling the parliament just a little of one person's story—an elegant, eloquent and wonderful woman in her 80s, full of life, full of funny stories, despite what has happened in her life's journey, a woman who has travelled a long way to be with us today, a member of the Stolen Generation who shared some of her story with me when I called around to see her just a few days ago. Nanna Nungala Fejo, as she prefers to be called, was born in the late 1920s. She remembers her earliest childhood days living with her family and her community in a bush camp just outside Tennant Creek. She remembers the love and the warmth and the kinship of those days long ago, including traditional dancing around the camp fire at night. She loved the dancing. She remembers once getting into strife when, as a four-year-old girl, she insisted on dancing with the male tribal elders rather than just sitting and watching the men, as the girls were supposed to do.

But then, sometime around 1932, when she was about four, she remembers the coming of the welfare men. Her family had feared that day and had dug holes in the creek bank where the children could run and hide. What they had not expected was that the white welfare men did not come alone. They brought a truck, two white men and an Aboriginal stockman on horseback cracking his stockwhip. The kids were found; they ran for their mothers, screaming, but they could not get away. They were herded and piled onto the back of the truck. Tears flowing, her mum tried clinging to the sides of the truck as her children were taken away to the Bungalow in Alice, all in the name of protection.

A few years later, government policy changed. Now the children would be handed over to the missions to be cared for by the churches. But which church would care for them? The kids were simply told to line up in three lines. Nanna Fejo and her sisters stood in the middle line, her older brother and cousin on her left. Those on the left were told that they had become Catholics, those in the middle Methodists and those on the right Church of England. That is how the complex questions of post-reformation theology were resolved in the Australian outback in the 1930s. It was as crude as that. She and her sister were sent to a Methodist mission on Goulburn Island and then Croker Island. Her Catholic brother was sent to work at a cattle station and her cousin to a Catholic mission.

Nanna Fejo's family had been broken up for a second time. She stayed at the mission until after the war, when she was allowed to leave for a prearranged job as a domestic in Darwin. She was 16. Nanna Fejo never saw her mum again. After she left the mission, her brother let her know that her mum had died years before, a broken woman fretting for the children that had literally been ripped away from her.

I asked Nanna Fejo what she would have me say today about her story. She thought for a few moments then said that what I should say today was that all mothers are important. And she added: "Families—keeping them together is very important. It's a good thing that you are surrounded by love and that love is passed down the generations. That's what gives you happiness." As I left, later on, Nanna Fejo took one of my staff aside, wanting to make sure that I was not too hard on the Aboriginal stockman who had hunted those kids down all those years ago. The stockman had found her again decades later, this time himself to say, "Sorry." And remarkably, extraordinarily, she had forgiven him.

Nanna Fejo's is just one story. There are thousands, tens of thousands, of them: stories of forced separation of Aboriginal and Torres Strait Islander children from their mums and dads over the better part of a century. Some of these stories are graphically told in bringing them home, the report commissioned in 1995 by Prime Minister Keating and received in 1997 by Prime Minister Howard. There is something terribly primal about these firsthand accounts. The pain is searing; it screams from the pages. The hurt, the humiliation, the degradation and the sheer brutality of the act of physically separating a mother from her children is a deep assault on our senses and on our most elemental humanity.

These stories cry out to be heard; they cry out for an apology. Instead, from the nation's parliament there has been a stony and stubborn and deafening silence for more than a decade; a view that somehow we, the parliament, should suspend our most basic instincts of what is right and what is wrong; a view that, instead, we should look for any pretext to push this great wrong to one side, to leave it languishing with the historians, the academics and the cultural warriors, as if the Stolen Generations are little more than an interesting sociological phenomenon. But the Stolen Generations are not intellectual curiosities. They are human beings; human beings who have been damaged deeply by the decisions of parliaments and governments. But, as of today, the time for denial, the time for delay, has at last come to an end.

The nation is demanding of its political leadership to take us forward. Decency, human decency, universal human decency, demands that the nation now step forward to right an historical wrong. That is what we are doing in this place today. But should there still be doubts as to why we must now act, let the parliament reflect for a moment on the following facts: that, between 1910 and 1970, between 10 and 30 per cent of Indigenous children were forcibly taken from their mothers and fathers; that, as a result, up to 50,000 children were forcibly taken from their families; that this was the product of the deliberate, calculated policies of the state as reflected in the explicit powers given to them under statute; that this policy was taken to such extremes by some in administrative authority that the forced extractions of children of so-called "mixed lineage" were seen as part of a broader policy of dealing with "the problem of the Aboriginal population."

One of the most notorious examples of this approach was from the Northern Territory Protector of Natives, who stated: Generally by the fifth and invariably by the sixth generation, all native characteristics of the Australian aborigine are eradicated. The problem of our half-castes — to quote the Protector — will quickly be eliminated by the complete disappearance of the black race, and the swift submergence of their progeny in the white ...

The Western Australian Protector of Natives expressed not dissimilar views, expounding them at length in Canberra in 1937 at the first national conference on Indigenous affairs that brought together the Commonwealth and state protectors of natives. These are uncomfortable things to be brought out into the light. They are not pleasant. They are profoundly disturbing. But we must acknowledge these facts if we are to deal once and for all with the argument that the policy of generic forced separation was somehow well motivated, justified by its historical context and, as a result, unworthy of any apology today.

Then we come to the argument of intergenerational responsibility, also used by some to argue against giving an apology today. But let us remember the fact that the forced removal of Aboriginal children was happening as late as the early 1970s. The 1970s is not exactly a point in remote antiquity. There are still serving members of this parliament who were first elected to this place in the early 1970s. It is well within the adult memory span of many of us. The uncomfortable truth for us all is that the parliaments of the nation, individually and collectively, enacted statutes and delegated authority under those statutes that made the forced removal of children on racial grounds fully lawful.

There is a further reason for an apology as well: it is that reconciliation is in fact an expression of a core value of our nation—and that value is a fair go for all. There is a deep and abiding belief in the Australian community that, for the Stolen Generations, there was no fair go at all. There is a pretty basic Aussie belief that says it is time to put right this most outrageous of wrongs. It is for these reasons, quite apart from concerns of fundamental human decency, that the governments and parliaments of this nation must make this apology—because, put simply, the laws that our parliaments enacted made the stolen generations possible. We, the parliaments of the nation, are ultimately responsible, not those who gave effect to our laws. The problem lay with the laws themselves. As has been said of settler societies elsewhere, we are the bearers of many blessings from our ancestors, and therefore we must also be the bearer of their burdens as well.

Therefore, for our nation, the course of action is clear, and therefore, for our people, the course of action is clear: that is, to deal now with what has become one of the darkest chapters in Australia's history. In doing so, we are doing more than contending with the facts, the evidence and the often rancorous public debate. In doing so, we are also wrestling with our own soul. This is not, as some would argue, a black-armband view of history; it is just the truth: the cold, confronting, uncomfortable truth—facing it, dealing with it, moving on from it. Until we fully confront that truth, there will always be a shadow hanging over us and our future as a fully united and fully reconciled people. It is time to reconcile. It is time to recognize the injustices of the past. It is time to say sorry. It is time to move forward together.

To the Stolen Generations, I say the following: as Prime Minister of Australia, I am sorry. On behalf of the government of Australia, I am sorry. On behalf of the parliament of Australia, I am sorry. I offer you this apology without qualification. We apologise for the hurt, the pain and suffering that we, the parliament, have caused you by the laws that previous parliaments have enacted. We apologise for the indignity, the degradation and the humiliation these laws embodied. We offer this apology to the mothers, the fathers, the brothers, the sisters, the families and the communities whose lives were ripped apart by the actions of successive governments under successive parliaments. In making this apology, I would also like to speak personally to the members of the Stolen Generations and their families: to those here today, so many of you; to those listening across the nation—from Yuendumu, in the central west of the Northern Territory, to Yabara, in North Queensland, and to Pitjantjatjara in South Australia.

I know that, in offering this apology on behalf of the government and the parliament, there is nothing I can say today that can take away the pain you have suffered personally. Whatever words I speak today, I cannot undo that. Words alone are not that powerful; grief is a very personal thing. I ask those non-Indigenous Australians listening today who may not fully understand why what we are doing is so important to imagine for a moment that this had happened to you. I say to honorable members here present: imagine if this had happened to us. Imagine the crippling effect. Imagine how hard it would be to forgive. My proposal is this: if the apology we extend today is accepted in the spirit of reconciliation in which it is offered, we can today resolve together that there be a new beginning for Australia. And it is to such a new beginning that I believe the nation is now calling us.

Australians are a passionate lot. We are also a very practical lot. For us, symbolism is important but, unless the great symbolism of reconciliation is accompanied by an even greater substance, it is little more than a clanging gong. It is not sentiment that makes history; it is our actions that make history. Today's apology, however inadequate, is aimed at righting past wrongs. It is also aimed at building a bridge between Indigenous and non-Indigenous Australians—a bridge based on a real respect rather than a thinly veiled contempt. Our challenge for the future is to now cross that bridge and, in so doing, to embrace a new partnership between Indigenous and non-Indigenous Australians.

Australians—embracing, as part of that partnership, expanded link-up and other critical services to help the Stolen Generations to trace their families if at all possible and to provide dignity to their lives. But the core of this partnership for the future is the closing of the gap between Indigenous and non-Indigenous Australians on life expectancy, educational achievement and employment opportunities. This new partnership on closing the gap will set concrete targets for the future: within a decade to halve the widening gap in literacy, numeracy and employment outcomes and opportunities for Indigenous Australians, within a decade to halve the appalling gap in infant mortality rates between Indigenous and non-Indigenous children and, within a generation, to close the equally appalling 17-year life gap

Chapter 1
The Aboriginal History

between Indigenous and non-Indigenous in overall life expectancy.

The truth is, a business as usual approach towards Indigenous Australians is not working. Most old approaches are not working. We need a new beginning—a new beginning which contains real measures of policy success or policy failure; a new beginning, a new partnership, on closing the gap with sufficient flexibility not to insist on a one-size-fits-all approach for each of the hundreds of remote and regional Indigenous communities across the country but instead allowing flexible, tailored, localapproaches to achieve commonly-agreed national objectives that lie at the core of our proposed new partnership; a new beginning that draws intelligently on the experiences of new policy settings across the nation. However, unless we as a parliament set a destination for the nation, we have no clear point to guide our policy, our programs or our purpose; we have no centralized organizing principle.

Let us resolve today to begin with the little children—a fitting place to start on this day of apology for the Stolen Generations. Let us resolve over the next five years to have every Indigenous four-year-old in a remote Aboriginal community enrolled in and attending a proper early childhood education centre or opportunity and engaged in proper preliteracy and prenumeracy programs. Let us resolve to build new educational opportunities for these little ones, year by year, step by step, following the completion of their crucial preschool year. Let us resolve to use this systematic approach to building future educational opportunities for Indigenous children and providing proper primary and preventative health care for the same children, to beginning the task of rolling back the obscenity that we find today in infant mortality rates in remote Indigenous communities—up to four times higher than in other communities.

None of this will be easy. Most of it will be hard—very hard. But none of it is impossible, and all of it is achievable with clear goals, clear thinking, and by placing an absolute premium on respect, cooperation and mutual responsibility as the guiding principles of this new partnership on closing the gap. The mood of the nation is for reconciliation now, between Indigenous and non-Indigenous Australians. The mood of the nation on Indigenous policy and politics is now very simple. The nation is calling on us, the politicians, to move beyond our infantile bickering, our point-scoring and our mindlessly partisan politics and elevate this one core area of national responsibility to a rare position beyond the partisan divide. Surely this is the unfulfilled spirit of the 1967 referendum. Surely, at least from this day forward, we should give it a go.

Let me take this one step further, and take what some may see as a piece of political posturing and make a practical proposal to the opposition on this day, the first full sitting day of the new parliament. I said before the election that the nation needed a kind of war cabinet on parts of Indigenous policy, because the challenges are too great and the consequences too great to allow it all to become a political football, as it has been so often in the past. I therefore propose a joint policy commission, to be led by the Leader of the Opposition and me, with a mandate to develop and implement—to begin with—an effective housing strategy for remote communities over the next five years. It will be consistent with the government's policy framework, a new partnership for closing the gap. If this commission operates well, I then propose that it work on the further task of constitutional recognition of the first Australians, consistent with the longstanding platform commitments of my party and the pre-election position of the opposition. This would probably be desirable in any event because, unless such a proposition was absolutely bipartisan, it would fail at a referendum. As I have said before, the time has come for new approaches to enduring problems. Working constructively together on such defined projects I believe would meet with the support of the nation. It is time for fresh ideas to fashion the nation's future.

Mr. Speaker, today the parliament has come together to right a great wrong. We have come together to deal with the past so that we might fully embrace the future. We have had sufficient audacity of faith to advance a pathway to that future, with arms extended rather than with fists still clenched. So let us seize the day. Let it not become a moment of mere sentimental reflection. Let us take it with both hands and allow this day, this day of national reconciliation, to become one of those rare moments in which we might just be able to transform the way in which the nation thinks about itself, whereby the injustice administered to the Stolen Generations in the name of these, our parliaments, causes all of us to reappraise, at the deepestlevel of our beliefs, the real possibility of reconciliation writ large: reconciliation across all Indigenous Australia; reconciliation across the entire history of the often bloody encounter between those who emerged from the Dreamtime a thousand generations ago and those who, like me, came across the seas only yesterday; reconciliation which opens up whole new possibilities for the future.

It is for the nation to bring the first two centuries of our settled history to a close, as we begin a new chapter. We embrace with pride, admiration and awe these great and ancient cultures we are truly blessed to have among us—cultures that provide a unique, uninterrupted human thread linking our Australian continent to the most ancient prehistory of our planet. Growing from this new respect, we see our Indigenousbrothers and sisters with fresh eyes, with new eyes, and we have our minds wide open as to how we might tackle, together, the great practical challenges that Indigenous Australia faces in the future.

Let us turn this page together: Indigenous and non-Indigenous Australians, government and opposition, Commonwealth and state, and write this new chapter in our nation's story together. First Australians, First Fleeters, and those who first took the oath of allegiance just a few weeks ago — let's grasp this opportunity to craft a new future for this great land, Australia. Mr. Speaker, I commend the motion to the House.

New Words

mistreatment	n.	虐待,苛待	descendant	n.	后代
statute	n.	法规,条令	progeny	n.	子孙,后裔
blemished	a.	有污点的	degradation	n.	衰退,退化
eradicate	v.	连根拔起	expound	v.	解释,详细说明
inflict	v.	造成,把……强加给	harness	v.	利用
			antiquity	n.	古代
submergence	n.	下沉,淹没	endure	v.	忍耐

abiding	a.	持久的		systematic	a.	系统的
stake	n.	赌注		rip	v.	撕,扯
outrageous	a.	粗暴的,可恶的		obscenity	n.	猥亵(的行为)
reconcile	v.	和解		extraordinarily	ad.	非凡地
rancorous	a.	怀恶意的		premium	n.	额外费用
assemble	v.	集合		graphically	ad.	生动地
black-armband	a.	带着黑色臂章的		bickering	n.	争吵,争论
reconciliation	n.	和解,和谐		primal	a.	主要的
crippling	a.	造成严重后果的		infantile	a.	幼稚的
commencement	n.	开始		searing	a.	强烈的,灼热的
symbolism	n.	象征,象征主义		partisan	a.	党派的
eloquent	a.	有口才的		humiliation	n.	耻辱
clanging	a.	发出叮当声的		referendum	n.	全民公决
kinship	n.	亲属关系		brutality	n.	无情,暴行
numeracy	n.	计算能力		cabinet	n.	内阁
strife	n.	冲突,争吵		assault	n.	攻击
halve	v.	二等分,减半		mandate	n.	命令
stockwhip	n.	牧人用短柄长鞭		stony	a.	无情的
appalling	a.	可怕的		implement	v.	实施,执行
herd	v.	使成群;放牧		suspend	v.	暂停
infant	a.	初期的		constitutional	a.	本质的;宪法的
Catholic	n.	天主教徒		instinct	n.	本能,直觉
enroll	v.	登记		bipartisan	a.	代表两党的
crude	a.	粗鲁的		pretext	n.	借口
preliteracy	n.	学前书写教育		audacity	n.	大胆而无畏
Methodist	n.	卫理公会派教		languish	v.	凋萎,失去活力
prenumeracy	n.	学前计数教育		clenched	a.	紧握的
prearranged	a.	预先安排的		sociological	a.	社会学的
crucial	a.	重要的		reappraise	v.	重新评价
fret	v.	担心				

Exercises

1. **True or false judgments**
   (1) Rudd said sorry especially for the removal of Aboriginal and Torres Strait Islander children from their families, their communities, and their country.
   (2) When Nanna Nungala Fejo was about five in 1920, she was captured by two white men and an Aboriginal stockman on horseback.
   (3) Nanna Fejo and her sisters were sent to a Catholic mission.
   (4) Howard admitted that Australia did wrong to "the Stolen Generations," but he refused to make an apology because he held that the mistakes were made by the

previous governments.

(5) The Western Australian Protector of Natives expounded them at length in Canberra in 1937 at the second national conference on Indigenous affairs that brought together the Commonwealth and state protectors of natives.

(6) Rudd thinks that today's apology is a national apology which can solve the problems of Australian Aborigines effectively.

2. Term interpretations

(1) Nanna Nungala Fejo
(2) Tennant Creek
(3) Catholics
(4) Methodist
(5) Keating
(6) Howard
(7) the Northern Territory Protector of Natives
(8) a fair go
(9) 1967 referendum
(10) the Dreamtime

3. Essay questions

(1) Why did Rudd mention Nanna Nungala Fejo in his speech?

(2) What is happiness in the eyes of Nanna Nungala Fejo?

(3) What are the attitudes of the previous governments towards "the Stolen Generations"?

(4) Why did Rudd decide to deliver this speech?

(5) What would Rudd like to convey to Australians through this speech?

1.4　Reading Passage: Australian Cinema and Settler-Colonial Imagination: *Rabbit-Proof Fence*
by Greg McCarthy[①]

Australian cinema provides the space for addressing the notion of an imagined community. This imagination is derived from Australian historical engagement with the world. As a settler-colonial society, Australia represents a conflicted imagination, as its origins are caught, on the one hand, between the vision of a seemingly peaceful settlement and on the other, of a violent colonial conquest of the Indigenous peoples. An imagination wedged between pride and shame, between triumphalism and a "black-arm band" view of history (McCarthy, 2004). The contestation over Australia's colonial origins has become deeply embedded into the nation's mindset and emerges in multiple forms, which are overlaid by claims that Australia is integrated into a Western superior form of civilizations due to its Anglosphere roots and institutions. However, to achieve this level of confidence Australia has had to find a national identity that is distinct from that of Britain or America. The struggle for a distinct national identity and addressing the stain of a racial past have been two important tropes in Australian cinema. This chapter will address but the second of these themes, the perpetuation of a settler racial mentality toward Aboriginal peoples, which challenges the belief of a superior civilization. The argument will be that as films engage the audience in both a conscious and subconscious manner they evoke the disturbing undercurrent of Australia's racial past and question its present. The case study for this argument will be the Philip Noyce's film *Rabbit-Proof Fence* (2002). To explain how this film confronts not just Australia's racial history but also the ideology of an Australian society being the yardstick of advancement, it is important to give two important contextual factors. The first context, is the *Bringing Them Home Report*[1], which provides the necessary background to the history of Aboriginal children taken from their parents, called the Stolen Generation; secondly, to the Doris Pilkington-Garimara's novel (1996)[2] on which the film takes its inspiration. Both texts destabilize the assertion of Australia's advancement to a higher civilization as a march of progress.

The Stolen Generation Report

The *Bringing Them Home Report* (1997) by the Australian Human Rights Commission[3], led by Sir Ian Wilson[4] inquired into Aboriginal children taken from their parents. The Commission took the testimonies from a wide range of Indigenous witnesses of their experience of being taken from their mothers, from all States and Territories in Australia. The Report was the first systematic and official documentation of children

---

[①] Professor McCarthy holds a Personal Chair of Australian Studies at the University of Western Australia. He is concurrently the BHP Billiton Chair of Australian Politics at Peking University. This prestigious chair was established in 2012 with support of the Australia-China Council, the Foundation for Australian Studies in China (FASIC), Australian Department of Foreign Affairs and Trade (DFAT), the Australian Embassy in China and funded by BHP Billiton.

"stolen" from their mothers to be assimilated into white society. Whilst previously there had been evidence of the loss of land, language and culture, and the deprivation of liberty, this was first evidential basis of a systematic state-based racial program to breed out the Indigenous culture. In his introduction to the volume, Commissioner Wilson invoked the 1948 United Nations genocide convention[5], categorizing the stolen generation practice as genocide. The *Bringing Them Home Report* represented the taking of Aboriginal children as not merely isolated incidents but a multitude of incidents; not an individualized but a whole of People's account. The Report, which contains testimonies from 535 witnesses, sent shock waves through the nation when it was first released. The testimonies were heart-wrenching, evoking emotional response and this was evident in the Opposition Leader Kim Beazley[6] tearfully read out examples of the Report's testimonies to the parliament. It also revealed how systematic the assimilation process was by government authorities and Christian institutions. The Report called for a national apology to the Indigenous People. The Prime Minister of the day John Howard refused such a request, saying this was but historical events and not the responsibility of contemporary Australians. However, his successor, Prime Minister, Kevin Rudd, did apologize to the Stolen Generation in 2014. Critically, the importance of the *Bringing Them Home Report* was that it gave official legitimacy to the life-stories of dispossession, loss of family and kinship ties, loss of language, and the dispossession of one's country—and critically the ongoing effects of these losses. The sheer accumulation of so many stories, told through first-person narrative and grouped together thematically through the Report, unsettled the white Australian people's sense of a higher civilization.

Indigenous Life Stories

Although the report stunned the nation, much of the detail it contains had been presented before through Indigenous autobiographies and life-story narratives (Schaffer, 2001). The *Bringing Them Home Report*, however, placed these earlier stories into a racialized context, not as tales of Indigenous women as "batters," just like white mothers, but as racialized victims. A prominent example of these life-stories was that of Doris Pilkington-Garimara's account of her mother and aunt's life in the book *Follow the Rabbit-Proof Fence* (1996). The telling of the story of her mother and aunt's forced removal from their Aboriginal family and their subsequent 1,500-mile trek home was a powerful testimony at the *Bringing Them Home* inquiry. Pilkington-Garimara wrote the book based on her mother's (Daisy's) recollection of how in 1931 government agents forcibly took, Molly, then 14 years old, her 11-year-old sister Daisy (Pilkington-Gamkira's mother), and 9-year-old cousin Gracie, from their mothers, in the small settlement of Jigalong in Western Australia. The three girls were transported on a 1,500 miles' journey to a Christian mission at the Moore River Native Settlement. The book details how the three girls immediately ran away from the Mission, heading East before they found the rabbit-proof fence (built across Australian in 1901), then following the fence-line, the girls travelled the arduous journey through desolate country back to their mothers. The book was then adapted to the film.

The Film *Rabbit-Proof Fence*

The film *Rabbit-Proof Fence* dramatically tells this "true story". Phillip Noyce directed the film. He was an experience and renown director, having become famous in Hollywood and returned to Australia specifically to make the film. His outstanding directorial skills were evident in the films' aesthetics, its plot, and its theatrical effects. The movie vividly retells the tale of the three Aboriginal children from their kidnapping to return home. In the opening scene, the film informs the audience, that as so-called "half-caste" daughters, the State had the power to legally kidnap them. The audience is also made aware that the Indigenous mothers knew that Molly (Everlyn Sampi), her sister Daisy (Tianna Sansbury) and cousin Gracie (Laura Monaghan) might be targets and be taken by the police. In the traumatic opening act, the girls are forced into a police car and driven away from their distraught and desperate mothers. The film shows how the girls are then taken to the Moore River Native Settlement, around 1,500 miles to the north. But they escape and follow the rabbit-proof fence home, a journey of almost unconceivable adversity. On the way, Gracie is captured but Molly and Daisy continue their journey home. The tension of the film is heightened by the pursuing of the girls by the Aboriginal tracker Moodoo (David Gulipilil), who comes to respect their endeavor and determination. The film captures the heroism of the journey home, moreover, it presents a broader settler-colonial focus by interspersing the journey-home with other tales of racial oppression, including rape and domestic servitude of Aboriginal girls (McCarthy, 2004). However, *Rabbit-Proof Fence* explores not just the heroic story of these girls but of the genocidal ideology and practices of the day. The film depicts genocide, through its portrayal of A. O. Neville, the Western Australian Protector of Aborigines, shown as a single-minded bureaucrat dedicated to civilizing the natives by breeding out their black blood. The actor Kenneth Branagh[7] depicts Neville, as a man on a mission to assimilate Aboriginal girls into white civilization via eugenics.

Response to the Film

The film was a box-office success, grossing over $16 million (McCarthy, 2004). It was also praised by film critics as a fine work of cinematic art. However, the film provoked diverse political responses from those who attacked it as a slur on Australia's history of advancement, as opposed to those who defended its portrayal as accurately reflecting the evidence before the *Bringing Them Home* inquiry and true to Indigenous life-stories. For example, on the former, Bolt (2002) criticized the film as supporting "Stolen Generation" activism and the black-arm band view of Australian history. In contrast, Manne (2002) defended the film, saying the central point of the film is that "in interwar WA 'half-caste' children were seized by the state exclusively based on race — and this was incontrovertibly true" (p. 1). Manne argued that there is overwhelming documentary evidence that from 1899 to the 1940s "half-caste" children were removed from their families on the orders of the respective Western Australian Chief Protector of Aborigines (e. g. Neville). Manne notes that as the film is true to both the broad historic record of Aboriginal experience and accurately represents it; it passes the basic cinematic test of truth. Manne concludes his review with the following appraisal:

> *Rabbit-Proof Fence* is not only a remarkable accurate account of a dark episode in our history. As it suggests, a simple story of the seizure and the escape of three young "half-caste" girls can take us, if we are willing to open our eyes, to an understanding of the racial fantasies and phobias and to the genocidal thoughts that masqueraded as policies for the welfare of Aborigines in Australia's interwar years. (Manne, 2002, p. 2)

Lydon (2004), goes beyond the political and judicial controversy over the actual extent of stolen generation numbers, (estimated between 50,000 to 180,000; see: Attwood & Magowan, 2001; Manne, 2001), to contend that the film stands above these debates. She writes:

> In my view, Noyce has accomplished a fine thing in transcending the narrowly forensic terms of this debate so far, instead attempting to represent the experience of families torn apart under assimilation. He brings a range of cinematic strategies to bear on telling a story which will touch as many people as possible. A central element in the film's box-office success has been its universality, the ease with which viewers translate a local historical event into immediately personal terms. While the factuality of the events re-told is important, as director Philip Noyce explained, "halfway through reading the screenplay, they ceased to be black or white, they were just children wanting to return to their mothers. And I thought, this is a film that has to be made." (Lydon, 2004, p. 147)

In part, the film's strength is in its refusal to reduce assimilation to some judicial category but to personalize it. Moreover, it opens up layers of political affect over colonization and systemic racism. There is an uncomfortable political parallel here in that the "genocide" occurred in Australia in the 1930s at the same time as it was occurring in Nazi Germany[8]. As such[9], behind the spectre of the "Stolen Generation" is a profound questioning of Australian society, politics and history. For some the personal and family story of the film's central motif can be criticized for disguising the systemic genocide that was evident in the stolen generation process. This is the very point made by Hughes-d'Aeth[10] (2002) who prefers Steven Spielberg's *Schindler's List*[11] as a film that brings the personal and the systemic together. He writes that both movies are "based on non-fictional accounts (by Pilkington-Garimara and Keneally) of traumatic events that were founded on survivor testimony ... they are both survivor stories that take place against a backdrop of non-survival, or alternatively escape stories that confound a more general condition of imprisonment" (Hughes d'Aeth, 2002). It is documented (McCarthy, 2004) that Noyce drew on the cinematic history of the holocaust but was more concerned to concentrate on telling the "true story" from the girls' point of view. For example, whilst the film has the girls transported by train in a cage to the settlement, in fact they were transported by ship. It is the train that the audience, knowingly or subconsciously, recognises as the Nazi means of transporting the Jews, however, overwhelmingly the film draws us into the personal trauma of the young girls. For Hughes-d'Aeth (2002), the film's aesthetic sutures the audience into an all too easy empathetic subjectivity with the children, especially Molly, while simultaneously asking the audience to distance itself from the overall cruelty of generational assimilation (Hughes-d'Aeth, 2002). In contrast, Emily Potter[12], and Kay Schaffer[13] (2004) contend that whilst the film's aesthetic does emphasise the children's heroic tale, however, it is inescapable for the audience not to see the multiple subjectivities summoned up by the film, thereby challenging the audience to question Australia's racist past.

In general terms, the film's depiction of Neville and his Office enters into the historical puzzle over what the administrative conditions are for genocide. This is the very conundrum postulated by Bauman when he writes that: "Modern genocide is genocide with a purpose. Getting rid of the adversary is not an end in itself. It is means to an end ... The end itself is a grand vision of a better, and radically different, society" (Bauman, 1989, p. 91). Bauman contends that the rationalisation of modern bureaucracy has the potential for producing the "silencing morality," as the process removes the bureaucrat from the outcome of their polices (Bauman, 1989, 29). In the Australian colonial setting, the potential of a dehumanising outcome is reinforced by an ideology of racial superiority based on a notion of the march of western progress (Smith, 1999, p. 58). In this sense, the spirit of modernist genocide that emerges from the film *Rabbit-Proof Fence*, is a combination of colonialism and modernism (McCarthy, 2004). The removal of children from their families via a routine bureaucratic procedure is reinforced by the idea that the result of breeding out black-blood will lead in three generations to whiteness; the basis of a superior civilization.

Conclusion

This chapter has placed the film *The Rabbit Proof Fence* into its contemporary and historical setting. The film emerged out of indigenous life-stories and these were given legitimacy by the *Bringing Them Home Report*. The film struck a sympathetic cord in Australian and international audiences as a story of State-based kidnapping and the bravery of the girls to return home to their mothers. The girls' performances, have a deep and universal emotional quality, giving us insights into how to understand the Australian past and present and the lasting effects of the Stolen Generation. The film equally raised the serious question of genocide in Australian history. If the film opens with the police forcibly taking the girls from their hysterical mothers, the film ends on a dual note of reunion but also of questions for the present. As the child draw near to Jigalong there is the following dialogue between two policemen: "[W]hat's that women's business? Been going all day, They're up to something." One officer goes looking in the dark, only to be confronted by Molly's mother and aunt, whose spirituality humiliations him (Lydon, 2004, p. 148). As Lydon notes the film ends movingly,

> The family is reunited. But not quite: for me, one of the film's most moving ironies is the contrast it makes between Neville's admonition to Molly to mind her duty, and Molly's own sense of her responsibility to her kin, expressed most poignantly as she is enfolded into her weeping mother's arms at the end of the film, sobbing "I lost one. I lost one." The missing

Gracie stands for a larger absence. The final footage of the elderly Molly and Daisy still living in their community brings the story firmly into the here and now[14], amplifying its intimations of unfinished business (Lydon, 2004, p.148).

As such, the film marked an important and indelible moment in Australian cinematography, as it turns a standard trope of white families into an Indigenous one, simultaneously raising the history of racial discrimination. The film also carved a space for Indigenous cinema in Australia and was followed by Indigenous film makers, such as Ivan Sen's *Beneath Clouds*[15] (2002) and Warwick Thornton's *Sampson and Delila*[16] (2009), both gaining international acclaim. The film *Rabbit-Proof Fence* stands as a moment of clarity and progress in Australian cinema, which has stood the test of cinematic time.

References

Bain Attwood and Fiona Magowan (2001) "Learning about the Truth: The Stolen Generations Narrative in *Telling Stories: Indigenous history and memory in Australia and New Zealand*", ends. Sydney: Allen and Unwin.

Bolt, Andrew, "Rabbit Proof Myths", *Herald Sun*, 14 February 2002.

Hughes-d'Aeth, Tony (2002). "Which Rabbit-Proof Fence? Empathy, Assimilation, Hollywood", *Australian Humanities Review*, September 2002, www.lib.Latrobe.edu.au/AHR/archives.

Lydon, J. (2004) "A Strange Time Machine: The Tracker, Black and White, and Rabbit-Proof Fence", *Australian Historical Studies*, 35:123, 137—148.

Manne, R. (2002) "In Denial: The Stolen Generation and the Right", *Australian Quarterly Essays*, 1, 2001, 1—113.

Manne, R. (2002) "The Colour of Prejudice", *Sydney Morning Herald*, 23 February.

McCarthy, G. (2004) "Australian Cinema and the Spectres of Post-Coloniality: Rabbit-Proof Fence, Australian Rules, The Tracker and Beneath Clouds". *London Papers in Australian Studies* No. 8, pp. 1—37.

Pilkington, Doris/Garimanugi. (1996) Follow the *Rabbit Proof Fence*. Queensland: University of Queensland Press.

Potter, Emily and Kay Schaffer. (2004) "Rabbit-Proof Fence, Relational Ecologies and the Commodification of Indigenous Experience", *Australian Humanities Review*, April.

Schaffer, Kay. "Manne's Generation: White National Response to the Stolen Generation Report", *Australian Humanities Review*, June 2001, www.lib.Latrobe.edu.au/AHR/archive.

Smith, A. T. (1999) *Decolonizing Methodologies: Research and Indigenous Peoples*, Snelling Michael (ed.). London: Zed Books.

Wilson, Ronald. Sir. (1997) "Bringing Them Home: Report of the National Inquiry into the Separation of Aboriginal and Torres Strait Islander Children from Their Families".

Sydney: *Human Rights and Equal Opportunity Commission*, 1997.

Notes

[1] the *Bringing Them Home Report*: the report of the National Inquiry into the Separation of Aboriginal and Torres Strait Islander children from their families from 26 May 1997.
[2] the Doris Pilkington-Garimara's novel (1996): the book *Follow the Rabbit-Proof Fence*, written by Doris Pilkington-Garimara (1937—2014), an Australian Indigenous author.
[3] the Australian Human Rights Commission: a national human rights institution, established in 1986, and renamed in 2008.
[4] Ian Wilson (1932—2013): Australian politician and solicitor.
[5] The 1948 United Nations genocide convention is the Convention on the Prevention and Punishment of the Crime of Genocide, which was adopted by the United Nations General Assembly on 9 December 1948. The Convention entered into force on 12 January 1951.
[6] Kim Beazley (1948—): the Deputy Prime Minister of Australia from 1995 to 1996, and subsequently the Leader of the Australian Labor Party (ALP).
[7] Kenneth Branagh (1960—) is a Northern Irish actor, director, and producer. In the film *Rabbit-Proof Fence*, he is an actor of A. O. Neville.
[8] Nazi Germany: the common English name for the period in German history from 1933 to 1945.
[9] as such: with respect to its inherent nature.
[10] Hughes-d'Aeth (1972—): a teacher in the English Department at the University of Western Australia and is the co-editor of the Australian chapter of Annotated Bibliography of English Studies (ABES).
[11] Steven Spielberg's *Schindler's List*: a 1993 American epic historical period drama film directed and co-produced by Steven Spielberg (1946—), an American director, producer, and screenwriter.
[12] Emily Potter: an ARC Postdoctoral Fellow in the Faculty of Architecture, Building and Planning, University of Melbourne.
[13] Kay Schaffer: an Emerita Professor in Gender Studies and Social Inquiry, Faculty of Arts at the University of Adelaide.
[14] here and now: at this time.
[15] *Beneath Clouds*（《云层以下》）: a 2002 film by Australian director Ivan Sen(1972—), an Australian indigenous filmmaker.
[16] Warwick Thornton's *Sampson and Delila*: a 2009 Australian film directed by Warwick Thornton. The film won the Caméra d'Or at the 2009 Cannes Film Festival.

New Words

seemingly	*ad.*	表面上看来		multitude	*n.*	大量，许多
bureaucrat	*n.*	官僚		personalize	*v.*	带有个人感情
wedge	*v.*	挤进		heart-wrenching	*a.*	令人心痛的
eugenics	*n.*	优生学		spectre	*n.*	幽灵
contestation	*n.*	主张		enfold	*v.*	围住
gross	*v.*	总共收入		fictional	*a.*	虚构的
mindset	*n.*	思维倾向		legitimacy	*n.*	合法；合理
slur	*v.*	诽谤		backdrop	*n.*	背景
overlay	*v.*	覆盖		dispossession	*n.*	剥夺
activism	*n.*	行动主义		alternatively	*ad.*	二者择一地
Anglosphere	*a.*	英语圈的		critically	*ad.*	批判性地
incontrovertibly	*ad.*	无疑地		confound	*v.*	使混淆
stain	*n.*	污点		ongoing	*a.*	进行的
overwhelming	*a.*	压倒一切的		imprisonment	*n.*	监禁
trope	*n.*	修辞		sheer	*ad.*	完全地
appraisal	*n.*	评价		holocaust	*n.*	大屠杀
perpetuation	*n.*	永存，不朽		group	*v.*	分类
episode	*n.*	插曲		cage	*n.*	笼子
mentality	*n.*	心理		thematically	*ad.*	主题地
seizure	*n.*	夺取		knowingly	*ad.*	故意地
evoke	*v.*	唤起		unsettle	*v.*	扰乱
fantasy	*n.*	想象		trauma	*n.*	创伤
undercurrent	*n.*	潜在的影响		stun	*v.*	使大吃一惊
yardstick	*n.*	尺度		suture	*n./v.*	缝合
masquerade	*n.*	伪装		autobiography	*n.*	自传
inspiration	*n.*	灵感		empathetic	*a.*	移情的
controversy	*n.*	论战		narrative	*n.*	叙述
destabilize	*v.*	使失去稳定性		simultaneously	*ad.*	同时地
transcend	*v.*	超越		prominent	*a.*	突出的
testimony	*n.*	证明		summon	*v.*	召唤
forensic	*a.*	论争的		subsequent	*a.*	随后的
whilst	*conj.*	同时		conundrum	*n.*	难解的问题
universality	*n.*	普遍性		trek	*v.*	长途跋涉
invoke	*v.*	祈求		postulate	*v.*	提出要求
factuality	*n.*	实在性		recollection	*n.*	回忆
genocide	*n.*	种族灭绝		grand	*a.*	重要的
screenplay	*n.*	电影剧本		forcibly	*ad.*	强有力地
convention	*n.*	习俗		dehumanize	*v.*	使失去人性
judicial	*a.*	明断的		mission	*n.*	布道所；使命

reinforce	v.	强化		footage	n.	长度；距离	
detail	v.	详述		unconceivable	a.	不能想象的	
breed	v.	繁殖		amplify	v.	增强	
arduous	a.	艰巨的		adversity	n.	逆境	
cord	n.	绳		intimation	n.	正式宣告	
desolate	a.	荒凉的		indelible	a.	不可磨灭的	
hysterical	a.	情绪激动的		intersperse	v.	散置，散布	
renown	n.	名望		cinematography	n.	电影术	
humiliation	n.	羞辱		rape	n.	掠夺	
aesthetics	n.	审美学		carve	v.	开创	
movingly	ad.	感人地		servitude	n.	奴役	
traumatic	a.	创伤的		clarity	n.	明确	
admonition	n.	告诫		heighten	v.	加强	
distraught	a.	心神错乱的		agent	n.	代理人	
poignantly	ad.	令人辛酸地		phobia	n.	恐惧	
desperate	a.	绝望的					

Exercises

1. **Ture or false judgments**
   (1) This paper mainly talks about Australia's distinct national identity.
   (2) The author discusses Australia's racial past by analyzing the film *Rabbit-Proof Fence* (2002) as the case study.
   (3) The *Bringing Them Home Report* (1997) is regarded as the first systematic and official documentation of children "stolen" from their mothers to be assimilated into white society.
   (4) The stolen generation children are considered as isolated incidents and an individualized account in the history of Australia.
   (5) Based on the 1948 United Nations genocide convention, the Australian stolen generation practice would be defined as genocide.

2. **Essay questions**
   (1) Why does the author think the *Bringing Them Home Report* is important?
   (2) What did the book *Follow the Rabbit-Proof Fence* describe?
   (3) How did the film *Rabbit-Proof Fence* depict genocide?

Chapter 2
Australian National History

2.1 Background

In 1778, the Australian continent entered a period of colonization. The British government transported their convicts to Australia; therefore, Australia became a penal colonization of the Great Britain. The economic mainstay in the Australian convict settlement chiefly depended on the sheep industry. In 1851, gold was discovered in Australia, which stimulated economic activities in all the south-eastern colonies. In 1852, the economy of the nation boomed. The colonies were strong enough to break from Britain's control and become independent. Economic development and political independence accelerated the process of the formation of the Commonwealth of Australia.

Before the federation, the six colonies were self-governing. In 1870, foreign military forces at sea threatened the Australian continent. The six colonies recognized the value of establishing a collective national defense. Meanwhile, the United States and Canada declared their national independence, which inspired the six colonies to discuss the formation of a federation. On January 1, 1901, the Commonwealth of Australia was formally proclaimed based on "One People, One Flag, One Destiny"(Knightley, 2000: 50—57).

In 1914 when World War I broke out, Australia, a newly-established nation, soon got involved. For one thing, 98% of Australia's population was of British descent, and they had close ties to the "mother country." In their eyes, the First World War was the British war, and they needed to show loyalty to Britain. For another, Australia aimed to show itself off as a new-born country on the international stage. Though there was opposition to conscription, the nation, however, was in high spirits participating in the war.

In September 1914, the Australian and New Zealand Army Corps (ANZAC) was established. A total of 331,814 Australians joined the Australian Imperial Force (AIF) and were sent overseas. The major campaign was the Battle of Gallipoli against the Turks in 1915, but this battle resulted in a disastrous defeat. Australia suffered a great loss. The failure at Gallipoli motivated Australia to reflect on the following issues: "Why did we join up?""Whom did we, Australia, fight for?" "What did the First World War mean to Australia?" In 1914 the male population of Australia was less than 3 million, yet almost

400,000 of them volunteered to fight in the war. 60,000 died and tens of thousands were wounded.

As a percentage of those involved, Australian losses were among the highest of any country in the world. In the years after the First World War, Australia suffered the Great Depression (1929—1933) and was thought to have been one of the hardest-hit countries in the Western world. The economy was at its nadir (Wang Zhijin, 2004: 57).

In 1939 when the Second World War broke out, Australia fought two wars, although not on the Australian mainland. Australian soldiers joined one war against Germany and Italy, and then after Pearl Harbor attack and the fall of Singapore, joined another war against Japan. The unforgettable battle was the Kokoda Trail campaign as part of the Pacific War of World War II to attack the Japanese. Australian soldiers fought valiantly. Australian forces made a significant contribution to the allied victories in Europe, Asia, and the Pacific during the Second World War.

World War II accelerated the process of industrialization. After WWII, hundreds of thousands of refugees and migrants arrived in Australia in the immediate post-war period. The effects of the war also fostered the development of a more diverse and cosmopolitan Australian society. After 1945, Australia entered a boom period. The post-war prosperity brought about economic progress in almost every aspect of society.

2.2 The Film *Gallipoli*

Gallipoli is a 1981 Australian war film directed by Peter Weir. The film described the enthusiasm and devotion of Australian young people involving themselves in World War I and the failure of the Gallipoli campaign.

Australia as an independent country was established in 1901. A new nation was born, but people had a weak sense of national identity. When the First World War broke out, Australia immediately was at war because Britain, as Prime Minister Menzies said, was at war. Australia should show its loyalty to its "mother country," Britain. Australia and New Zealand co-organized the Australian and New Zealand Army Corps(ANZAC) to fight against the Turks on the peninsula of Gallipoli.

During the war, Australian soldiers displayed reckless valor and never admitted defeat. In the film, two young men with different personalities, Archy and Frank, were brave in facing the fire and guns of the cruel enemy. During the course of the movie, the young men slowly lost their innocence about the purpose of war. The climax of the movie occurs on the ANZAC battlefield at Gallipoli. Because of the failure in the strategies of the British military officers, they were defeated by the Turks. Facing the great losses, Australians started to reflect on their reasons for joining up and the purpose of the war. The film aroused in Australia the self-awareness of nationalism.

2.2.1 Director Peter Weir

Peter Weir (1944—) is a great Australian film director. In his youth, he majored in arts at the University of Sydney. At the age of 21, he went to London for a fresh perspective from which to contemplate what it means to be an Australian, a question that would inform all his early full-length features. Peter Weir helped to define the rebirth of Australian cinema, while addressing some of the most pressing concerns of the nation in the 1970s and 1980s. Weir's signature films, such as *Picnic at Hanging Rock*, *The Last Wave*, *Gallipoli*, *The Year of Living Dangerously*, etc., move the audience beyond the commonplace while keeping them in an unsettled state to the end. In the late 1980s, he shifted to Hollywood and directed many successful films, such as *Witness*, *The Mosquito Coast*, *Dead Poets Society*, *Green Card*, etc. Weir has managed to combine his arthouse sensibility within generic Hollywood expectations (Bliss, 2000: 56). In his life up to now, he has won 30 awards and 12 nominations, including his personally accrued six Academy Award nominations as either a director, writer, or producer.

Gallipoli is his 1981 Australian film. The screenplay, based on a story by Weir and written by David Williamson, takes on one of the founding myths of Australian nationalism: the 1915 Gallipoli campaign of the First World War in a hopeless battle against the Turks. *Gallipoli* was internationally received as a statement on the irrationality of warfare; and in Australia, it was also received as a statement about the damaging results of British arrogance on the Australian psyche (Olivier Eyquem, 1987: 29—31).

2.2.2 Main Characters

(1) Archy Hamilton is an 18-year-old stockman and an aspiring sprinter. He enlisted as a Light Horseman in the army. In the battle of Gallipoli, Archy sacrificed his young life.
(2) Frank Dunne is an unemployed railway laborer. He has little desire to fight for the British Empire. Persuaded by Archy, he finally enlisted in the infantry. He saw with

his own eyes when Archy was hit by bullets.
(3) Colonel Robinson is a British commander in charge of the Gallipoli campaign. He insists that the ANZAC attack proceed. Due to his failure in military strategies, ANZAC was defeated at Gallipoli.
(4) Major Barton is a responsible Australian officer. During the Gallipoli battle, he was ordered by a British commander to push on. He was disappointed with Colonel Robinson.

2.2.3 Plot

The film *Gallipoli* contains the following three parts:

The first part is set in Western Australia in May 1915, as the first news of the Gallipoli landings was published. Archy was a stockman under 18 years of age. With idealism, he enlisted in the Australian Imperial Force as a Light Horseman. Frank was a laborer who had run out of money. He was a realist, reluctant to join in. Influenced by Archy and other friends, he enlisted in the infantry with three co-workers from the railway. All soldiers embarked on a transport ship bound for Cairo. Australian soldiers enlisted for these motives: to serve the King and Empire, to have an adventure, to see the world, and to do the right thing.

The second part of the movie is set in Egypt. After landing, the soldiers took interest in the outside world, having a wonderful time drinking and playing. The military training in Cairo prior to the war seemed relaxed and loose. They survived several small fights, and some soldiers were wounded.

The final part of the movie takes place at Gallipoli. Frank was sent to deliver messages from Barton, an Australian Major, to British Colonel Robinson. The Australian Light Horse attacked Turkish machine gunners three times. The British Colonel insisted the attack continue and ordered Australian soldiers to push on. Archy joined the last wave and went over the top. The bullets hit his chest and head. He sacrificed his young life.

2.2.4 Theme Analysis

Australia became a Federation in 1901. The First World War broke out in 1914. More than 10 years had passed, but Australia possessed a weak sense of the nation. In its eyes, Australia was closely attached to its mother country, Britain, as a proud junior partner. Australians joined up with idealism and enthusiasm out of loyalty to Britain. "Give England a hand," Australian soldiers shouted in an innocent and naïve way. On the battlefield, these young soldiers fought bravely and ultimately suffered great losses. Thousands of brilliant young men like Archy were buried at Gallipoli, a remote place far from home. Gallipoli, a place people had never heard of before, became a moving story people would never forget! The Gallipoli campaign has become a "founding myth" for Australia.

Before the First World War, when introducing themselves to foreigners, Australian people responded: "I am from Victoria," or "I am from New South Wales." After the First World War, when introducing themselves to foreigners, people would say: "I'm an

Australian." The high cost and meaningless deaths provoked Australians to ponder on their innocence. The failure at Gallipoli stimulated the growth of a self-conscious Australian nationalism. Gallipoli was said to mark the birth of Australia: Australia became Australians' Australia rather than Britain's Australia. It is considered to be the beginning of national identity.

Within the context of the First World War, the film centers around the mateship which is an old Australian concept and value. Images of mateship appear throughout the film. In the beginning, Archy and Zac, an Aboriginal stockhand, splash each other in the horse trough. Archy says to him: "We are mates," displaying their friendship. At the medical examination, the doctor finds Snow's bad teeth, and Frank says to the doctor: "If you do not pass him, you lose all four of us." This kind of "togetherness" is depicted everywhere when they are in Cairo. The mateship between Archy and Frank can also be viewed from start to finish: developing as rivals in athletic competitions, deciding to enlist together, and eventually becoming part of the same Light Horse unit. All these reflect the nature of an established relationship.

New Words

spring	n.	弹簧		outback	n.	（澳大利亚远离城市、人烟稀少的）内地
hurl	v.	向……扑过去				
leopard	n.	豹；美洲豹				
bastard	n.	臭小子		register	v.	登记
bet	n.	赌注		scratching	n.	刮伤
reckon	v.	估计；认为		guinea	n.	基尼（英国旧时金币名）
sonny	n.	孩子，小伙子（用于称呼男孩或比自己年轻得多的男子）				
				quid	n.	一英镑；一镑金币
				lad	n.	小伙子
scram	v.	跑开，迅速离开		scrape	n.	碎片；残余物
gallivant	v.	闲逛		certificate	n.	证明；证书
furiously	ad.	猛烈地；狂暴地		baptism	n.	洗礼
howl	v.	咆哮；狂嚎		rocky	a.	摇晃的
entanglement	n.	铁丝网		slope	n.	斜坡
pit	n.	坑		crook	v.	让……弯曲
spike	v.	扎入		cockatoo	n.	凤头鹦鹉
bloke	n.	家伙；小子		mob	n.	民众
hell	n.	极其糟糕的情况		infantry	n.	步兵团
giddap	v.	快跑		gotta	ad.	必须
preserves	n.	果酱；蜜饯		bloody	ad.	很
proceed	v.	继续进行		coward	a.	胆小的，懦弱的
handicapping	n.	障碍；不利条件		ally	n.	同盟国
				crucify	v.	折磨

kitten	n.	小动物	
toff	n.	花花公子；爱打扮的人	
stirrup	n.	马镫	
swing	v.	摇摆；转向	
bugger	n.	家伙	
wreck	n.	残骸	
nonsense	a.	荒谬的	
fella	n.	伙计；小伙子	
singlet	n.	汗衫，单衬衣	
damn	ad.	很，非常	
drought	n.	干旱	
galah	n.	桃红鹦鹉	
lofty	a.	崇高的	
steak	n.	肉排	
pelican	n.	鹈鹕	
inhabitant	n.	居民	
etrnally	ad.	永恒地，永远地	
antiquity	n.	古物	
liquor	n.	烈酒	
contemplate	v.	思忖	
horizontal	a.	同水平的	
proverbial	a.	众所周知的	
legacy	n.	遗产；遗赠	
jumbo	n.	庞然大物	
piaster	n.	比索（埃及、西班牙、墨西哥的硬币单位）	
chap	n.	小伙子；家伙	
encounter	v.	遇到，遭遇	
biz	n.	行业	
shalom	int.	您好；再见	
diplomat	n.	外交官	
flatten	v.	击败；摧毁	
sailing	n.	航行	
snowflake	n.	雪花	
peeper	n.	眼睛	
bob	n.	先令（旧时的英国硬币）	
halt	v.	停止	

frontal	a.	正面的	
assault	n.	袭击，攻击	
trench	n.	沟，战壕	
presumably	ad.	大概	
ass	n.	屁股；驴子	
warfare	n.	战争，冲突	
chuck	v.	抛掷	
crouching		蜷缩，蹲下	
pyramid	n.	角锥体	
sprinter	n.	短跑选手	
telegram	n.	电报	
douse	v.	弄熄；脱掉	
porridge	n.	粥	
bully	a.	一流的；特好的	
pin	v.	栓；压住	
champagne	n.	香槟	
shortcut	n.	捷径	
midget	n.	侏儒，矮人	
eyeful	n.	满眼，满眶	
crikey	int.	哎呀！（表惊讶的感叹语）	
nope	ad.	不；没有	
flask	n.	酒瓶	
bunker	n.	沙坑	
diversion	n.	转移	
secrecy	n.	保密，秘密	
fortress	n.	要塞	
point-blank	a.	断然的	
barrage	n.	弹幕	
bombardment	n.	轰炸，炮击	
morale	n.	士气，斗志	
ointment	n.	药膏	
lavender	a.	淡紫色的	
talcum	n.	滑石	
morphine	n.	吗啡	
chrome	n.	铬合金	
shelling	v.	去壳	
bayonet	n.	刺刀	

cease	v.	停止		colonel	n.	陆军上校
lure	v.	诱惑,引诱		gangway	int.	让路
damn	v.	谴责		knotty	a.	棘手的,难解决的
rifle	n.	步枪,来复枪		thy	a.	你的(旧)
stretcher	n.	担架		rod	n.	惩罚;权力

Exercises

1. **True or false judgments**
   (1) The Australian soldiers knew what they were doing before the war.
   (2) The Australians were eager to earn a reputation for themselves and their country.
   (3) The Australians possessed a strong sense of national identity in their hearts before the war.
   (4) At the beginning, Frank was not willing to join up because he was afraid of death.
   (5) Archy was hit by bullets because Frank arrived too late.
   (6) The major themes of the film are the loss of innocence and the coming of age of the Australian soldiers and of their country.

2. **Term interpretations**
   (1) the Light Horse   (2) Archy
   (3) Frank   (4) Barton
   (5) ANZAC   (6) AIF

3. **Essay questions**
   (1) Why were Australians so happy to join up?
   (2) What kind of army is AIF?
   (3) Why did the Australian troops die in such large numbers?
   (4) How did the battle of Gallipoli awake Australia's self-awareness of national identity?
   (5) What is the ANZAC spirit?

2.3 The Film *Kokoda*

The film *Kokoda* is a 2006 Australian film directed by Alister Grierson and is based on the real experiences of Australian troops fighting Japanese forces in the Kokoda Track, located in the rugged mountain areas of New Guinea. Hot, humid days with intensely cold nights and the risk of endemic tropical diseases such as malaria made fighting extremely hard.

Chapter 2
Australian National History

    The objective of the Japanese forces was to control the Kokoda Track and then invade the Australian mainland through the trail. Therefore, Australia had to launch a deadly battle with the Japanese in order to defend the country. From July to November in 1942, Australian soldiers fought the Japanese forces, first to keep them from reaching Port Moresby and then to push them back over the Owen Stanleys to their north coast strongholds at Buna, Gona, and Sanananda in appalling conditions. Australian forces, under-trained, under-provisioned, and under-equipped, finally beat battle-hardened Japanese soldiers to save Australia. More than 600 Australians were killed and some 1680 wounded during perhaps the most significant battle fought by Australians in World War II. As a result, within the collective Australian psyche, the campaign has become a key part of modern notions of the ANZAC legend.

    The film received 6 nominations: Two 2006 Australian Film Institute (AFI) nominations for best costume design and best visual effects, one nomination from the Film Critics Circle of Australia for best cinematography, and three from the Inside Film Awards (now known as the IF Awards) for best cinematography, best editing, and best production design. Some critics went so far as to say that *Kokoda* could be compared to Peter Weir's film *Gallipoli*.

2.3.1 Director Alister Grierson

    Alister Grierson (1969—) is an Australian film director and scriptwriter. He graduated from the Australian National University majoring in Economics and Arts and gained a Master of Arts in Directing at the Australian Film, Television, and Radio School (AFTRS), which is Australia's national screen arts and broadcasting school. This school is an Australian Commonwealth government statutory authority. He has shot 15 short films, winning three Tropfest awards, which is the world's largest short film festival. Tropfest has also become known as the world's first global film festival. Besides, being a director and writer, he is also famous for the films *Sanctum* (2011) and *Bomb* (2005).

2.3.2 Main Characters

(1) Max is a lance-corporal. During the battle, he is badly wounded by a gunshot and finally survives.
(2) Blue is a soldier of the 39th Battalion and is killed by the Japanese.
(3) Darko is a soldier of the 39th Battalion and sees the final victory.
(4) Jack is a soldier of the 39th Battalion and sees the final victory.
(5) Sam is a soldier of the 39th Battalion and is wounded during the battle.
(6) Johnno is a soldier of the 39th Battalion who suffers severe dysentery and is finally killed by the Japanese.
(7) Burke is a soldier of the 39th Battalion and is killed by the Japanese.

2.3.3 Plot

The story centers on an infantry section of the 39th Battalion. The soldiers of the 39th Battalion in the dense jungle are surrounded by Japanese forces. Their friend Blue is killed by a Japanese, which makes them hopeless and causes them to remain hidden until nightfall. Later they decide to make their way to Iurava, where another group of the 39th Battalion are fighting a desperate battle. The wounded Sam avoids troubling other soldiers, hiding himself in a hollow tree stump. After a serious fighting with the Japanese, Max is also wounded and is carried by all the men. Johnno has severe dysentery, and Max wants to stay with him at the New Guinea village. Jack, Darko, and Burke head off to Isurava. At the village, a few Japanese arrive and kill Johnno. When a New Guinea tribesman comes back to inspect the village, he finds a badly wounded Max in the hut. After a hard climb, Jack, Darko, and Burke arrive at Isurava with the help of the AIF.

One AIF officer asks for any available men from the 39th to help hold the line. Jack, Burke, and Darko volunteer and are assigned to a position held by men of the 2/16th Infantry. After a heavy fighting, the Japanese ended the assault and the battle is over. Burke sacrifices his life. The next day, Jack and Darko receive the news that they will be taken off the line. The Australians withdraw from Isurava to take up positions at Brigade Hill. Max is sent to an aid station and survives. The Japanese give up fighting. The Australian Infantry have saved their own country.

2.3.4 Theme Analysis

The film *Kokoda* describes the 1942 fight between Australian militiamen, or "chocos," from the 39th Battalion and the Imperial Japanese forces as part of the Pacific War of World War II in Papua, New Guinea. The Japanese forces intended to attack the Australian mainland. The Kokoda Track was a jungle pathway across the rugged mountains used to invade Australia. Australian soldiers, viewed as "chocos" and expected to melt in the heat of battle, are not regularly trained but rather, ill-equipped volunteers. Every day they were beset by tropical diseases. But it is during four months from July to November that these soldiers kept the Japanese from reaching Port Moresby, pushing them back over the Owen Stanleys until the AIF arrived to relieve them. The victory was not won easily. The film depicts an honest portrait of the young men who fulfill an almost impossible task.

During the battles, we can see the spirit of the old Australian concept—mateship among the soldiers. Sam is wounded and hides himself so as not to slow down others. Max is shot and carried by all. No one wants to leave him behind. When Johnno, with severe dysentery, cannot go further, Max decides to stay with him and let others continue their way. The spirit of mateship, which gives a helping hand to others when necessary or closely relies on each other for all sorts of help, has become the essence of the Australian spirit.

The victory of the Kokoda Track Campaign forced Japan to abandon its attempt to attack Australia. The Kokoda Track embodies the pride of Australians, which enhances national self-identity and loyalty to their own nation. Australia fought at Britain's side from the outset of World War I and World War II and came under attack from the Empire of Japan. These wars profoundly affected Australia's sense of nationhood, and a proud military legend developed around the spirit of Australia's ANZAC troops, who came to symbolize the virtues of mateship, courage, and endurance for the nation. We can conclude that from the failure of Gallipoli in the First World War to the victory of the Kokoda Track Campaign, Australian national identity went through a formative and intensifying process.

New Words

relentless	*a.*	不屈不挠的
fleet	*n.*	船队,舰队;车队
Pearl Harbour	*n.*	珍珠港
trail	*n.*	小路;路线;踪迹
colonel	*n.*	上校
relieve	*v.*	接替……的职位
melt	*v.*	融化
riddle	*v.*	使满是弹孔
malaria	*n.*	疟疾
quinine	*n.*	奎宁,金鸡纳霜（治疗疟疾等）
slaughter	*v.*	杀戮;屠宰
bloke	*n.*	〈俚〉家伙
quartermaster	*n.*	军需官
skipper	*n.*	队长;船长
rehab	*n.*	疗养院;康复

trench	n.	壕沟,战壕		pounce	v.	猛扑,突袭
charcoal	n.	木炭		spry	n.	(尤指老人)充满活力的
budge	v.	让步;改变主意				
miraculously	ad.	不可思议地;超自然地		convent	n.	女修道院
				seminary	n.	神学院
bastard	n.	坏蛋		heathen	n.	没有宗教信仰的人
creek	n.	小海湾;小河				
commissioner	n.	长官,要人		fella	n.	小伙子
repute	n.	名誉		wharf	n.	码头
copper	n.	警察;铜;铜币		battalion	n.	(陆军的)一营;一大群
patrol	n.	巡逻队				
bluff	n./v.	欺骗,虚张声势		stretch	v.	延伸;耗尽
juncture	n.	特定时刻,(尤指)重要关头		gallantry	n.	英勇;殷勤
				conviction	n.	坚定的信念;定罪
fallback	a.	退守的;备选的		exaltation	n.	兴奋,得意洋洋
stink	n.	臭味;(引人注意地)发怒		transcendent	a.	卓越的
				fiery	a.	熊熊燃烧的;(感情)激烈的
prick	n.	笨蛋;刺痛感				
ridge	n.	山脊		crucible	n.	熔炉,坩埚;严峻的考验
gut	n.	内脏;本能				
stretcher	n.	担架		fortitude	n.	刚毅,坚忍
ventilation	v.	使空气流通		rearguard	n.	后卫部队
dawdle	v.	闲逛		bloodshed	n.	杀戮,流血事件
scrounge	v.	索要;乞讨		retreat	n.	离开;(军队)撤退
ammo	n.	〈俚〉军火,武器		chisel	n.	凿子

Exercises

1. **True or false judgments**

   (1) Early on patrol, a camouflaged Japanese soldier slits the Lieutenant's throat, before tackling Wilstead, and is shot by Dan.

   (2) Blue was bayoneted in the eye by a Japanese soldier.

   (3) Jack was promoted as the Lance-corporal after the Lieutenant died.

   (4) After Max was badly wounded, his mates didn't give him up.

   (5) The number of Japanese soldiers was almost ten times as large as Australian soldiers.

   (6) Max was killed by the Indigenous people.

   (7) The injured chose to support the 39th instead of having a break from the action.

   (8) Jack didn't see Max again at the end of the film.

2. **Term interpretations**

   (1) the Kokoda Track campaign   (2) Jack
   (3) Max   (4) Blue

(5) the 39th Battalion (6) fuzzy-wuzzy angels
(7) Isurava
3. **Essay questions**
   (1) Why did Japan send its forces to capture the territory of New Guinea in the Second World War?
   (2) What kind of geographical conditions exist at the Kokoda Track, as shown in the film *Kokoda*?
   (3) What impressions does the film leave you of Australian soldiers?
   (4) What are the differences between the Gallipoli battle and the Kokoda Track Campaign in Australian national history?
   (5) What profound historical significance does the Kokoda Track campaign have?

2.4　Reading Passage: War and National Survival
by Stephen Alomes[①]

Having neither land borders nor linguistic or cultural boundaries, white Australia had lacked two of the main traditional forces for the creation of a sense of nationality. Although Australians had oddly tried to rectify this deficiency with exaggerated fears of invasion since the early 1800s, it was not until the 1940s that the threat of invasion became a real possibility. The beginning of a European war in September 1939 brought both traditional and new responses. Unlike Canada, which examined the situation for a week before committing itself, Australia immediately declared itself on Britain's side. Australia, Prime Minister Menzies[1] declaimed, was at war simply because Britain was at war. The twin drums[2] of proud Britishness and hatred of the Hun[3] had a familiar sound. Nor was geographical confusion missing from the rhetoric[4] as Menzies declared that "our frontiers were not only here but on the Rhine and on the east coast of England..."

Jingoism's appeal[5], however, had been weakened by the horrors of the Great War, horrors that had appropriately been symbolised by the Limbless Soldiers Ball[6] in the 1938 celebrations. Even Menzies found it to be his "melancholy duty" to make the announcement. Artist Norman Lindsay[7] drew not a violent cartoon, as in the Great War, but pictured "The Old Firm" of the soldier and the profiteer standing before a newsbanner reading "War—Business as Usua—Prices Up"[8]. The last quarter century had reduced popular support for an imperial dominion culture more than had been readily apparent on the eve of the war. Fears of Japan also reduced enthusiasm for a European war except for those Australian men, some unemployed, who saw in the army the prospects of income or work, service or adventure after the grey 1930[9].

The period of the "phoney war[10]", when little was happening in Europe, and the

---

① Stephen Alomes: Professor of School of History Heritage and Society, Faculty of Arts and Education, Deakin University, Victoria, Australia. "War and national survival" by Stephen Alomes. 1998. *National At Last? The Changing Character of Australian Nationalism 1880—1988* [M]. Sydney: Angus & Robertson. pp. 112—123.

delay in raising an Australian force contributed to a business-as-usual indifference towards the war well into 1940, despite the evocation of the Anzac tradition[11] by troop marches through the capital cities. Business, sport and entertainment went on as before, as one "patriot" lamented:

> What's the matter with the spirit of this nation ... has patriotism gone out of fashion?
> "The Empire is in deadly danger" means nothing to Bill Smith[12] with his safe job in the city, his surf over the weekends and "pitchers Sat'dee night[13]" ...
> Young Brown who joins up is a "mug"[14]; Young James who says he is not going to "rush into anything[15]" is regarded as shrewd and steady.

In these comfortable days of expeditionary war, sport and patriotism could be mixed: a AFL knockout competition[16] raised £2500; "La Marseillaise" was played at Randwick and the Sydney Cricket Groundas[17] a tribute to France. Despite a sense of continuity between the first and second AIF[18], the Empire mattered little to many Australians and after the Depression experience "looking after yourself first" seemed to have become the basic law of everyday life. It was to be an enduring principle in twentieth-century Australia.

Not until May 1940, when the German advance across Europe meant that Britain itself was under threat, did Australian imperial patriotism reappear with almost the dedication and vigour of twenty-five years before. The rhetoric of "Home"[19], both genuine and a product of imperial indoctrination, still had a compelling appeal. Imagesof British stoicism, of the dedication of the King and Queen and their two daughters, the British bulldog-like pugnacity of Churchill[20] and reports of bombing around the famed buildings of London all stimulated Australia's alleged Britishness. The rhetoric of the "British character" and "the British spirit" particularly appealed to preachers and editorialists, to politicians and older Australians who wished to return to the enthusiastic unity of 1914. Traditional loyalty or the opportunities for adventure or both did have an effect in increasing the flow of recruits for the new 7th Division.

The involvement of the 6th, 7th and 9th Divisions[21] in the Middle East and the Greece campaign in 1940—41 might have suggested a replica of World War 1 with ghosts of the Light Horse and Gallipoli. The Gallipoli disaster was also echoed in British blunders and defeats, including the retreat through Greece when Australian troops almost totally lacked air cover[22]. Events in the Pacific, however, were to make the role of "spear-carrier to the Chief" a superfluous colonial indulgence[23]. Japan's bombing of Pearl Harbour on 7 December 1941[24] reminded Australians that their country and their defence lay in the Pacific not in Europe, whatever their racial and cultural fantasies of Britishness.

The rapid Japanese advance into China and through South-East Asia in the following months posed the fundamental question of how Australia would be defended. Would the British play a traditional role through the Royal Navy and the Singapore base[25], or would Australia have to stand alone with a potentially large army but limited naval and air resources?

The sinking of the British battleships Prince of Wales and Repulse[26] three days after

Pearl Harbour and the revelation that the Singapore base (hitherto the imaginary keystone of Australian defence), had grossly inadequate fortifications made it clear that Britain would be of little, if any, help. On 8 December 1941 the Labour prime minister of just over two months, John Curtin[27], declared that "this is the gravest hour in our history" and appealed to Australians to face the challenge "with full vigour and courage." It was "our darkest hour"—"the nation itself is imperilled":

> Men and women of Australia, the call is to you for your courage, your physical and mental ability, your inflexible determination that we as a free people shall survive. My appeal to you is in the name of Australia, for Australia is the stake[28] in this contest.

Australia's first line of defence was not the Rhine or Afghanistan, South Africa or Suez, but the islands of the Dutch East Indies and NewGuinea to its north. The call was not to imperial jingoism but to the real national interest.

It was again the paradox of Australian nationalism that Australiandefence on the one occasion it mattered was, as before, conceived in relation to a Great Power. On 27 December Curtin made his call to the US. Recognising that to the British the war in the Pacific was of secondary importance—"Australia can go and Britain can still hold on"—he looked to America, "free of any pangs"[29] of traditional links of kinship with the UK, to ensure the defence of Australia. It was hard for a "loyal" colony to face reality. Many conservatives were disgusted. Menzies said that Curtin had made "a great blunder" if he thought that Australia's ties with Britain were merely "traditional," for they were "real and indissoluble." In hundreds of letters-to-the-editor, writers challenged Curtin. One asked of Australians, "Who lives if England dies?"declaring that "England is recognized the world over as the bulwark of democracy and freedom." The contradictions between imperial rule and democracy, between Britain's over-pressed forces and the demanding Pacific situation escaped this ardent idealist of Empire.

In practical terms, placing Australia's national interest firstmeant bringing back Australian army divisions from the Middle East to halt the rapid Japanese advance. Churchill reluctantly agreed that the 6th and 7th Divisions should return to Australia, the 9th remaining. When on the water, Churchill diverted the convoys to Burma without prior consultation. During an acrimonious exchange of cables Churchill cabled with headmasterly presumption "we could not contemplate that you would refuse our request and that of the President of the United Sates for diversion of the leading Australian division to Burma." Curtin did refuse, placing the defence of Australia before traditional loyalties to Great Powers. It was a rare occasion when the allegedly aggressive Australians actually stood up for themselves against a larger power.

Loyalty to Britain and the Empire could still blind some Australians to their own national interests. In London and Washington those servants of empire and nation S. M. Bruce, Earle Page and R. G. Casey[30] did not always see things from an Australian point of view; too often these "imperial statesmen" had a London, not a Canberra perspective. Page even offered written advice for Churchill's use in the dispute over the diversion of the 7th

Division and exercised direct censorship in handling messages from Canberra to London. H. V. Evatt, the Minister for External Affairs, condemned Page, who seemed to have acted in opposition to his instructions. He remarked to Bruce of the government's embarrassment at having "our decisions over AIF ignored," concluding that "you are out of touch with the home defence position here." In her excellent study of the role of the trio, F. J. Garner[31] cites another case of a failure to express government objections, this time to a London base for a proposed Far Eastern Council, although Bruce later revised his position. In Washington, R. G. Casey was another good boy scout for the Empire; he usually visited the US administration with the British ambassador; was more concerned with bringing America into the war (as Britain wanted) than with avoiding a Pacific war (as Australia wanted); did not pass on all relevant information to Canberra; and altered an Australian request to Roosevelt[32], also providing copies to the British chiefs of staff. When Australia was under immediate threat of invasion in March 1942, Casey, the lover of Empire and admirer of Churchill, chose—despite the Australian government's objections—to leave Washington to serve as the United Kingdom's minister of state in Cairo.

Given the servility of the imperial boy scouts, it might be asked whether Casey served his country well in making the move. The dutiful imperialists believed that the Australian government had, as Bruce explained it to Churchill, a "somewhat ill-advised and certainly irritation tone" due to inexperience in government. That cliche has often been repeated by the polite practitioners of foreign affairs commentary in Australia. Such views failed to recognise that the politesse of the English headmasterly style (with Australia cast in an obedient, respectful rule as during Niemeyer's visit[33] was inappropriate when Australia was under threat and Britain's interests were elsewhere. In Evatt's words[34] "the stage of gentle persuasion has passed." It is a sign of the conservative imperial deference of the foreign policy history community that the imperial boy scouts are usually seen as more effective than the impatient Labour larrikins. In reality they were honoured only with the job of opening the doors of the black limousines of Westminster[35], and it seems that they could not detect the courteous indifference with which they were being received.

In later years Bruce and Casey became English lords, and in his last days in office Menzies, now Sir Robert[36], anachronistically created a Churchill Trust. Both the honours and the trust symbolised traditional Australian middle-class upper-middle-class links to Britain. No Churchill Awards have been given for the study of Churchill's strategy in Greece, his focus on the Middle East or his stress on Burma. And John Curtin's role as saviour of Australia received no official recognition nor memorial.

The American role in the defence of Australia was significant, but it came slowly and with the terms that larger countries impose on smaller ones. Not until April 1942 was General Douglas MacArthur[37] appointed Supreme Commander for the South West Pacific, based in Australia. He arrived in Australia in characteristically regal fashion with a large entourage, setting himself up in the best of quarters in grand hotels. However, he brought more in the way of ego than troops in the first instance. The crucial early American role was in naval defence; the May 1942 and June 1942 Coral Sea and Midway victories ended Japan's naval dominance in the region, but it was also essential to rebuff the Japanese on land. In

August 1942 when Japanese troops were 80 kilometres from Port Moresby[38] and launching a seaborne attack on Milne Bay[39] at the south-east tip of New Guinea, the major defence role was Australian; 54,000 Australians and 30,000 Americans forced the Japanese back along the Kokoda Trail[40], and a small and almost entirely Australian force broke the assault on Milne Bay-the first defeat of Japanese land forces. Even in April 1943 there were four Australians fighting in the South West Pacific for every American, although this changed dramatically by 1944 when over half of the one million servicemen fighting in the area were American. Even in the short term, American demands were dramatic. MacArthur treated the Australian government and army with indifference if not veiled contempt, preferring the leadership of his own inexperienced officers to that of the battle-hardened Australians. During the Japanese retreat, Americans led the advancing forces, increasing US diplomatic and economic opportunities in any post war division of spoils.

In economic spheres too, the Americans looked after their own interests. America sought to weaken imperial preference and to extend American markets at the expense of Britain during the war. Under Lend Lease[41], an American-originated scheme to fund wartime production, Australia exported much primary produce to the US and imported secondary industry materials; in simple terms, from 1941—42 to 1944—45 over 40 per cent of Australian imports came from the US. The Americans rejected most Australian attempts to import industrial machinery for producing new defence equipment, preferring the traditional view of Australia as a farm in the larger scheme of things. In historian Michael Dunn's calculations, the Australian contribution to Lend Lease and to Reverse (or Reciprocal) Lend lease[42] was MYMA113 per head of population compared with MYM96 from the US and MYM84 from Britain. The industrialist Laurence Hartnett[43] noted that the American saw the Australian role as a traditional one of "growing food and supplying troops." The role of America in postwar Australia was being clearly signalled.

In popular historical myth, war is seen as a force for national unity, a force for nation-building. In Australia World War 2 can be seen as a total war which galvanised the nation into action, demanding the development of every scientific, economic, administrative and military resource. The contribution of the war to industry, to science and to communications helped develop secondary industry and government; it strengthened the federal government and further integrated the states into a larger national economy. The demands of a total war effort could only be made it a better Australia was promised in the future and indeed the war did stimulate a new sense of Australia as well as movements for social reform. Such myths, however, are often overstated. Wars, like depressions, bring more disunity than unity. World War II brought divisions between the middle class and working class; between profiteers and those whose everyday necessities were rationed; between civilians and soldiers; between American and Australian servicemen; between men and women over types of work and rates of pay; between older Australians and ethnic minorities; between workers, whose conditions occasionally drove them to absenteeism or to strikes, and middle-class patriots; between dreams of a better society and the images and reality of modern evil produced by the turmoil and corruption of war; and finally between the rhetoric of liberty and the often needless repression of opinion by the authorities.

Many middle-class Australians were displeased at the deprivations of the war. They were sure that they had a mortgage on patriotism[44]. One letter-to-the-editor writer from Neutral Bay in Sydney believed that rewards should follow from social position: "People of the middle-class do not feign superiority in the social sense, but claim, and rightly, recognition of, and proportionate recompense for, their greater contribution to the social order." One Toorak[45] lady was particularly miffed at losing her domestic servant. Could she carry on maintaining a large servantless house without neglecting her children and husband, or would the situation lead to a breakdown? She was answered by another mother, from north of the Yarra[46], with eight rather than two children, who did not seem to find life abnormally hard.

Earnest patriots who beat their breasts[47] in letters columns were sure that absentee women workers and striking workers are undermining the war effort. Their own comfortable situations did not allow them to understand the difficulties faced by women whose working hours had not been adjusted to allow for the demands of child-care, or the feelings of male or female workers worn down by sixty hours work per week in munitions factories. In Bishop E. H. Burgmann's words[48], "People who write letters about strikes make very few guns or bombs. We can at least give our gratitude to those who do." In the Blue Mountains[49] leisure resorts the hotels were full and one observer saw no "visible lack of golf and tennis balls and tennis shoes."

In a time of food and clothing rationing and of Manpower Regulations[50] which pressed workers into essential industries, neither the wealth of the Americans nor the corrupt wealth of the profiteers aided national morale. Americans received twice the pay of Australian soldiers and more generous food and alcohol allowances in their camps. While most Australian soldiers were fighting in the jungles of Asia, Americans in Australia had presents of chocolate, Coca-Cola and nylon stockings for Australian women. Their association with Hollywood stars meant that they were received with enthusiasm by many Australians dazzled by visitors from another world. On the other hand there was understandable resentment against these flash foreigners who seemed able to live so lavishly. American money also meant access to the black market-although American soldiers were not alone there. The world of profiteering disillusioned those Australians who were donating to patriotic appeals, subscribing to Victory Loans[51] and wearing their Austerity suits. But when all goods were in short supply, a Christmas present for the kids sometimes made the black market more appealing. It was not the stuff, however, of which a new social order was made.

The dangers, disruptions and dislocations of war generated changing sexual morals, greater juvenile freedom and sometimes delinquency. Sudden marriage, equally rapid divorce and marital infidelity became common as troops came and went from the war zones. The painters captured this new urban Australia. In Albert Tucker[52]'s *Night Image and Others* in his "Images of Modern Evil" series, in John Perceval[53]'s *Hornblower at Night* and in Arther Boyd's *St Kilda* paintings the end of Australian innocence was vividly, and alarmingly, depicted.

The instinct for survival aroused by wartime turbulence had national as well as individual expressions. In three spheres there was a new awareness and an attempted remarking of Australia. Firstly, there was a popular discovery of Australian life; it was nurtured both by the improvisation required by the war and by the organs of government publicity[54] which sought to build up national morale for the war effort. Secondly, and in a related way, intellectuals and critical commentators discovered Australia in its weaknesses as well as its strengths in their painting, writing and analysis. Thirdly, the reorganisation of government for the war effort was directed not only at immediate needs but at building the institutions of a modern nation and, in some respects, a better society. These areas of self-awareness and positive action were mirrored in a more nature and independent approach to foreign policy in the war years and after. In an uncharacteristically dramatic response, the engine of war motivated a new Australian nationalism, concerned not just with the rhetoric of national identity as in World War I, but rather with new definitions and perceptions of the role of Australia in the world and of the character and direction of Australian society.

Notes

[1] Prime Minister Menzies (1894—1978): Australian politician and the sixteenth Prime Minister of Australia. His second term saw him become Australia's longest serving Prime Minister.
[2] drum: emotion.
[3] Hun: Germany, and it is used here as a pejorative slang.
[4] Nor was geographical confusion missing from the rhetoric: the geographical descriptions were confusing.
[5] jingoism's appeal: great powers of Europe.
[6] the Limbless Soldiers Ball: a dance to raise money to help people who lost arms and legs in WWII.
[7] Artist Norman Lindsay (1879—1969): a prolific artist, sculptor, writer, editorial cartoonist and scale modeler, as well as being a highly talented boxer.
[8] War—Business as Usual—Prices Up: a headline.
[9] the grey 1933: the Great Depression of 1930s.
[10] the "phoney war": the name given to the period of time in World War Two from September 1939 to April 1940 when, after the blitzkrieg attack on Poland in September 1939, seemingly nothing happened. Many in Great Britain expected a major calamity—but the title "Phoney War" sums up what happened in Western Europe—near enough nothing.
[11] the Anzac tradition: ANZAC stands for Australian and New Zealand Army Corps. On 25 April every year, Australians commemorate ANZAC Day. It commemorates the landing of Australian and New Zealand troops at Gallipoli on 25 April 1915. The date, 25 April, was officially named ANZAC Day in 1916.
[12] Bill Smith: an ordinary man.
[13] pitchers Sat'dee night: pictures or movies in a Saturday night.

〔14〕 Young Brown who joins up is a "mug": Young Brown who joins up in the army is regarded as an idiot.

〔15〕 "rush into anything": in a hurry to join up the army.

〔16〕 a AFL knockout competition: the Australian Football League competition.

〔17〕 "La Marseillaise" was played at Randwick and Sydney Cricket Ground a tribute to France. "La Marseillaise": the national anthem of France. Randwick: a suburb in south-eastern Sydney, in the state of New South Wales, Australia. The Sydney Cricket Ground (SCG): a sports stadium in Sydney.

〔18〕 the first and second AIF: The First Australian Imperial Force (1st AIF): the main expeditionary force of the Australian Army during World War I. The Second Australian Imperial Force (2nd AIF) was the name given to the volunteer personnel of the Australian Army in World War II.

〔19〕 "home": Britain.

〔20〕 Churchill (1874—1965): a British politician known chiefly for his leadership of the United Kingdom during World War II. He served as Prime Minister of the United Kingdom from 1940 to 1945 and again from 1951 to 1955.

〔21〕 the 6th, 7th, and 9th Divisions: The 6th Division of the Australian Army: a unit in the Second Australian Imperial Force (2nd AIF) during World War II. It served in the North African campaign, the Greek campaign and the New Guinea campaign, including the crucial battles of the Kokoda Track, among others. The 7th Division of the Australian Military Forces was raised in February 1940 to serve in World War II, as part of the Second Australian Imperial Force (2nd AIF). The 9th Division: a division of the Australian Army that served during World War II.

〔22〕 air cover: protective use of military aircraft during ground operations.

〔23〕 the role of "spear-carrier to the Chief" a superfluous colonial indulgence: chief's enforcer.

〔24〕 Pearl Harbour on 7 December 1941—The attack on Pearl Harbor, the Battle of Pearl Harbor by some Americans, was a surprise military strike conducted by the Imperial Japanese Navy against the United States naval base at Pearl Harbor, Hawaii on the morning of December 7, 1941. It resulted in the United States' entry into World War II.

〔25〕 the Royal Navy and the Singapore base: the oldest of the British armed services. From the mid-18th century to the middle of the 20th century, it was the most powerful navy in the world, playing a key part in establishing the British Empire as the dominant world power from 1815 until the early 1940s. The Singapore naval base was built and supplied to sustain a siege long enough to enable Britain's European-based fleet to reach the area. By 1940, however, it was clear that the British fleet and armed forces were fully committed in Europe and the Middle East and could not be spared to deal with a potential threat in Asia.

〔26〕 the British battleships Prince of Wales and Repulse: a World War II naval engagement which illustrated the effectiveness of aerial attacks against naval forces that were not protected by air cover and the resulting importance of including an aircraft carrier in

any major fleet action.
[27] John Curtin (1885—1945): Australian politician and 14th Prime Minister of Australia, led Australia when the Australian mainland came under direct military threat during the Japanese advance in World War II. He is widely regarded as one of the country's greatest Prime Ministers.
[28] in stake: in danger.
[29] "free of any pangs": without pain.
[30] S. M. Bruce, Earle Page and R. G. Casey: regarded as the trio in WWI in Australia—S. M. Bruce (1883—1967): businessman, prime minister and public servant. Earle Page (1880—1961): Australian politician, was the eleventh Prime Minister of Australia, and is to date the second-longest serving federal parliamentarian in Australian history with 41 years, 361 days in Parliament. R. G. Casey (1890—1976): an Australian politician, diplomat and 16th Governor-General of Australia.
[31] F. J. Garner: Australian commentator.
[32] Roosevelt (1882—1945): the thirty-second President of the United States. He was a central figure of the 20th century during a time of worldwide economic crisis and world war. Elected to four terms in office, he served from 1933 to 1945 and is the only U. S. president to have served more than two terms.
[33] Niemeyer's visit—Sir Otto ErnstNiemeyer (1883—1971): financial controller at the Treasury and a director at the Bank of England. He was also treasurer of the National Association of Mental Health (UK) post World War II. In July 1930, during Australia's Great Depression, he travelled to Melbourne to advise James Scullin's government. There, he devised the "Niemeyer statement," a monthly statement of commonwealth government financial transactions.
[34] Evatt (1894—1965): the Minister for External Affairs, politician and writer. He was President of the United Nations General Assembly in 1948—49 and helped draft the United Nations Universal Declaration of Human Rights (1948). He was leader of the Australian Labor Party from 1951 to 1960.
[35] the black limousines of Westminster: 威斯敏斯特的黑色豪华轿车。
[36] Sir Robert: Sir Robert Gordon Menzies.
[37] General Douglas MacArthur (1880—1964): an American general and Field Marshal of the Philippine Army. He was a Chief of Staff of the United States Army during the 1930s and later played a prominent role in the Pacific theater of World War II.
[38] Port Moresby: the capital and largest city of Papua New Guinea (PNG). The city is located on the shores of the Gulf of Papua, on the southeastern coast of the island of New Guinea.
[39] Milne Bay: a large bay in Milne Bay Province, southeastern Papua New Guinea. The area was a site of the Battle of Milne Bay in 1942. The bay is named after Sir Alexander Milne.
[40] the Kokoda Trail: a single-file foot thoroughfare in a straight line—through the Owen Stanley Range in Papua New Guinea (PNG). The track is the most famous in PNG and is renowned as the location of the World War II battle between Japanese and Australian

forces in 1942.

〔41〕 Lend Lease(租借法案): the name of the program under which the United States of America supplied the United Kingdom, the Soviet Union, China, France and other Allied nations with vast amounts of war material between 1941 and 1945 in return for, in the case of Britain, military bases in Newfoundland, Bermuda, and the British West Indies.

〔42〕 Reverse (or Reciprocal) Lend Lease: a reciprocal aid agreement of the United States with Great Britain, Australia, New Zealand, and the Free French was announced. Under its terms a "reverse lend-lease" was affected, whereby goods, services, shipping, and military installations were given to American forces overseas. Other nations in which U. S. forces were stationed subsequently adhered to the agreement.

〔43〕 the industrialist Laurence Hartnett (1898—1986): an engineer who made several important contributions to the Australian automotive industry.

〔44〕 a mortgage on patriotism: to make subject to a claim or risk.

〔45〕 Toorak: a suburb of Melbourne, Victoria, Australia.

〔46〕 Yarra: an inner Melbourne municipality.

〔47〕 beat their breasts: angry.

〔48〕 Bishop E. H. Burgmann (1885—1967): Anglican bishop and social critic.

〔49〕 the Blue Mountains: a section of the Main Western railway line in New South Wales, Australia. It serves the Blue Mountains region to the west of Sydney.

〔50〕 Manpower Regulations: a notice of regulations comprising of a cream cardboard rectangle, printed on one side with black and filled-in with blue typing. The notice is titled "National Security (Man Power) Regulations 1943" and the regulations have been issued from the "Director-General of Man Power."

〔51〕 Victory Loans: government appeals for money to finance the war effort in WWI and WWII. The first domestic war loan was raised in November 1915, but not until the fourth campaign of November 1917 was the term "Victory Loan" applied.

〔52〕 Albert Tucker (1914—1999): an Australian artist, pivotal in the development of 20th century Australian Expressionist painting.

〔53〕 John Perceval (1923—2000): Australian painter and potter. He was one of a group of artists who brought radical innovations of style and subject-matter to Australian painting in the 1940s.

〔54〕 the organs of government publicity: organizations or institutions which promote the government's work. 政府宣传机构。

New Words

rectify	v.	矫正,调整	rhetoric	n.	花言巧语
cliche	n.	陈词滥调	larrikin	n.	恶棍
deficiency	n.	不足,缺乏	jingoism	n.	沙文主义
obedient	a.	服从的	limousine	n.	轿车

appeal	n.	吸引力,要求
detect	v.	发现,察觉
melancholy	a.	忧郁的,悲伤的
anachronistically	ad.	时代错误地
newsbanner = poster	n.	海报,招贴
saviour	n.	救助者
phoney	a.	骗人的
regal	a.	帝王的
lament	v.	悲哀,悲伤
entourage	n.	随从
surf	n.	海浪
rebuff	v.	回绝
mug = idiot	n.	傻瓜
seaborne	a.	海运的
shrewd	a.	精明的
veil	v.	盖住
	n.	面罩
indoctrination	n.	灌输,教导
galvanise	v.	刺激
preacher	n.	传道人
ration	v.	配发
recruit	v.	征募新兵
turmoil	n.	混乱
replica	n.	复制品
repression	n.	镇压,压抑
grossly	ad.	大略
displease	v.	使生气
fortification	n.	防御工事,要塞
deprivation	n.	剥夺
imperil	v.	危害
mortgage	v.	抵押
imperial	a.	帝王的
feign	v.	假装
paradox	n.	自相矛盾
proportionate	a.	成适当比例的
conceive	v.	考虑,构思
recompense	n.	报酬
blunder	n.	大错
mif	v.	发脾气
indissoluble	a.	不能分解的
resort	n.	常去之地
bulwark	n.	壁垒
nylon	n.	尼龙
ardent	a.	热烈的,热心的
dazzle	v.	使目眩,使眼花
halt	v.	停止,踌躇
flash	a.	浮华的
divert	v.	转向,转移
disillusion	v.	醒悟
acrimonious	a.	严厉的
subscribe	v.	订阅
cable	n.	电缆
juvenile	a.	青少年的
headmasterly	ad.	监督地
delinquency	n.	行为不正
presumption	n.	假定
marital	a.	婚姻的
contemplate	v.	注视,沉思
depict	v.	描述
allegedly	ad.	依其申述
turbulence	n.	骚乱
aggressive	a.	好斗的,有侵略性的
improvisation	n.	即席创作
condemn	v.	谴责;处刑
perception	n.	理解,感觉
trio	n.	三人组
pragmatism	n.	实用主义
scout	n.	侦察
encroachment	n.	侵犯
servility	n.	卑屈
equator	n.	赤道

Exercises

1. **True or false judgments**
   (1) Prime Minister Menzies called for Australians to join the Second World War, because Britain was at war.
   (2) Most Australian men responded rapidly to Prime Minister Menzies' call.
   (3) John Curtin turned to the US for help in one of the milestones of Australian history, and finally he received his official recognition from Churchill's Awards.
   (4) S. M. Bruce, Earle Page and R. G. Casey are regarded as the imperial Boy Scouts in following British policy and showing their loyalty to Britain.
   (5) MacArthur demonstrated his strong love for Australia after he arrived in this Southern continent.
   (6) After the Second World War, Australia entered the economic boom, but the social divisions began to emerge.

2. **Essay questions**
   (1) What were Australians' reactions to the prospect of a Second World War in only a short period after the first one?
   (2) What characterized Australian relations with Britain and America during World War II?
   (3) What were some of the effects of World War II on Australia?

Part Two
Australian Multiculturalism

Australian history can be traced back to Aboriginal and Torres Strait Islander peoples, who inhabited the oldest landmasses for an estimated 60,000 years. Australia's European history is short. Its European settlement was established in 1788 by Great Britain. Australia's particular history has determined its cultural features. Australian culture includes the white culture as an Anglo-Celtic core, the Aboriginal culture and the immigrant culture. Most Australians today are immigrants or descendants of immigrants. Australia is home to citizens from some 200 countries, making it the most multilingual workforce in the Asia-Pacific region. Australian culture has grown to be one of the most diverse cultures in the world. It is a multicultural nation. In the 21st century, this country is viewed as a stable, diverse and democratic society with a skilled workforce and a strong, competitive economy.

By 1970, the word "multiculturalism" had been introduced from Canada. Now it has progressed to the point where it is central to Australian society. Australian multiculturalism summarizes the way the nation deals with the challenges of its diversity. It accepts and respects the right of all Australians to express and share their individual cultural heritage. Today the success of Australian multiculturalism has deep roots in Australian history.

The history of multiculturalism in Australia reflects a journey. From 1901 to the mid-1960s, Australian culture experienced a stage of cultural assimilation, a monocultural phase based on the "Anglo-Celtic" core culture. To Aboriginal people, Australia implemented the "purifying" or "breeding out" policy so as to maintain its racial purity. Aboriginal children as "half-castes" were removed from their families to receive Christian training in a re-education camp to prepare them for lives as domestic servants and turn them into white. To the immigrants from non-European countries, the government imposed a poll-tax (Zhang Xianping, 2007: 255—256). Meanwhile, all non-European immigrants were expected to assimilate to an English-speaking society.

In the 1960s, with immigrants pouring in, Australia started to adopt an integration policy in the migrant settlement. The living conditions of immigrants were improved and expenditure on migrant assistance and welfare increased (Reynolds, 1987: 84—99). The Australian government advocated a view of mutual respect and understanding.

After the 1970s, Australia entered a stage of multiculturalism. In general, encouraging multiculturalism has been a bipartisan policy. It is a collective phenomenon of shared meanings within a community of mutual understanding. Immigrants from over 200 countries in the world have settled in Australia bringing their own languages, cultures and religions, which are reflected on the streets, at schools, at football stadiums. They have experienced the processes of cultural shock, conflict, adaptation, reconciliation, and finally gained their identity as Australians. Today being an Australian is to be accepting of other people and other cultures. No one feels that he is an outsider because everyone is so different. Every immigrant is considered a cultural outsider. To be a good citizen of this diverse nation is to have the skills to deal with difference. This is consistent with a dominant concept that Australian national identity embraces multiculturalism (Moran, 2011: 134—167).

Multiculturalism has served a variety of goals over the past 50 years, including the pursuit of social justice, the recognition of identities, the integration of migrants, appreciation of diversity, and maintenance of social cohesion. In this part, we will analyze how Australian multiculturalism is constructed and how immigrants struggle to find themselves in the process of cultural conflicts and cultural integration through four Australian cultural movies: *Crocodile Dundee* (1986), *Looking for Alibrandi* (2000), *Strictly Ballroom* (1992), and *The Castle* (1997). Successful films are often taken as evidence that a mature, sophisticated Australian culture has arrived. Australian cinema plays a major role in creating images of national identity (Carter, 2006: 190).

Chapter 1
Cultural Clash

Cultural clash is a type of conflict that occurs when different cultural values and beliefs encounter. Differences in cultural values and beliefs place people at odds with one another. Different cultures are like underground rivers that run through the lives and relationships of people, giving them messages that shape their perceptions, attributes, judgments, and ideas of self and others (Duryea Michelle LeBaron, 1993: 105).

1.1 Background

The first cultural film, *Crocodile Dundee*, reveals cultural conflicts, between a stereotypical Australian bushman, naïve but honest, and American brash New York arrogance. It is a conflict between two forms of national identity, the Australian down to earth (bush legend) and the American (big city) over confidence. This is a cultural conflict between two Anglophone countries, showing how national identities are different and can come into conflict.

In the film *Crocodile Dundee*, the two following backgrounds deserve further explanations. One is the crocodile. Many plots revolve around this Australian endemic animal. Crocodiles live in lakes, swamps and the upstream areas of small rivers. The bigger and aggressive saltwater crocodile attacks people with its sharp teeth, inflicting serious wounds (Johnson, 2009: 181). In the Australian outback, bushmen like Dundee are crocodile hunters, good at handling saltwater crocodiles. Dundee himself once survived a vicious crocodile attack in the bush, which aroused the interest of the New York Newspaper reporter, Sue. Another natural scene depicted in the film is typical Australian outback or the bush, which is a vast, and remote interior area in Australia. Although often called the bush, the outback refers to the areas which are more remote than those called the bush. Both are far away from urban areas. Whether called the outback or the bush, the soil is arid and dry with poor vegetation. From a cultural perspective, the outback is deeply ingrained in Australian heritage, history and folklore (Lewis, 2005). Dundee, as a crocodile hunter, is full of bush cultural qualities: honest, good-hearted, and humorous. Sue, as a professional woman, is full of metropolitan superiority and cultural confidence.

Chapter 1
Cultural Clash

1.2　The Film *Crocodile Dundee*

Crocodile Dundee is a 1986 Australian-American comedy film set both in the Australian outback and in New York City. The film does not only tell a romantic story between Sue and Dundee, but also reveals the changing process from cultural conflict, cultural adaptation and cultural tolerance between the bush and the metropolitan cultures. When Sue reaches the remote areas of the outback, she is amazed at the native wildlife and surprised by bushmen subduing them. The outback's cultural environment makes her tense and worried. Obviously, she is not used to this life. With the help of Dundee, she gradually understands the outback and gets along with Dundee's friends like Walter and the Aboriginal people.

When Dundee is in New York City, he encounters many unfamiliar city affairs from the very beginning. He is perplexed by local behaviors and customs. He greets the New Yorkers on seeing them, but no one responds to him, feeling he is strange and different. At night clubs, due to his different way of treating people, he is attacked by wrongdoers. After conflicts and adaptations, he overcomes problematic situations including two encounters with a pimp and two attempted robberies. Many New Yorkers tend to respect him, and he also makes friends with them. Sue realizes her true feelings for him, and selects him as her boyfriend rather than Richard, a New York gentleman.

Dundee and Sue can appreciate each other and tolerate their different cultures. The love between them transcends the cultural boundaries and complexities.

1.2.1　Director Peter Faiman

Peter Faiman (1944—　) is an Australian film director, producer, and coordinating director for the opening and closing broadcasts of the Sydney 2000 Olympic Games.

He worked in the UK as creative and management consultant for BSkyB and in the USA for the Fox Network as Vice President of Fox Circle Productions and later as President of

Programing and Production for 20th Century Fox Television. These accomplishments earned him much acclaim.

Faiman directed the 1986 blockbuster film *Crocodile Dundee*, which was a world-wide hit. The Dundee "phenomenon" attracted the attention of the audience. Before *Crocodile Dundee* was released, Americans knew little about Australia and its bush. It is this film that aroused Americans' interest in the Australian outback.

1.2.2 Main Characters

(1) Michael Dundee is a bushman and crocodile hunter. He is invited by Sue to visit New York, which is a totally different environment from the Australian outback. He is welcomed by New Yorkers. Finally he and Sue fall in love.
(2) Sue Charlton is a feature writer for the New York newspaper, *Newsday*. She corresponds with Dundee in the Australian outback and is attracted to him later. Out of gratitude, she invites Dundee to visit New York City.
(3) Richard Mason is Sue's boyfriend and colleague at *Newsday*.
(4) Walter Reilly is Dundee's business partner in the Australian outback. He is also Dundee's teacher and friend.

1.2.3 Plot

Sue, a feature writer for the New York newspaper *Newsday*, travels to the Australian outback to report about Mick "Crocodile" Dundee who survives a crocodile attack as an Australian bushman. After she arrives in the outback, she is amazed to see with her own eyes Dundee subduing a water buffalo and killing a snake with his bare hands. She admires Dundee and tries to go out in the bush alone to show she is also brave. Dundee follows her secretly. When she approaches a billabong, a large crocodile attacks her. At this dangerous moment, Dundee comes and rescues Sue.

Out of gratitude, Sue invites Mick to visit New York City. Once in New York, Dundee is troubled by local behaviors. What's more, Sue's boyfriend Richard treats Dundee rudely. New Yorkers think Dundee is strange. With good adaptability and adjustability, Dundee handles problematic situations. What Dundee does in New York City deeply moves Sue. Finally, they kiss each other.

At a dinner party, Richard proposes marriage to Sue openly. Dundee is sad and leaves the party early. Sue changes her mind, deciding not to marry Richard but Dundee. When Dundee is at the subway station, ready to leave New York City, Sue hurries to the subway and expresses her love to this bushman.

1.2.4 Theme Analysis

Crocodile Dundee reveals three cultural processes, that is, cultural conflict, cultural adaptation, and cultural tolerance. The film is set in the Australian outback and in New York City. The two places possess totally different cultures.

First, the story starts by developing a picture of cultural conflicts. When Sue, a New

York newspaper reporter, arrives at Walkabout Creek, she is not used to the life in the wild bush. What impresses her deeply is that bushmen are rude and clumsy. They get drunk and fight at the local pub. Meanwhile, Dundee is not as legendary as she imagined before she arrives. Sue gets into trouble when cast into an unfamiliar outback. She believes that a woman can live alone as well as a man in the outback, but when she is really alone, stopping by the river, she is attacked by a large crocodile, making her frightened. Dundee in New York City is shocked by the local behaviors and customs. Despite his expert knowledge of living outdoors, he knows little of city life. He greets New Yorkers on the streets, and is ignored. At New York night clubs, he is laughed at because of his "strange" way of greeting people. Both characters experience cultural shock and cultural misfit when confronted with the different cultural values and beliefs.

Secondly, Sue and Dundee try to keep an open mind when facing the different cultural environments, learn to adapt, and try to accept them. In the wild bush, Sue is amazed by Dundee's skills of killing a snake with his bare hands. She becomes acquainted with the Aboriginal people, enjoying their tribal dance ceremony. Sue begins to eat raw food in the outback. The bushmen impress her deeply. They are honest, humorous and warm-hearted. While in New York City, Dundee would like to learn how to open the TV set at the hotel room and study how to use a bidet which he has never seen in his life. Gradually, Dundee becomes used to talking at night clubs. He is eager to help others in need, which wins him respect and appreciation. Cross-cultural adaptation or accommodation is a process of changing perspectives and reconciling values of people.

Lastly, the film *Crocodile Dundee* shows us the process of cultural understanding and tolerance. At the very beginning, when Sue meets Dundee at the local pub, she thinks Dundee is rude. Dundee pulls her up to dance without inviting. She is moved by him for the first time when sue is saved by him from the attack of a large crocodile. In New York City where she is threatened by robbers on the street, Dundee comes in time to drive them away. She kisses Dundee and is touched by him for the second time. At the family banquet, Sue agrees to marry Richard, but later she changes her decision and chooses Dundee. She chases Dundee to the subway station to express her love after Dundee decides to leave New York City. Sue and Dundee with different cultural backgrounds finally fall in love and get together in the end. Both of them overcome all obstacles. Love can not only transcend the cultural boundaries but also goes beyond race.

New Words

terrific	a.	极好的	walkabout	n.	(澳洲土著)短期丛林流浪
crocodile	n.	鳄鱼			
territory	n.	领域;领土	creek	n.	小溪
crawl	v.	爬行	nail	v.	钉;使固定
safari	n.	旅行	arrangement	n.	安排

chopper	v.	乘直升机飞行
assure	v.	保证；担保
spill	v.	溢出；漏出
breed	n.	种类
reserved	a.	高冷的；话不多
legend	n.	传奇
giant	a.	巨大的
toe	n.	脚趾
snake-infested	a.	布满蛇的
swamp	n.	沼泽
bugger	n.	家伙
stuffed	a.	假的
exaggeration	n.	夸大
harsh	a.	严酷的
mighty	a.	强有力的，强大的
reckon	v.	猜想；认为
poacher	n.	偷猎者
tribal	a.	部落的
bushman	n.	居住于丛林地的人
ashore	a.	在岸上的
sheila	n.	小姐；姑娘
ledge	n.	暗礁
jam	n.	困境
tenderize	v.	使肉嫩化
grip	v.	抓住
rebel	v.	反抗
march	v.	示威游行
anti-nuke	n.	反核人士
women's lib	n.	妇女运动
ratbag	n.	怪人
protest	v.	抗议
roam	v.	漫步
rifle	n.	步枪
spotlight	v.	聚光照明
cheeky	a.	无耻的
rugged	a.	崎岖的
emptiness	n.	空虚
escarpment	n.	悬崖
skin	v.	剥皮
scratch	n.	擦伤
septic	a.	败血症的；流脓的
sneak	v.	偷偷地做
render	v.	实施
scrub	v.	擦洗
corroboree	n.	土人的夜间祭祀；狂欢会
spirit	n.	灵魂
lens	n.	镜头
taboo	v.	禁止
turnout	n.	到场人数
telepathic	a.	心灵感应术的
busybody	n.	爱管闲事的人
goner	n.	已死者
apostle	n.	使徒，信徒
mineral	n.	富含矿物质的
poke	v.	刺，捅
goanna	n.	巨蜥
yam	n.	甘薯
grub	n.	幼虫
fella	n.	伙伴
wrap	n.	外套
horizon	n.	视野
stunning	a.	极好的
backwoods	n.	偏僻的森林地区
riot	n.	暴乱
dial	v.	拨号
nitwit	n.	傻子
dunny	n.	〈澳〉厕所
bidet	n.	坐浴盆
novelty	n.	新奇的事物
gent	n.	（假）绅士
gourmet	n.	美食家
lash	v.	讽刺

Chapter 1
Cultural Clash

boozer	n.	酒馆
widow	n.	寡妇
froth	v.	吐白沫
lizard	v.	蜥蜴
flat out	v.	竭尽全力;疲惫
lonesome	a.	寂寞的
hanker	v.	向往;追求
swear	v.	发誓
dopey	a.	迟钝的,呆笨的
pelican	n.	鹈鹕
pepper	n.	胡椒粉
sauerkraut	n.	一种德国泡菜
encounter	v.	遇到
hardhearted	a.	无情的,心肠硬的
sniff	v.	嗅;用力吸
buzz	n.	嗡嗡声;迷乱状态
shove	v.	挤,猛推
bonzer	a.	优秀的,极好的
cattle	n.	牲畜
buffalo	n.	水牛
lunatic	n.	疯子
asylum	n.	收容所,救济院
uptight	a.	心情焦躁的
psychiatrist	n.	精神病医生
liquor	n.	酒
medicinal	a.	药用的,治疗的
hop	v.	跳跃

Exercises

1. **True or false judgments**
   (1) The journalist Sue Charlton arrives at Australia by train.
   (2) Walter Reilly is Mr. Dundee's business partner.
   (3) In the bush, the time and date are not of vital importance.
   (4) Sue invites Mick to return with her to New York City.
   (5) Dundee greets strangers warmly on New York streets, and they respond to him warmly in return.
   (6) Richard attempts to make a fool of Dundee at the Italian restaurant.
   (7) Richard's proposal to Sue at the party is refused.
   (8) Dundee leaves the hotel and decides to go walkabout without telling Sue.

2. **Term interpretations**
   (1) Dundee   (2) Sue
   (3) Richard   (4) Walter
   (5) Walkabout Creek   (6) *Newsday*

3. **Essay questions**
   (1) Why does Sue insist on going to Australia?
   (2) What do Australian bushmen look like in Sue's eyes after she is about to leave Australia?
   (3) How does Sue fall in love with Dundee?
   (4) Describe a plot set in New York City reflecting Dundee's conflicts with New York's local culture.
   (5) Is Dundee similar to Sue's boyfriend Richard in personality? State in detail.

1.3 Reading Passage: Cultural Attitudes and Aussie Communicative Style

by Cliff Goddard[1]

This section reviews a selection of values and attitudes which influence traditional Aussie communicative style. Needless to say, it is not exhaustive. One purpose of this reviewis to establish some of the more obvious and distinctive characteristics of the Aussie speech culture, in implicit contrast with major English-speaking countries such as the USA and Britain. In choosing specific topics, however, I have kept one eye on the matter of deadpan jocular irony[1], and we will see in due course that most of the following discussion bears directly or indirectly on that more subtle practice.

"Thou shalt not try to be better than others."

Many commentators have identified something like "egalitarianism"[2] as an Australian social ideal, and despite the widening gap between rich and poor, most commentators recognize that an "egalitarianism of manners," to use historian John Hirst's[3] phrase, is still an important part of Australian social life. Needless to say, however, a sophisticated label like this represents the perspective of a sophisticated outsider, the perspective of a sociologist, a historian or a political scientist. A description which comes closer to an insider's perspective, because it is framed in terms which are recognizable to insiders, is offered by Donald Horne in his classic work The Lucky Country[4]. "Australians like people to be ordinary," Horne says. They have "a deep belief in the essential sameness and ordinariness of mankind." "They think that all people are the same, that what is good for oneself is good for anyone else," even to the point that "they seek similarity where often it does not exist—even among themselves." Sharp[5] illustrates this attitude by way of an incident in 1991. The then prime minister Bob Hawke[6] was interviewed for television in the back of his limousine. Unfortunately for him, viewers could plainly see that he had neglected to fasten his seatbelt, as is compulsory under Australian law. The switchboard was jammed with more than 1000 calls. Sharp explains Hawke's reaction and the aftermath:

> He said he was very sorry and asked the police to treat him like any other citizen. He was duly fined AMYM100 for his lapse. In some societies, such public criticism would be unthinkable. But Australians were quite happy to put the matter out of their minds once justice had been done, the leader leveled. Besides, they prefer their leaders that way: ordinary men, capable of peccadillos.

---

[1] Cliff Goddard: Chair in Linguistics, School of Behavioral, Cognitive and Social Sciences; Language and Cognition Research Centre, University of New England, New South Wales, Australia. "Cultural attitudes and Aussie communicative style" by Cliff Goddard. 2006. "Lift your game Martina!": Deadpan Jocular Irony and the Ethnopragmatics of Australian English. In C. Goddard (ed.). *Ethnopragmatics: Understanding Discourse in Cultural Context* [M]. Berlin: MOUTON DE Gruyter. pp. 65—99.

Chapter 1
Cultural Clash

Wierzbicka[7] has proposed the simple cultural script[8] in [A] to capture the core idea.

[A] A cultural script for a characteristically Aussie social attitude

People think like this: it is good if other people can think like this about a person: "This person is someone like me."

The attitude portrayed in [A] is only the beginning, however. Wierzbicka argues that there is a suite of[9] related attitudes, which can be captured in related cultural scripts. For example, since "being like other people" is socially desirable it follows that thinking of oneself as better than others, and hence as not like others, will be disapproved of. This distaste for feeling of self-importance can be stated as in script [B1]. Taking things a step further, it is only natural that any one appears to want other people to think that he or she is superior and unlike others will be disapproved of as stated in script [B2].

[B1] An Aussie cultural script discouraging feelings of self-importance

People think like this:

It is bad if someone thinks like this:

"I am someone very good

I am not like other people"

[B2] An Aussie cultural script discouraging wanting other people's admiration

People think like this:

It is bad if someone thinks like this:

"I want other people to think like this about me:

'this person is someone very goodthis person is not like other people'"

As one would expect from this set of scripts, conspicuous self-promotion, efforts to impress, or merely seeking recognition of one's special achievements are likely to win only scorn in the Aussie ethos (cf. Peeters[10] on the "tall poppy syndrome"[11]), while conversely efforts at modesty and self-deprecation are admired.

The Australian humorist Robert Treborlang (originally from Hungary) has satirized the "Low Key" style of self-presentation as follows:

Low key has to do with pretending that you're a lot less than what others think you are (if this is possible)... Achievements, assets, attitudes, should only be referred to with badly constructed... you know... lots of punctuation marks... sort of ... obliquely... and how can one put it... Ambition must also be heavily played down[12] and its hard-earned fruit should always be attributed to... err... luck?

There is lexical evidence for the validity of these and related scripts in the existence of, on the one hand, colloquial pejorative terms such as wanker, smartarse and big head, negative speech act verbs[13] such as big-noting oneself, and descriptors such as up oneself, on oneself, and uppity; and on the other hand, positive social categories such as mate and mateship, and solidarity practices such as altered surnames (like Thommo for Thompson, Gibbo for Gibson) and "anti-diminutive" first name forms, such as Shaz for Sharon, Lozaa for Laurie, and so on.

There are of course numerous behavioral implications. McFayden[14] includes "thou shalt not try to be better than others" as one of his three "Australian cultural commandments"[15], and Sharp has a similar observation: "The Australian does not want to appear too good at what he or she does, lest this in some way offend or put down other people around him or her." According to Sharp, this helps explain why "an Australian worker will sometimes look and sound much less competent or professional than he really is." Her advice to new comers: "Remember, you must play the game if you are to get on with Australians. If you are successful or intelligent, hide it, or at least actively play it down."

Beal suggests that the "egalitarian" ideal helps explain a notable tendency she found in Australians' responses to the typically Australian Monday morning routine "did you have a good weekend?" In her recordings and interviews of employees in a French company, based in Australia, Beal observed that whereas the French tended to play up[16] the dramatic and unusual, the Australians preferred to give brief and unexciting factual replies about predictable activities, such as going the beach or countryside, eating and drinking, watching TV, socializing, and the like. Even when weekend activities had been quite special, there was a tendency to downplay it by describing the weekend as merely "good." Beal suggests the following explanation: "typical weekend activities that everybody does are preferred to anything that might give the impression that one thinks oneself special or superior." Further illustration the "laconic" Australian style, Beal mentions Rwanda[17] where she saw the famous gorillas. On the day she returned to work, she was asked about her trip. "'Well,' she said, 'it was interesting... a bit strenuous... it was... different.'"

Notes

[1] deadpan jocular irony: defining a fairly widespread communicativepattern. 不动声色的诙谐讽刺。
[2] "egalitarianism": the doctrine of the equality of mankind and the desirability of political and economic and social equality.
[3] John Hirst: a widely respected historian and social commentator. He wrote the official history of Australia for new citizens.
[4] Donald Horne in his classic work The Lucky CountryDonald Horne (1921—2005): an Australian journalist, writer, social critic, and academic who became one of Australia's best known public intellectuals. The lucky country has a particular resonance. Donald Horne's famous words have been used in numerous ways to describe everything that is great about our nation. The phrase has been used to describe the weather, the lifestyle and the history. It is often invoked to describe the nation's good fortune, from gold booms to economic booms.
[5] Sharp (Rhonda Sharp): Adjunct Professor, University of South Australia Adelaide Area, Australia.
[6] Bob Hawke: the 23rd Prime Minister of Australia and longest serving Australian Labor

Party Prime Minister.
〔7〕Wierzbicka (Anna Wierzbicka): a linguist at the Australian National University.
〔8〕cultural script: a pattern of social interaction that is characteristic of a particular cultural group.
〔9〕a suite of: a group of related things intended to be used together.
〔10〕Peeters—Bert Peeters: a professor of University of Tasmania.
〔11〕"tall poppy syndrome": a pejorative term used to describe a social phenomenon in which people of genuine merit are resented, attacked, cut down, or criticized because their talents or achievements elevate them above. 高罂粟花综合症。
〔12〕play down: to minimize the importance of.
〔13〕speech act verbs: 行为动词。
〔14〕McFayden—Stuart McFadyen: a professor of University of Alberta, Canada.
〔15〕"Australian cultural commandments": The "must-do's" of Australian culture.
〔16〕play up: to emphasize something; to be a booster of something.
〔17〕Rwanda: 卢旺达。

New Words

Aussie	a./n.	澳大利亚的/澳大利亚人	colloquial	a.	口语体的
scorn	n.	轻蔑	plainly	ad.	明白地
exhaustive	a.	全面的	pejorative	a.	轻蔑的
conversely	ad.	相反地	seatbelt	n.	座位安全带
implicit	a.	含蓄的	wanker	n.	手淫的人
self-deprecation	n.	自我贬低	switchboard	n.	接线总机
deadpan	a.	毫无表情的	uppity	n.	自负
Hungary	n.	匈牙利	aftermath	n.	后果
jocular	a.	滑稽的	solidarity	a.	团结一致
satirize	v.	讽刺	peccadillo	n.	小过失
subtle	a.	微妙的	diminutive	a.	微小的
asset	n.	资产	script	n.	脚本
commentator	n.	评论员	commandment	n.	戒律
obliquely	ad.	转弯抹角地	characteristically	ad.	典型地
egalitarianism	n.	平等主义	laconic	a.	简明的
lexical	a.	词汇的	distaste	n.	厌恶
frame	v.	设计	gorilla	n.	大猩猩
validity	n.	有效性	conspicuous	a.	显而易见的
limousine	n.	豪华轿车	strenuous	a.	费力的

Exercises

1. **True or false judgments**
   (1) Australians seek similarity to the point that even where similarity does not exist among themselves, they believe it does.
   (2) The feeling of self-importance is highly appreciated.
   (3) Self-importance is not popular but ambition is encouraged.
   (4) Follow these communicative styles, as the author advises, if newcomers want to get on with Australians.
   (5) Australians like brevity.

2. **Essay questions**
   (1) How do you understand the simple cultural script in [A] proposed by Wierzbicka?
   (2) What kind of lifestyle is mainly recommended by the author?
   (3) Does the sentence "thou shalt not try to be better than others" mean that you should always be worse than others?

Chapter 2
Cultural Recognition

After World War II, Australia entered a boom period. Hundreds of thousands of refugees and migrants arrived in Australia, mainly from Britain and Europe, and then after the 1970s, immigration from Asia grew and embraced their new lives. Since then, Australia has always had a culturally diverse population. Every person who lives in Australia, with the exception of Aboriginal and Torres Strait Islander Australians, is either a migrant or a descendent of a migrant. Between 1945 and 2011, some 7.2 million immigrants have arrived and Australia's population has increased from about seven million in 1945 to almost twenty three million today (OAM, 2012: 10).

Mass migration required changes to immigration and related laws. The successive governments have commenced the development of multicultural policies to maintain the languages, cultures, and religions of immigrants, creating a cohesive and tolerant environment. Australian diverse cultures have extended liberty, equality and economic wealth to waves of migrants who join Australian society that offers them a sense of belonging, unparalleled opportunities, and integration into democratic institutions (Dixon, 2002: 57—98).

However, in the minds of Australians, immigrants are still considered as second class citizens. They experience racial prejudice, having difficulties in integrating into the Anglo-Celtic culture and being accepted by society. The racial distinctions are obvious. Immigrants feel themselves excluded from the mainstream culture. In order to get a better life, they settle down in the new world but they keep wondering what they want and who they are, searching for inner selves. Immigrants are struggling within the gap between home cultural identity and the Australian cultural identity.

Many Australian novels and films in this period record and reveal the process of the identity transformation of immigrants. These literary works show both a need and desire to seek out "New Australians." Both *Japanese Story* (2003) and Clara Law Cheuk-Yu's *The Goddess of 1967* (2000) deal with slowly developing Japanese-Australian male-female relationships. Richard Roxburgh's *Romulus, My Father* (2007, adapted from the memoir by Raimond Gaita) deals with a Romanian-Australian family; Kate Woods's *Looking for Alibrandi* (2000) deals with the Italian-Australian community, in particular growing-up in it; Baz Luhrhman's *Strictly Ballroom* (1992) deals with the Spanish-Australian; and Ana Kokinos's *Head On* (1998), an adaptation of Christos Tsolkas's first novel, *Loaded*, deals with the Greek-Australian.

The film *Looking for Alibrandi* (2000) discusses the issue of growing up in Australia between two cultures. The main character, Josie Alibrandi, is born in Australia into a family with strong Italian cultural links and battles to find her self-identity. The film *Strictly Ballroom* (1992) tells about a Spanish immigrant girl, Fran, who transforms from an ugly duck to a beautiful swan in the alien land Australia. She backs Scott, a ballroom dancer, in breaking through rigid rules of dance traditions and creating a free representation in the dancing field. Later she becomes Scott's dancing partner. They integrate Spanish Pasodoble steps into traditional ballroom dance and finally get acclaim from the audience. Fran also grows up from a girl looked down upon because of her immigrant background to a respectable ballroom dancer. Their story transcends the barriers of the only dancing type dominating the whole Australian dancing field and breaks through Australian cultural stereotypes abound in the traditional ballroom dance world. Immigrants, like Josie and Fran, in Australia experience prejudice and marginalization, worrying about their recognition and belonging. Through efforts and struggles, they have achieved their inner self-realization and self-revealation.

Australia in the 21st century is a culturally, ethnically, and racially diverse and tolerant country. It has learnt more about some 200 migrant cultures and has experienced a journey from a society based on racial prejudice and intolerance to a contemporary multicultural Australia embracing diversity. Every immigrant needs to find himself/herself in this new world. Everyone is tolerable, warm-hearted, and equal, which makes up what this country is and what everyone is. Today Australians see no contradiction between being Australian and maintaining immigrant cultures and identity.

2.1 Background

Looking for Alibrandi, directed by Kate Woods, is based on the novel of the same name written by Melina Marchetta. Both the novel and the film reveal the process of growing up of an immigrant girl, Josie. The background of Australia as an immigrant country brings about many social issues to immigrants, for example, racial prejudice, the sense of identity and belonging, etc. The second and third generations of immigrants may keep asking the following questions:

> Who am I?
> Who, really, am I?
> Where, really, is my home?
> Can this new place where I live be my home?
> Will my home always be the place I have left behind?
> Am I Australian?
> Am I Italian-Australian?
> Where is my own cultural background?
> Where are my roots?

Chapter 2
Cultural Recognition

> Do I have any roots?
> What is my identity?
> Have I been intellectually colonized?...

These questions reflect their needs for emotional reassurance. They will search for the answers. Immigrants may painfully struggle to comprehend who they are between the self as defined by national culture and the self as defined by the alien cultural environments (Marchetta, 1992: 106). Josie makes great efforts to change her status and image as a second class citizen. She attends an upper class private school due to her intelligence and diligence, however, she does not get well-deserved respect from schoolmates and teachers. Josie endures racial prejudice. Through many things taking place around her, finally, Josie comes to realize what she is and finds her identity. Josie is proud of her Italian background. Josie's story is representative of the immigrant experience in Australia.

2.2 The Film *Looking for Alibrandi*

Looking for Alibrandi is a 2000 Australian film directed by Kate Woods. The film tells the story about the growing-up experience of an Italian-immigrant high school girl, Josie, through her interactions with her friends and family. The main character, Josie, comes from an immigrant and single-mother family, which causes discrimination from people around her. At school, the upper-class Australian schoolmates despise her because of her family background. At home, her grandmother with old-world values talks about her family's past almost every day. She feels inferior at home and loses herself at school. At the same time, Josie longs for the attentions and friendship from her schoolmates and looks forward to a better life.

During her later school years, she experiences issues such as the suicide of her friend, the care from a 'bad boy', the appearance of her natural father. At the end of the film, Josie realizes what she comes across in life is the universal human condition. What's more, she feels proud as a second-generation-migrant. Although her grandmother is garrulous and her mother is single, she never feels her family background is inferior any more, instead she loves them more than ever. She finds herself and knows clearly what she wants and what she has got as a new-generation immigrant. Josie's soul is set free totally. The last scene of the film shows Josie happily enjoying "Tomato Day," a traditional Italian festival.

The film *Looking for Alibrandi* won five awards at the 2000 Australian Film Institute (AFI) Awards including Best Film, Best Lead Actress, Best Supporting Actress, Best Adapted Screenplay, and Best Film Editing.

2.2.1 Director Kate Woods

Kate Woods (1981—) is an Australian film and television director. In 2000, she directed *Looking for Alibrandi*, which is based on the novel by Melina Marchetta. The film *Looking for Alibrandi*, as her first feature, won numerous awards and critical acclaim.

Kate Woods is a productive director. Her directing career spans almost 30 years, and includes a number of mini series, telemovies, pilots, television series and a multi award-winning feature film. She is the only director to have appeared on both Australia's top Film Directors and top Television Directors' lists.

2.2.2 Main Characters

(1) Josephine Alibrandi is a teenage Australian girl at a wealthy Catholic high school, she is of Italian descent.
(2) Michael Andretti is Josie's natural father, who left her and her mother before Josie's birth and finally returned to her life.
(3) Jacob Coote is Josie's boyfriend and is described as a "bad boy."
(4) Katia Alibrandi is Josie's grandmother.
(5) Christina Alibrandi is Josie's mother.
(6) John Barton is a handsome boy whom Josie loves and who finally commits suicide because of the pressure.

2.2.3 Plot

Josie is a scholarship student at a posh private school and a second-generation immigrant. In the film *Looking for Alibrandi*, the development is driven by the daily traumas in Josie's school years which is seen as a confusing time.

Josie's parents separated with each other before her birth. She lives in a one-parent family in the Italian immigrant neighborhood. Being considered an illegitimate child, she is looked down upon by Carly, who is a racist and a popular girl at school. She loves John Barton, a handsome boy from an established background, and dreams of becoming his wife, but John is attracted by a freewheeling girl. At the wealthy Catholic high school, Josie is the only non-Australian student, longing for the acceptance from her schoolmates.

To her grief, John commits suicide because of lost freedom. Josie finds her spiritual comfort from Jacob Coote, a caring person. Jacob Coote's miserable life exerts an influence on Josie.

Josie feels inferior about her own family and immigrant background. Her Italian grandmother is garrulous about her birth and the family's past, which troubles Josie a lot. By chance, she meets her long-lost natural father Michael Andretti. Their relationship is awkward at first, but they finally get to know each other and recognize themselves in each other.

At the end of the film, Josie joins the Italian Tomato Day and enjoys talking with people in her ethnic community, where she is growing up. Josie's world is full of pain as well as happiness. She becomes confident in herself.

2.2.4 Theme Analysis

Looking for Albrandi describes the experience of growing up as a 17-year old Australian of Italian descend in Sydney during the 1990s. It is a simple coming-of-age story. There are so many themes explored in this film: cultural identity, class division, suicide, and relationship with parents. The issues are all woven into the experiences of the main character, Josie, as she progresses through her final year at a private school. It is a time in her life when Josie needs to face struggles to form her identity. Although she is born in Australia, she has an Italian immigrant background. Immigrant Australians were considered then as second class citizens. They lived in immigrant communities, belonging to the working class in Australia.

Josie grows as a smart student and she wants to get a scholarship in order to be recognized by Australians. She longs for acceptance from schoolmates. Unluckily, at that time, her intelligence does not change the reality that she comes from an Italian immigrant family. As a result, she does not make many friends at school. She cannot transform her identity as an Italian immigrant no matter how hard she tries, which upsets her.

Josie is in teenage or adolescent stage. Generally speaking, the adolescent stage is the stage of "identity versus role confusion." This stage is the stage when adolescents try to find their identity on their own. They have to struggle to find their identity while interacting with the social environment (Ferdi, 2016: 150). Therefore, the transformation of her identity is viewed as the most important theme of many issues presented in the film, for we can see finally that an Italian immigrant girl in Australia struggles to discover who she is.

The film is adapted from the novel of the same name written by Melina Marchetta. In the last chapter of this novel, there is a part where Joise tells about her nationality, "If someone comes up and asks me what nationality I am, I'll look at them and say that I'm an Australian with Italian blood flowing rapidly through my veins." (Ferdi, 2016: 153) At the end of the film, Josie no longer worries about her identity, whether being seen as an Italian or Australian. She thinks of herself as an Italian and Australian as a whole. Her pride of family as an Italian and her pride to be born in Australia are combined into her nationality as an "Australian with Italian blood." It is not important any more whether she is seen as an Australian, or as an Italian or as an inbetween (Bhabha, 1994: 98). Finally, she sets herself free. Overcoming challenges allows the self-growth of an individual.

New Words

chunk	v.	终止（活动）	curse	v.	诅咒
dickhead	n.	笨蛋	salon	n.	客厅
fig	n.	无花果	Easter	n.	复活节
rave	v.	胡言乱语	intern	v.	拘留
bloke	n.	〈俚〉家伙	Pasta	n.	意大利面条
punch-up	n.	打架	signore	n.	意大利式对人的尊称
dubious	a.	可疑的			
pageant	n.	庆典	disgrace	n.	耻辱
morgue	n.	太平间	devil	n.	魔鬼
scandal	n.	流言蜚语	bush	n.	灌木丛
barrister	n.	律师	tile	n.	墙砖
immaculate	a.	无瑕的	dirt	n.	灰尘
virgin	n.	处女	sin	n.	罪孽
gypsy	n.	吉卜赛人	penance	n.	苦行
slap	v.	打耳光	disgusting	a.	令人厌恶的
tablet	n.	药片	despise	v.	鄙视

Exercises

1. **True or false judgments**

   (1) *Looking for Alibrandi* is the story of Josie Alibrandi's experience during her second year at St Martha's girls' school.

   (2) Josie learns to cope with her feelings of insecurity and be more comfortable at the end of the film.

   (3) Nonna often talks of the past with Josie and goes through her photo album with her.

   (4) Josie used to believe that one day she will grow up and be free of all the traditions and culture that seem to suffocate her.

   (5) Josie never wants to be a part of the privileged world of middle-class Australia that Carly belongs to.

   (6) John Barton has a strange relationship with Josie where they both have an affection for each other but nothing develops in the end.

   (7) Jacob and Josie ride on Jacob's motorbike, during which time, Josie goes from being petrified to enjoying it.

   (8) At the end of the film, Michael and Josie get to know each other. Josie can confide in Michael, her natural father.

2. **Term interpretations**

   (1) Josie Alibrandi   (2) Michael Andretti
   (3) Nonna Katia   (4) Carly Bishop
   (5) John Barton   (6) Jacob Coote

3. **Essay questions**
   (1) How is Josie different at the beginning of the film from herself at the end of the film?
   (2) Why does Josie feel inferior about her Italian immigrant background?
   (3) What are the differences between John Barton and Jacob Coote?
   (4) What are Josie's attitudes towards her mother and grandmother in the film?
   (5) What is Josie's attitude towards her newly acquired father?

2.3　The Film *Strictly Ballroom*

Strictly Ballroom is a 1992 Australian romantic comedy film directed and co-written by Baz Luhrmann. The film examines appropriation, modification and adaptation of musical styles within a multicultural society.

The main character, Scott, is a ballroom dancer. Because he dances his own steps without following the prescribed standards of the Pan-Pacific Grand Prix Dancing Championship, he loses the championship. He hates the traditional and rigid dancing rules of the competition, struggling instead to give the steps a free representation. Through his struggles, the arrogant Scott throws off his airs, selects the Spanish Pasodoble steps and mix them with ballroom dance. Such a blending turns out to be accepted by the audience in the later Pan-Pacific Grand Prix Dancing Championship.

Another character, Fran, has a Spanish immigrant background; and therefore, she is excluded from the dancing field. When Scott is low in spirit, she encourages him and becomes his dancing partner. They make efforts to gain acceptance finally. Fran also gets respect from people and gains confidence and pride.

In 1992, the film won Australian Film Institute (AFI) Award for Best Director and Best Screenplay; London Critics Circle Film Award (ALFS Award) for Newcomer of the Year; and was nominated British Academy Film Award (BAFTA) for Best Adapted Screenplay.

2.3.1 Director Baz Luhrmann

Baz Luhrmann (1962—) is a distinguished Australian film director, screenwriter, and producer. So far Baz Luhrmann has won 73 awards including Oscar award nominations. His famous works are *Strictly Ballroom* (1992)(《舞国英雄》), *Romeo ＋ Juliet* (1996)(《罗密欧与朱丽叶》/又名:《罗密欧与朱丽叶后现代激情篇》) and *Moulin Rouge* (2001)(《红磨坊》), which are viewed as The Red Curtain Trilogy.

Strictly Ballroom (1992) is the first of his theatre-motif-relations films. This romantic comedy film revolves around ballroom dance, which comes from his childhood experience. When he was a boy, he was a ballroom dancer and his mother was a ballroom dance teacher, which was an inspiration for this story.

In 2008, he directed a romantic epic *Australia*, which explores Australia's relationship with England and with its Indigenous population. Luhrmann says this film depicts "a mythologised Australia" (Fox, 2008). *Australia* was successful in both the USA and Europe. It is the third-highest grossing Australian film of all time, after *Crocodile Dundee* and *Mad Max: Fury Road*. This film won the Satellite Award for Best Original Screenplay and the Australian Film Institute (AFI) Members' Choice Award. In 2013, Baz Luhrmann directed the film *The Great Gatsby*, which is primarily concerned with a young millionaire, Jay Gatsby and his quixotic passion for the beautiful former debutante Daisy Buchanan during an era of loose morals. At the 86th Academy Awards, the film won in both of its nominated categories: Best Production Design and Best Costume Design.

In addition to his contributions to film making, Baz Luhrmann's accomplishments cover many fields including television series, screen actor, stage actor, music producer, and advertisement planning.

2.3.2 Main Characters

(1) Scott Hastings is an Australian ballroom dancer in the film. He hates the traditional and rigid judging criteria of ballroom dancers. He struggles to find his own niche and finally gets acceptance from the audience.
(2) Liz Holt is Scott's former dance partner.
(3) Fran is a Spanish immigrant and a beginner dancer. Later she becomes Scott's new dance partner. She falls in love with Scott. They mix the Pasodoble steps with traditional ballroom dance.
(4) Shirley Hastings is Scott's mother, a ballroom dance teacher at her own studio.
(5) Doug Hastings is Scott's father. He handles maintenance chores at his dance studio.
(6) Rico is Fran's father and a Spanish Pasodoble dancer.
(7) Ya Ya is Fran's grandmother and a Spanish Pasodoble dancer.
(8) Barry Fife is the president of the Australian Dancing Federation.

2.3.3 Plot

Strictly Ballroom tells the story of an Australian ballroom dancer, Scott Hastings, and his struggle to establish his own personal style of ballroom dance on his way to win the Pan-

Chapter 2
Cultural Recognition

Pacific Grand Prix Dancing Championship.

Scott comes from a family with a history of ballroom dancing as his parents used to be famous dancers. Scott starts dancing his own steps at the competition, and his dancing partner Liz Holt leaves him alone because he loses the competition. His family helps him find a new partner, but Scott secretly begins practising with a Spanish dancer, Fran, as a partner at his parents' studio. Scott has a skeptical attitude towards Fran initially, but later realizes her potential. By chance, he gets to know Fran's family and learns a lot about Spanish culture and the Pasodoble steps. Scott decides to mix his ballroom dance with Spanish Pasodoble styles, creating his own free ballroom dance, which is different from the traditional one.

When Scott returns to the dance studio, he finds out that Barry Fife, the conniving president of the Australian Dancing Federation has lied to him. This impels him to dance with Liz using the formal and regular steps.

At the Pan-Pacific Grand Prix, after hearing his father's revelation about his family's past, Scott asks Fran to dance with him. Fife tries to cut the music but eventually fails. The dance steps of Scott and Fran bring down the house. Scott's parents and the audience join them on the floor.

2.3.4 Theme Analysis

The film *Strictly Ballroom* examines modification and adaptation of musical styles within ballroom dancing field in the context of a multicultural society. It emphasizes the importance of the sence of belonging and understanding oneself before gaining acceptance from the audience. One's struggle to belong can often involve challenges to their identity and inner self.

Ballroom dancing was initially popularized in the 18th and 19th century England, and was appreciated by the privileged and restricted to the upper class. The criteria for ballroom dancing performances are strict with rigid rules, what is more, they are thought as the sole (mono-) criteria.

Scott hates rigid rules. He wishes to create a free representation of dance steps and search for the steps he wants to dance. The voice Scott is in search of is none other than his inner self. He resists the pressures of his family and the traditional ballroom dancing world to explore alternative forms of belonging, by learning the Pasodoble from Fran's family, and blending the Pasodoble steps into traditional ballroom dance steps. When the audience accept their dance steps and give them acclaim, his mother shows her acceptance by dancing with them. This convinces the elite that the mixed dance steps can be recognized widely in the Australian dancing field. Scott finds the steps he searches for, that is, he finds his inner self and he gains a strong sense of belonging in the ballroom dancing realm. People embrace their steps. Meanwhile, he realizes that the spirit of ballroom dance is by no means to "dance to win" but "dance from the heart," which is what Fran's father taught him. Scott is a winner in the film, for he transcends the barriers of the only dancing type dominating the whole Australian dancing field and breaks through Australian cultural stereotypes in a traditional dance context.

Fran's story in the film reflects a new generation of immigrant struggling for success. She is a Spanish immigrant dancer. With no confidence at first, she is timid. On hearing that she is Scott's partner, people mock her with clichés and prejudice. As a second-generation immigrant, Fran is also in a quest for belonging and recognition in an alien environment. She wonders what her identity is. Fran keeps her birth country's customs and traditions. Through great efforts, she gains acceptance from the audience. Fran's persistence convinces Scott to dance their own steps in the Pan-Pacific Championship, which breaks the competition conformity. We have seen an ugly duckling turn into a beautiful swan in the alien land Australia. Baz Luhrmann comments that Fran in this case as the ugly duckling is a misunderstood universal myth. It is not about turning into a blonde Barbie doll or becoming what she dreams of being, instead it is about self-revelation and becoming who she is (Luhrmann, 2008). In a multicultural context, people tend to enjoy cultural adaptation and mix.

New Words

trophy	n.	奖杯；纪念品	shenanigan	n.	恶作剧
prix	n.	大奖赛，大奖	stir	n.	轰动
ambassador	n.	大使	sourpuss	n.	讨人嫌的家伙
ballroom	n.	跳舞场，舞厅	farewell	a.	告别的
ballroom dance	n.	交谊舞	exhibition	n.	表演
block in		使受限制，受阻	devil	n.	小恶魔
resort	v.	诉诸；采取；凭借	fruity	a.	古怪的
			rond	n.	绕圈
spin	v.	旋转；纺纱	crescent	a.	新月形的
toner	n.	化妆水	arced	a.	弧形的
choreography	n.	舞蹈编排	inconceivable	a.	不可想象的
fiancé	n.	未婚夫	nasty	a.	令人讨厌的
tryout	n.	选拔赛；试用	bruise	n.	失误；挫伤；意外
pathetic	a.	可怜的；差劲的；软弱的	clumsy	a.	愚蠢的
gutless	a.	怯懦的	scorecard	n.	记分卡
musicality	n.	音乐性；音感	terrific	a.	极好的
tubby	a.	肥胖的	available	a.	合适的
compatible	a.	能共处的	barrel	n.	桶
whisper	n.	私语	beginner	n.	初学者
shuffling	a.	支吾的，曳步的	pasodoble	n.	斗牛舞
proverb	n.	谚语	bravo	v.	喝彩
pretend	v.	假装	rhythm	n.	节奏；韵律
advantageous	a.	有利的	sacrifice	n.	牺牲

Chapter 2
Cultural Recognition

rot	v.	使腐烂	self-obsessed	a.	自恋的
overreact	v.	反应过度	improvise	v.	即兴创作、表演
jazzy	a.	奔放的；爵士乐的	vow	v.	发誓
			crawl	v.	缓慢地前进
bailar	v.	（西）跳舞	tack	v.	附加
unequivocally	ad.	明确地	semblance	n.	外貌
comprende	v.	（法）明白	brewery	n.	啤酒厂
rumba	n.	伦巴舞	tick	n.	记号
potentially	ad.	可能地，潜在地	scrutineer	n.	检查人
magnificent	a.	华丽的	puff	v.	膨胀
chickie	n.	年轻女子，姑娘	peacock	n.	孔雀
scruff	n.	颈背，后颈	syncopate	v.	切分
awing	ad.	飞翔地	credibility	n.	可信性
gang	n.	群	spud	n.	挖掘
funster	n.	幽默家，喜剧演员	disqualification	n.	取消资格
			suspend	v.	禁赛

Exercises

1. **True or false judgments**

    (1) Scott is a ballroom dancer as a child.

    (2) Scott accepts Fran as his dancing partner without any hesitation.

    (3) Doug used to be a great dancer.

    (4) Fran is a Spanish immigrant, coming to Australia with her big family.

    (5) Scott's mother expects Fran to be Scott's partner.

    (6) Fran's Spanish immigrant family is full of passion towards dance and life.

    (7) Being cheated and convinced to win "for his father's sake," Scott changes his mind and decides to dance with Liz instead of Fran.

    (8) Barry is willing to accept new steps.

    (9) Scott's father never joins the Pan-Pacific Grand Prix Dancing Championship.

    (10) The audience is inspired by their new steps and everyone joins the dance happily and freely at the end of the film.

2. **Term interpretations**

    (1) Scott   (2) Doug
    (3) Barry   (4) Fran
    (5) Shirley   (6) Liz
    (7) Rico   (8) The Pasodoble

3. **Essay questions**

    (1) Among the dance types shown in the film, which one do you like most?

    (2) Why does Shirley insist Scott should dance in the regular way?

(3) Why does Doug support his son's decision to follow his own personal style of dance?
(4) In what ways does Fran influence Scott?
(5) How does the relationship between Scott and Fran develop at the end of the film?

2.4 Reading Passage: Is Australia a Multicultural Nation?
by David Carter[①]

Is Australia a multicultural nation? This might seem a strange question. Australia is known in many parts of the world as a successful example of multiculturalism, a model for other nations to emulate. It has one of the highest percentage of immigrants in its resident population, more than 25% by mid-2008, second only to Israel in global terms and so higher than the USA or Canada. Further, Australia has defined itself as multicultural since the mid-1970s, a policy that has had the support of both major political parties with only slight variations in emphasis. And, finally, there are many multicultural programs in place across the country: in all States, in primary and secondary schools, in universities, in community organizations and so on[1]. The occasional high-profile debate[2] about multiculturalism in Australia—from the Blainey debate[3] to Pauline Hanson[4] to the so-called Cronulla riots[5]—only seems to highlight the degree to which Australia is indeed a multicultural nation.

International immigration represented 65% of Australia's population growth in the year 2008—2009, a very high figure globally, and numbers in this range have been the pattern now for some time[6]. Yet as James Jupp, one of Australia's leading historians of immigration, has repeatedly argued, a high level of immigration does not necessarily mean a "multicultural society"—that is, a society characterized by cultural, linguistic, religious or ethnic diversity, demographically and in its institutional or policy structures[7].

Jupp has argued even more strongly that the common description of Australia as "one of the most multicultural societies in the world" is simply wrong. Although precision is impossible, it has been estimated that between 65% and 70% of Australians have an Anglo-Celtic[8] background. Australia, despite its high immigration intake, is probably "whiter" than either the USA or Canada. The figure of 25% overseas-born in the Australian population is often quoted not just as a fact but as a source of pride—as evidence of Australia's tolerant, democratic society, and of our commitment to multiculturalpluralism. What we don't often mention is the fact that the vast majority of migrants since World War II have come from the United Kingdom and Ireland—near to 50% of the total of new migrants in the 1960s, 25% in the seventies, and still between 11% and 18% of new immigrant arrivals today. This fact is often forgotten in our enthusiasm to celebrate ethnic diversity, or, from the opposite perspective, in fears about ethnic "dilution." Certainly, for

---

[①] David Carter: Professor of School of English, Media Studies and Art History, the University of Queensland, Brisbane, Australia. "Is Australia a multicultural nation?" by David Carter. 28 October 2010. A Key Speech in the 12th International Conference of Australian Studies in Shanghai, China.

a number of decades, immigration reinforced rather than undermined white Anglo-Celtic or Anglo-Australian—or more broadly "European"—demographic and cultural dominance.

In the final analysis, I want to argue that Australia is both more and less multicultural than official versions of Australian multiculturalism suggest. I will begin with five reasons why we should not consider Australia a multicultural nation. Then I will answer these points with five reasons as to why we should still see Australia as multicultural. First, then, let me put forward the less familiar evidence for Australia not being a multicultural nation.

First, the demographic points already indicated. The majority of the population is of British, "Anglo-Australian"[9] or "Anglo-Celtic" background, around 70% as suggested.

Second, the point about immigration patterns. The demographic majority has been reinforced by high levels of immigration from the UK since World War II, high levels which have continued right through to the present. Even though the percentage of UK immigration in the overall immigration mix has been declining on an annual basis[10], it is still one of the largest source countries for new migrants, usually in the top two or three, alongside New Zealand, South Africa, China and India. Those born in the UK remain the largest group of overseas born in Australia, about four times larger than the Chinese born for example.

Third, the question of language. If Australia is a multicultural nation it is also, at the same time, largely monolingual in institutional terms despite the fact that the population speaks "almost 400 languages" according to the official Australian Year Book 2009—10[11]. Multicultural but monolingual: this is a key dynamic for understanding diversity in Australia. Of course this is due in part to forces[12] larger than those of national policy, to the global dominance of English. Nonetheless, despite a history of short-term policies for promoting foreign language maintenance or education, at a federal level mono rather than multi-lingualism has received the policy weighting in recent years. As in so many policy areas, it was John Howard as Prime Minister who set the tone[13]. His government not only insisted upon English-language ability among migration criteria but saw a shared language as the key to social "harmony" as it liked to call the goal of multiculturalism. Indeed it made a point of[14] defining English as Australia's "official language" although this is not stated anywhere in legislation or the Constitution. There is now little trace of the earlier principle, expressed by Prime Minister Keating[15] in 1995, of the right of individuals to "expression and sharing of their cultural heritage, including language and religion."

My fourth point also concerns demography, but this time settlement patterns. Ethnic, linguistic and religious diversity is very unevenly distributed across the nation—Melbourne, Sydney and Darwin more than the other capitals, all the capital cities more than smaller centers, and urban areas in general more than rural or regional Australia. Even within our most multicultural centers, within our cities, diversity is very unevenly distributed. While the language of "ghettos"[16] has never been appropriate to Australia despite its use in scare campaigns[17], there has been a predictable pattern of high concentration of first generation migrants in certain parts of the capital cities, while other areas show almost no trace of immigration or ethnic diversity.

This fact of the unequal presence of diversity in different parts of the nation has enormous and largely underestimated consequences for policy and politics in Australia. For what is an everyday and completely ordinary experience for some Australians (meeting with, working with, socializing with Australians of different ethnic backgrounds) is foreign, unfamiliar and so potentially threatening for many others. If multiculturalism makes good sense of everyday experience for the first group, to the second group it might well seem like a mysterious "plot," a form of enforced "social engineering," invented by bureaucrats in Canberra, something which does not speak at all to their everyday sense of being Australian.

The ethnic distribution of new migrants is also very uneven. In Victoria and NSW, the largest groups of new migrants are from China and India. But in Qld[18] and WA[19] they are from NZ[20], the UK and South Africa. Are we producing a newly divided Australia, the reverse of what it was in 1900, with an Asian multiracial south east and a white north and west? Probably not yet. But we can say that for some Australians, in some parts of the country, Australia is not a multicultural nation.

My fifth and final point, and perhaps the most important, concerns policy. To make the point dramatically we can say that multicultural policy itself is not very multicultural. It is surprisingly difficult to find any reference to multiculturalism on the website of the federal Department of Immigration and Citizenship[21]. A search on the website for "multiculturalism" produces a series of documents—but nothing beyond 2002—2003. A search for "multicultural" brings up[22] a link to the Australian Multicultural Advisory Council[23], which I'll discuss in a moment.

The Rudd and now Gillard[24] Labor governments have retained the name for the Department introduced by the Howard[25] government in 2006 to replace the previous "Department of Immigration and Multicultural Affairs"[26]. The change of name, replacing "multiculturalism" with "citizenship" reflects the unease which the Howard government felt about any notion of ethnic difference. The change to "citizenship" signaled a shift of[27] rhetoric whereby[28] the predominant discourse became that of "unity" and shared values, or simply "Australian values," in the language Howard preferred, and which continues in current policy documents. In the Howard government's official definitions of multiculturalism, the key words were not "diversity" or "difference" but "tolerance" and "harmony." Of course "tolerance" and "harmony" are good things, much better than "intolerance" and "disharmony," but the way these words are used has the effect of downplaying any sense of a society that is characterized by or that values difference. Multiculturalism becomes a way of talking about unity rather than diversity. It's what I call "white multiculturalism."

Little has changed under a Labor government. As indicated, the new name for the Department has been retained, as has the Statement of Australian Values[29] that migrants are required to declare, and the Citizenship Test[30] introduced by the Howard government in October 2007 (although this has been reviewed and modified, with a new focus on civic rather than cultural questions)[31]. The current Australian Values Statement makes no mention of multiculturalism. It is worded[32] in terms of abstract liberal-democratic principles such as the "equality of men and women," but the closest the Statement gets to proclaiming multiculturalism is a negative definition: "equal opportunity for individuals, regardless of their race, religion or ethnic background."

The booklet the Department publishes to accompany the Values Statement also makes no reference to multiculturalism. There are a few references to "cultural diversity": "Australia's cultural diversity is a strength which makes for a dynamic society." But every time "cultural diversity" is mentioned it is contained and, as it were[33], pacified: "An important feature of Australian society today is not only the cultural diversity of its people, but the extent to which they are united by an overriding and unifying commitment to Australia" (my emphasis). Or again: "One of the defining features of Australian society today is the cultural diversity of its people and the extent to which they are united by an overriding and unifying commitment to Australia" (my emphasis). Elsewhere, under "Australian values," the document states that "the English language, as the national language, is an important unifying element of Australian society." It's as if cultural diversity can't be trusted to be let out[34] on its own without being chaperoned by that defensive notion of an overriding and unifying commitment to Australia. In such statements, we can still hear the faint echoes of multicultural policy at its strongest[35], where an insistence on the rule of law and citizenship served as[36] a counter to ethnic definitions of the nation. But the notion of "diversity" has been leached of[37] any serious meaning, any fundamental sense of difference.

Of course these are all bureaucratic documents designed for specific ends within the administration of a migrant settlement program, so their emphases are perhaps not surprising, nor are the principles outlined exceptionable. Indeed the Values booklet is rather sophisticated in its discussion of Australian identity. Nonetheless the current documents provide strong evidence for my point: multicultural policy, if it can still be said to exist, is at best[38] a pale reflection of its former self; indeed in many ways it is anti-multicultural in spirit and effect.

The Rudd government did take one new initiative under the name of multiculturalism, establishing the Australian Multicultural Advisory Council in December 2008. Comprised of 16 individuals from diverse backgrounds (Anglo, immigrant, and Indigenous), its role is to advise the Minister on "social cohesion issues," overcoming intolerance and racism, communicating the social and economic benefits of diversity, and issues relating to social and civic participation. The Council[39] has produced a "statement on cultural diversity" called The Australian People which makes some strong statements of multiculturalism: "Multicultural Australia is this Australia, this democracy, the country we know. Australia is multicultural, it always has been and we can say with certainty that it will be in the future... We are multicultural because we choose to be and need to be." Despite the rather questionable history in this assertion, the statement is a forceful one, about as forceful as it can be in an environment where multiculturalism was, and remains, on the defensive[40]. It recommends that governments too should be more forceful in telling the story: "Our political leaders should have no difficulty in presenting 'multicultural Australia' as an important part of the 'national identity' they frequently invoke." At the same time the statement is defensive, a kind of minimalist definition of multiculturalism: "Multicultural Australia is not a vision or an ambition, much less an ideology or creed. It describes us as we are." Its recommendations are practical and positive, but again guarded and minimalist: a "sound multicultural policy... will encourage cultural diversity and celebrate it, but only within the broader aim of social harmony, national unity, and fundamental freedoms such as gender equality." While multiculturalism was always contained within the limits of the Australian law and political structures, the minimalism and defensiveness of this new document shows the effects of the Howard years. This is definitely multiculturalism post-9/11[41].

Having presented five arguments as to why Australia is not a multicultural country, or at least that it is less multicultural than we often assume, let me turn now to argue the opposing case and to answer each of my five negative points in turn.

First, demographics. While the majority of the population is indeed of "Anglo-Celtic" background, this percentage has been steadily declining since the 1980s, indeed ever since the late 1950s, from well over 90% to less than 70%, and the trend is increasing. The trend is decidedly towards ethnic diversity and "ethnic mixing." The latter is an important emphasis, because official statistics generally do not take account of[42] the high degree of intermarriage and "mixing" in Australia. There is a high level of "marrying out"—that is of people marrying out of their own ethnic community. Demographer Charles Price has shown that almost 80% of second-generation Chinese and more than 90% of Indians, for example, marry outside their own community[43]. There is also a high degree of intermarriage between Indigenous and non-Indigenous Australians.

Second, immigration patterns. While it is true that a significant percentage of Australia's new migrants continue to arrive from Britain, this figure has undergone a dramatic decline over recent decades. And if we look in terms of regions rather than countries we get an even stronger picture of fundamental change in the migrant intake: around 17% of new migrants still arrive from Europe, but almost 50% are from Asia, with another 16% from Africa and the Middle East. This shift has been progressive since the 1970s and rapid since the 1990s. Again, these statistics, just based on new migrants, do not take account of second, third and fourth generation children of one or more non-British backgrounds. In this sense, indeed, we can argue that Australia is more multicultural than the official statistics indicate, with their focus on migrant intake and numbers of overseas born, for these give little indication of ethnic diversity within the resident population across generations.

Third, language. Of course, with its global dominance, English is an irresistible force these days. At the same time, as Michael Clyne[44] has argued in his book Australia's Language Potential, Australia is much more linguistically diverse than most official statements show[45]. Our nation census records that around 16% of Australian households use a language other than English as the primary language, but this only registers the slightly unusual way the Australian Bureau of Statistics[46] asks the question. A much higher number of Australians speak languages other than English, primarily through inter-generational and inter-marriage transmission, but also, of course, through education or professional experience.

Although English does dominate our public institutions, it does not dominate everywhere in our private or everyday lives. There is a rich tradition of non-English language newspapers and, more recently, radio in Australia and, if less than previously, SBS TV still broadcasts significantly in languages other than English. So we can at least qualify the term "monolingual." There is substantial linguistic diversity in contemporary Australia although much of it remains unacknowledged, under-appreciated and under-utilized.

My fourth point was that ethnic or cultural diversity in Australia is very unevenly spread across the country. That is certainly the case, but at the same time the places where cultural diversity is most concentrated are also the places where the vast majority of Australians live-in the larger cities of one of the most highly urbanized countries in the world. And although we can point to specific "ethnic areas" in particular suburbs of these cities—Greek, Vietnamese, Lebanese[47], or Chinese suburbs—the overwhelming pattern in Australia has been dispersal rather than concentration. New migrants, of course, tend to cluster where housing is accessible, where work is available, and/or where others from their country or language group are already living: the Chinese in Sunnybank[48], in southern Brisbane, for example, where more than 40% of households use one or other Chinese as a primary language. Although these settlement patterns have been somewhat altered by Australia's current emphasis on professional and skilled migration, which has introduced a new mobility among recent arrivals, they remain common. While the first generation might stay in their place of arrival, the second generation moves out—and often the first generation, too, once they get established. In this sense, diversity is much more widely dispersed than the few highly visible, highly concentrated examples of "ethnic suburbs" suggest.

Finally, the policy area. This could be seen as the most serious charge against Australia's status as a multicultural nation[49]. If the national government can't take multiculturalism seriously, why should anyone else? Let me answer this point in two ways.

First, while multicultural policy has certainly been diluted at the federal policy level, most of the active programs and most of the funding made available under multicultural programs have always occurred at State and local government level. Theorists and critics of multiculturalism have tended to focus much too exclusively on the federal level, and on the level of explicit policy statements. For the most part these State and local programs have continued despite the change of rhetoric at the federal level. Australian schools, for example, are strong sources of "multicultural" education and experience. Further, even at the national level, government institutions, and cultural institutions, such as the Australia Council, almost always have "diversity" programs built into their recruitment and management strategies. In other words, multiculturalism is deeply embedded in[50] these institutions in a way that is not directly affected by changes in political fashion at the parliamentary or party level.

Second, as a number of commentators, including Jon Stratton[51] and Ghassan Hage[52], have argued, it is important to distinguish between what we might call "official" multiculturalism, on the one hand, and "everyday" or "ordinary" multiculturalism, on the other[53].

Official multiculturalism tells the story of Australia's successful multicultural society: we celebrate cultural diversity, harmony and tolerance as evidence of Australia's democratic traditions and our capacity to integrate peoples from diverse backgrounds without producing racial or religious conflict. In short, we celebrate multiculturalism as a national achievement, as evidence of our own virtue: it confirms rather than challenges ideas of national identity. This is the multiculturalism promoted on national occasions (such as in speeches on Australia Day) and less formally at multicultural festivals. This celebratory multiculturalism is the focus of a great deal of critical academic work, but in fact I don't want to criticize it as I think it performs a valuable function in our society. But it hardly reflects the reality of "multiculturalism on the street" — of ordinary, everyday multiculturalism.

What I mean by ordinary multiculturalism is the matter of fact, daily interactions that many, perhaps the majority, of Australians (of different ethnic or linguistic backgrounds) have with other Australians (of different ethnic backgrounds or identities). Such relations are often imagined as relations between white or Anglo-Australians and ethnic "others," but this is a failure of our multicultural imaginations because of course, in contemporary Australia, the interactions they are just as likely today to be interactions between Australians of mixed or non-Anglo backgrounds on both sides. Everyday multiculturalism, we might say, is both better and worse than official multiculturalism—"worse" in the sense that it will include examples of intolerance, disharmony, irreconcilable differences, conflict and racism (there are spectacular examples, like the Cronulla riots, but also everyday examples which pass under the radar). Ethnic diversity can't and won't be one happy folk festival. But everyday multiculturalism will also be "better" than the official version in the sense that it will include the very wide range of ordinary, mundane interactions with neighbors, workmates, customers, students, lovers, doctors and dentists, and so on, through which social and cultural interactions are transacted—the building of new kinds of relationships, new "Australian values" and, indeed, new cultures, that happens at this less spectacular but more fundamental level. At this level I'd want to say that Australia is in many ways more multicultural than we sometimes assume, and more than official policy acknowledges with its rhetoric of overriding and unifying commitments cares to admit. Much of the Australian experience of diversity and difference is so "ordinary," so everywhere and everyday, that we scarcely notice it.

So, is Australia a multicultural nation? Yes, but not necessarily in the ways we or our governments like to think it is. It is more multicultural than the notion of "Australian values" and "unifying commitments" want to acknowledge—diversity is already a great distance further down the track than these conservative fantasies of national management care to admit[54]. But it is less multicultural, if I can put it that way, than images of happy, harmonious "festival multiculturalism" project. Indigenous, settler, immigrant, Anglo, and mixtures of them all—both more and less, and better and worse, than the official version—this is the kind of multicultural Australia we need not just to define but perhaps also, today, to defend.

Chapter 2
Cultural Recognition

Notes

[1] "And, finally, there are many multicultural programs in place across the country: in all States, in primary and secondary schools, in universities, in community organizations and so on." See David Carter, *Dispossession, Dreams and Diversity: Issues in Australian Studies*, Sydney: Pearson, 2006, pp. 332—354.

[2] high-profile: attracting much attention and publicity.

[3] the Blainey debate: In 1984, Professor Blainey spoke of the Blainey debate on the size and composition of Australia's migrant intake. Geoffrey Blainey (1930—): an Australian historian.

[4] Pauline Hanson (1954—): an Australian politician. In 2006, she was named by The Bulletin as one of the 100 most influential Australians of all time.

[5] Cronulla riots: a series of racially motivated riots and mob violence originating in Cronulla, New South Wales and spreading, over the next few nights, to additional Sydney suburbs in 2005.

[6] Statistics here from the Australian Bureau of Statistics www.abs.gov.au.

[7] Yet as James Jupp, one of Australia's leading historians of immigration, has repeatedly argued, a high level of immigration does not necessarily mean a "multicultural society"— that is, a society characterized by cultural, linguistic, religious or ethnic diversity, demographically and in its institutional or policy structures. See James Jupp, *From White Australia to Woomera: The Story of Australian Immigration*, Melbourne: Cambridge University Press, 2002. James Jupp (1932—): a British-Australian political scientist and author.

[8] Anglo-Celtic: a macro-cultural term used to collectively describe the cultures native to Britain and Ireland.

[9] Anglo-Australian: Australians with British ancestral origins.

[10] on an annual basis: every year.

[11] the official Australian Year Book 2009-10: the official report from the Australian Bureauof Statistics.

[12] due in part to forces: due to: because of; in part: to some extent; partly.

[13] set the tone: to establish a particular mood or character for something. 定基调。

[14] make a point of: to be certain to do something that you think is important.

[15] Keating (1944—): the 24th Prime Minister of Australia.

[16] "ghetto": now described as an overcrowded urban area often associated with a specific ethnic or racial population; especially because of social, legal, or economic pressure.

[17] in scare campaigns: campaigns run by organizations to promote fear on an issue.

[18] Qld: Queensland, Australia.

[19] WA: Western Australia.

[20] NZ: New Zealand.

[21] the federal Department of Immigration and Citizenship (DIAC) has managed the arrival and settlement in Australia of nearly seven million migrants from 200 countries,

including more than 700,000 refugees under the Humanitarian Program since its establishment in 1945.

[22] bring up: introduce into discussion; mention.

[23] the Australian Multicultural Advisory Council: officially launched by the Minister for Immigration and Citizenship, Senator Chris Evans, on 17 December 2008 in Melbourne.

[24] Gillard (1961—): the 27th Prime Minister of Australia.

[25] Howard (1939—): the 25th Prime Minister of Australia.

[26] "Department of Immigration and Multicultural Affairs": Federal Government Department dealing with Immigration and Multicultural Affairs.

[27] a shift of: the change of.

[28] whereby: by or because of which.

[29] the Statement of Australian Values is that all applicants aged 18 years and over are required to sign a values statement when applying for selected visas. The statement requires applicants to confirm that they will respect the Australian way of life and obey the laws of Australia before being granted a visa.

[30] the Citizenship Test: a test that applicants for Australian citizenship who also meet the basic requirements for citizenship.

[31] (although this has been reviewed and modified, with a new focus on civic rather than cultural questions): See Department of Immigration and Citizenship, http://www.immi.gov.au/.

[32] It is worded: it can be expressed as...

[33] as it were: In a manner of speaking; as if such were so.

[34] let out: express audibly or make known.

[35] at its strongest: at its best.

[36] serve as: act as.

[37] leach of: to empty; drain.

[38] at best: at the most or under the most favorable conditions.

[39] the Council: the Australian Multicultural Advisory Council.

[40] on the defensive: prepared to withstand or attack.

[41] 9/11: suicide attacks by al-Qaeda upon the US on September 11, 2001.

[42] take account of: consider or pay attention to.

[43] marry outside their own community: cited in Stephen Fitzgerald, *Is Australia an Asian Country*? Sydney: Allen & Unwin, 1997, p. 66.

[44] Michael Clyne (1939—2010): an Australian linguist and academic.

[45] Australia is much more linguistically diverse than most official statements show: See Michael Clyne, *Australia's Language Potential*, Sydney: UNSW Press, 2005.

[46] the Australian Bureau of Statistics (ABS): Australia's national statistical agency.

[47] Lebanese: 黎巴嫩的。

[48] Sunnybank: a suburb in Brisbane, Queensland, Australia much reduced in size from the previous suburb of Sunnybank.
[49] This could be seen as the most serious charge against Australia's status as a multicultural nation. The sentence means this could be seen as the most serious challenge against Australia's status as a multicultural nation.
[50] embedded in: fix firmly.
[51] Jon Stratton: an Australian academic.
[52] Ghassan Hage (1957—): a Lebanese-Australian academic.
[53] it is important to distinguish between what we might call "official" multiculturalism, on the one hand, and "everyday" or "ordinary" multiculturalism, on the other: See Ghassan Hage, *White Nation: Fantasies of White Supremacy in a Multicultural Society*, Sydney: Pluto, 1998; Jon Stratton, *Race Daze: Australia's Identity Crisis*, Sydney: Pluto, 1998.
[54] It is more multicultural than the notion of "Australian values" and "unifying commitments" want to acknowledge — diversity is already a great distance further down the track than these conservative fantasies of national management care to admit. The sentence means that diversity is a longer way off than the conservative national managers would like to admit. Australian values and unifying commitments inhibit the creation of a diverse society.

New Words

emulate	v.	模仿		monolingual	a.	单一语言的
predominant	a.	主要的		register	v.	登记
Israel	n.	以色列		criteria	n.	标准（criterion 的复数）
downplay	v.	不予重视				
variation	n.	变化		dispersal	n.	分散
booklet	n.	小册子		unevenly	ad.	不均衡地
riot	n.	暴乱		cluster	v.	聚集
chaperon	v.	陪伴		urban	a.	城市的
demographically	ad.	人口学地		mobility	n.	移动
assertion	n.	声明		rural	a.	农村的
quote	v.	引述		explicit	a.	明确的
invoke	v.	祈求		potentially	ad.	潜在地
pluralism	n.	多元主义		irreconcilable	a.	不可调和的
decidedly	ad.	断然地		enforced	a.	实施的
dilution	n.	冲淡		mundane	a.	平凡的
irresistible	a.	不可抵抗的		bureaucrat	n.	官僚
undermine	v.	破坏		transact	v.	处理
census	n.	人口普查		reverse	n.	相反

Exercises

1. **True or false judgments**
   (1) According to James Jupp, given its high percentage of immigration, Australia can be defined without doubt as a multicultural society.
   (2) Nowadays about 50% of new Australian immigrants are from Asia.
   (3) Michael Clyne has supported the point of view that Australia is a multicultural country in his book *Australia's Language Potential*.
   (4) The Rudd government made no contributions to fostering a multicultural society.
   (5) The majority of Australians live in large cities where cultural diversity is most concentrated.

2. **Essay questions**
   (1) What makes Australia an example of a multicultural country?
   (2) Why does the author think Howard's official definition of multiculturalism means "white multiculturalism"?
   (3) What is the author's conclusion of Australian multiculturalism?

Chapter 3
Multicultural Oneness

Till the 1990s, Australian multiculturalism has not yet been fully accepted, that is, stress was on conformity and unity (Farnsworth, 1996: 348—459). The government, especially the former Prime Minister Julia Eileen Gillard, turned to an emphasis on everyday multiculturalism and daily interaction. Ordinary multiculturalism (Carter, 2006: 190) is like a day-to-day practice. What makes Australians feel that they belong to the neighborhood as well as the nation is their ability to be part of its diversity. Their strong attachment to their neighborhoods are often articulated in terms of high levels of social belonging to a functioning diverse environment (Visser, Bolt & Van Kempen, 2015: 36—52).

In Australia, therefore, multiculturalism exists as a collective phenomenon of shared meanings within a community of mutual understanding. The over 200 diverse cultural groups co-exist like a collage. In this context, the interactions between different peoples, groups, businesses and organizations are highly underlined and realized. Ms Gillard once said multiculturalism amounted to a civic virtue since it provided Australians with a way to share the public space, a common ground of inclusion and belonging for all the people.

3.1 Background

The story of *The Castle* takes place in a diverse neighborhood. The Kerrigans and neighbors as immigrants have a good relationship. Newcomers Farouk and Tabulah from Lebanon get along well with them. It is a friendly and peaceful neighborhood. Faced with unequal treatment from the Airlink Corporation, they hold meetings together to search for the solution, which suggests intercultural interdependence and a strong attachment to their neighborhoods to achieve high levels of social belonging to a functioning diverse environment (Visser, Bolt & Van Kempen, 2015: 36—52).

Australians find shared identity on the common ground of "a fair go." Darryl thinks that although the Airlink is a government authority, Australian Constitution gives everyone the common ground and equal right to possess the property of land and house. It makes no sense that an authority can violate the law in order to gain its own profit. Being working class, the Kerrigans and neighbors disdain people in power, which reveals the Australian spirit of a fair go in a multicultural context.

3.2　The Film *The Castle*

The Castle is a 1997 Australian comedy-drama film directed by Rob Sitch. The story takes place in a culturally diverse background, which is close to the airport. The neighbors are the Kerrigans, elderly Jack, divorcee Yvonne, and Farouk and Tabulah who are recent immigrants from Lebanon. They are the working class. The main character, Darryl Kerrigan, is depicted as a blue-collar hero. The film has become one of Australia's most widely quoted comedies.

The Airlink Corporation as a government authority attempts to pull down their houses to expand the airport runway. In order to protect his home, Darryl, as the backbone of his family, starts a fight against the Airlink. He appeals to the court. Though a rough process, Darryl wins at last. Like a battler, Darryl's victory suggests that "a man's home is his castle," based upon an English saying in a humorous way, but this humor just reveals the national self image, most notably the concept of working-class Australians and their place in multicultural Australia.

The film also refers to the land rights movement of the Australian Aborigines such as Mabo, with Darryl Kerrigan drawing an explicit parallel between his struggle and theirs. It also draws on one of the few rights protected in the Australian Constitution for subject matter, the right to just terms compensation for acquisition of property under section 51(xxxi).

The Castle won one Australian Film Institute Awards for Best Original Screenplay and three nominations: Australian Film Institute Award for Best Actor in a Leading Role, Australian Film Institute Award for Best Actress in a Supporting Role, and Australian Film Institute Award for Best Actor in a Supporting Role.

Chapter 3
Multicultural Oneness

3.2.1 Director Rob Sitch

Rob Sitch (1962—) is an Australian director, producer, screenwriter, actor, and comedian. He was born in Melbourne in 1962. His major in college was medicine. After graduation, he practised medicine for a short time, and then he shifted his interest to films and televisions.

Sitch produced television shows including *Frontline*, *A River Somewhere*, *The Panel*, *Thank God You're Here* and *Utopia*, and feature films *The Castle*, *The Dish* and *Any Questions for Ben?* He co-wrote and directed each of these films.

3.2.2 Main Characters

(1) Darryl Kerrigan is the father of the family. He defends his home by winning the law case of his house with the help of the lawyer Lawrence.
(2) Sal Kerrigan is Kerrigan's wife and the mother for four children. She takes care of the family without working outside the home.
(3) Dale Kerrigan is the youngest son of the Kerrigan family. He serves as the narrator of the film.
(4) Tracey Petropoulous is the family's only daughter and a newly-wed hair dresser.
(5) Dennis Denuto is a bumbling small-time lawyer who previously failed to defend Wayne on his charge.
(6) Farouk is the neighbor of the Kerrigan's family.
(7) Lawrence Hammill QC is a retired barrister who helps the Kerrigan's family to defend the law case of their house free of charge.

3.2.3 Plot

The Kerrigan home is located in the outer Melbourne blue-collar suburb of Coolaroois, beside an airport. In order to expand the airport runway, developers attempt the compulsory acquisition of their house. Darryl and his neighbors all receive a letter with the same content, informing them of the compulsory acquisition of their houses for a large sum of money. Darryl wants to fight the eviction because he believes that the government can defend his home. He hires an incompetent lawyer, Dennis Denuto who is actually unfamiliar with the law in court. During the time when they await the final decision outside the court, Darryl meets a retired lawyer Lawrence and talks with him about the conditions of his house. The result comes out and the court rejects the family's appeal and gives them two weeks to vacate. Lawrence shows sympathy and offers to argue before the High Court of Australia for them. In court, Lawrence points out that the Kerrigans have the right to just terms of compensation for acquisition of property under Section 51(xxxi) of the Australian Constitution. Finally, the court rules the Kerrigans have the right to keep their house and the developers lose the case.

3.2.4 Theme Analysis

The film *The Castle* reveals that small events also have their place in determining who we are and what we value as individuals and as a community in the Australian multicultural context. The Kerrigans are an Australian family, living in a low socioeconomic area near an expanding airport, against the Airlink Corporation, which takes advantage of the compensation terms for acquisition.

In the face of challenges and adversaries, Darryl and his neighbors are committed to their pursuit of the Australian Dream, for example, egalitarianism. They display enormous trust in the legal system, holding that the government cannot evict them against their will from their treasured home, and every Australian should enjoy the equal right of property, such as land and home. At last Darryl wins the case. This person has a role in the writing of history. The film, at the same time, suggests the triumphs of an ordinary working class family.

The film title *The Castle*, based on the English saying:"a man's home is his castle," is repeatedly used in the film. It foregrounds the importance of family and loyalty, which are considered significant in today's Australian society (Malone, 1997: 10—12). Home is a spiritual and cultural root of the family and all the emotional memories, which revolve around love. Therefore, Darryl as a husband and father defends it at all costs.

New Words

steal	n.	便宜的东西
real estate	n.	房地产
backbone	n.	支柱;脊梁骨
billiard table	n.	台球桌
axle	n.	车轴;轮轴
greyhound	n.	夜车
spray	n.	喷雾;浪花;装饰用的小树枝
apprentice	n.	学徒,新手
ergonomic	a.	人体工程学的
brake	n./v.	刹车
tumble	v.	翻滚;摔倒
hairdresser	n.	理发师
bride	n.	新娘
bust	v.	打碎,打破
black sheep		不肖子女;害群之马
close-knit	a.	紧密结合的
marvel	v.	赞叹,惊奇
snout	n.	动物的口鼻部
muzzle	n.	防止动物咬人的口套
ashtray	n.	烟灰缸
memento	n.	纪念品;遗物
aerial	n.	天线
valuation	n.	估价
overcapitalize	v.	对……估价过高;过分投资于
compulsory	a.	强制性的
freight	n.	货物,货运
ironclad	a.	铁定的,严格的
conveyance	v.	让渡,运送
magistrate	n.	地方法官
sprinkle	v.	洒;用……点缀
babble	v.	喋喋不休,胡言乱语;泄露
complimentary	a.	赠送的;赞美的,表示敬意的
moisture	n.	水分;降雨量
serenity	n.	宁静,安详
hulk	n.	残骸;外壳;笨重的人(物)
dispute	v.	就……进行争论;怀疑;抵抗

tribunal	n.	法庭；裁决	nullius	n.	无主地
iffy	a.	不确定的；可疑的，有问题的	ballpark	a.	大致正确的；运动场的
artillery	n.	炮兵部队	sensational	a.	绝妙的；耸人听闻的
barrister	n.	律师			
bloke	n.	家伙	outrageous	n.	粗暴的；无法容忍的；反常的
sermon	n.	布道			
interim	a.	暂时的；期中的；间歇的	gut	n.	肠，内脏；勇气
			disenchant	v.	使清醒，使不抱幻想
injunction	n.	强制令；禁令	gratis	a.	无偿的
rectify	v.	改变，校正			
spoil	n.	损坏；掠夺；变质	statute	n.	法令
pop	v.	突然出现，突然提出问题，突然行动	aviation	n.	航空
			obiter dictum		法官于判决中附带表示的意见
steward	n.	服务员，管家，理事	appellant	n.	上诉人；上诉
			eyesore	n.	难看的东西，碍眼
book	v.	立案控告			
contravene	v.	违反；否定；抵触	shortchange	v.	亏待；欺骗；少找零头
blatant	a.	公然的，明目张胆的			
			stun	v.	受刺激，大吃一惊；击晕
breach	v. / n.	违背；破坏			
vibe	n.	感应；氛围，环境	consortium	n.	财团
terra	n.	土地	eligible	n.	合乎条件的人

Exercises

1. True or false judgments

（1）Darryl makes some furniture for the family, and he's always planning extensions of the house.

（2）The neighbors are all local Australians.

（3）The developers attempt the compulsory acquisition of their house to expand the neighboring airport.

（4）Darryl has a strict rule: when the family starts to eat, the television is definitely turned down.

（5）The Kerrigans' family is an equal family.

（6）The Airlink Corporation is a government authority, but all the money is coming from Barlow Group in the film.

（7）Agents from the airport try to bribe and bully the family into giving up, which attracts Darryl initially.

（8）The "Mabo" decision pertains to the specific issue of native land title and *terra*

nullius.
(9) Dennis Denuto does local cases about conveyancing mainly, such as wills, petty theft and so on.
(10) Right after Darryl Kerrigan loses the case in federal court, he pulls himself together and encourages his family.

2. **Term interpretations**
   (1) Darryl   (2) Sal
   (3) Tracey   (4) Dennis Denuto
   (5) Lawrence   (6) Con
   (7) Wayne   (8) the Mabo Case

3. **Essay questions**
   (1) Does the Castle in the film refer to a large and stately mansion?
   (2) What differences do a house and a home have in Darryl's eyes?
   (3) What letter does Darryl receive after a property valuer inspects his house?
   (4) Why does Darryl go to court after hearing his house will be occupied to expand the airport?
   (5) What is the turning point in Darryl's rough case?

3.3 Reading Passage 1: Creative Nation: Approaching Australian Cinema and Cultural Studies
by Amit Sarwal and Reema Sarwal[①]

Introduction

It has often been said that Australia has no history, let alone a mythology. There has been a constant struggle over the representation, construction and reconstruction of "Australia." In the eyes of the world it is a new migrant nation or modern nation created by moving several million people across the world, with the majority of people from British origins along with a great hodge-podge of world cultures[1] (over 100 nationalities), a Great South Land[2], Wide Brown Land[3], a Cultural Desert, a Godforsaken Land[4], Land of the Fair Go[5], Antipodes[6] or just Down Under[7]. These fascinating, contradictory and diverse clichés, images, and stereotypes regarding Australia make one wonder about what to expect from its films- much needed to enhance the social unity of an underpopulated continent[8]. Well, it offers everything ranging from *Mad Max* (1979)[9] to *Crocodile Dundee* (1986); *They're a Weird Mob* (1966)[10] to *Rabbit-Proof Fence* (2002); *The Tracker* (2002)[11] to *Jammin' in the Middle E* (2005)[12]; *The Man from Snowy River*

---

① Amit Sarwal: Assistant Professor at the Department of English, Rajdhani College, University of Delhi, India. Reema Sarwal: Lecturer at Miranda House, University of Delhi, India. "Creative nation: approaching Australian cinema and cultural studies" by Amit Sarwal and Reema Sarwal. 2009. *Creative Nation: Australian Cinema and Cultural Studies Reader* [M]. New Delhi: Sports and Spiritual Science Publication. pp. xxvi-xlix.

(1982)[13] to *Happy Feet* (2007)[14]. The urban woman who finds herself at a station in the outback and wants to be a part of it unlike the men who wish to tame it in *We of the Never Never* (1982)[15], the old-fashioned picture show man travelling across the Australian landscape on a horse-cart, struggling against the new tide of talking films in *The Picture Show Man* (1977)[16], and the unusual comic patriarch of *The Castle* (1977) fighting the authorities to protect his dream house are just some of the striking examples of the delicate portraiture of human sensibilities that stick in our memory.

The reason to study Australian literature, cinema and culture may vary. Some people have visited Australia as tourists (both cultural and academic), some have seen or learnt about Australia from madia images and programmes such as those on the Discovery[17] or National Geographic channels[18], some have been lucky enough to watch and recognize an Australian film on television. The choice to study, engage or teach Australia is related to a highly personal investment. Reasons apart[19], any journey exploring Australian films is remarkably exciting, enjoyable and rewarding. The Australian film industry, as a social, economic and cultural institution, started with bushranger films and continued to produce hits[20] based on early Australian types-convicts, bushrangers and swagmen. Later, as the film production and technology grew in Australia, filmmakers not only adapted the conventional Hollywood forms but also changed to more serious, complex and diverse issues like those of suburbia, politics, societal idiosyncrasies, new ideologies and Australianness while discovering new ways exploring the old concerns with the outback, the bush and the unique Australian nature. It is a cinema which constructs and demolishes national myths at the same time-upholding the Australian dream of a family house in *The Castle* and *They're a Weird Mob* and shattering the myth of the Aborigines as belonging solely to the outback and not sharing any urban sensibilities in films as varied as *Crocodile Dundee*, *The Fringe Dwellers* (1986)[21], and *Black Talk* (2002)[22]. In fact, Australian identity today, particularly in tourism industry and cultural policies, is increasingly identified in terms of Aboriginal culture and cultural diversity presented within the boundaries of the modern city. The most reverberating national myths in Australia are the myths of identity such as the interconnection between landscape and character, the quest for home, and definitions of Australianness and these are all pervasive in both Australian cinema and culture, be it the film genres of comedy, tragedy, horror, drama, humor, documentary and so on or cultural expressions of music, theatre, mass art, photography, multiculturalism, educational institutes, etc[23].

Film Policy in Australia: "Combine" to "Creative Nation"

Australian cinema can be seen as part of an expanding chain of national cinemas, contributing to the global film industry in terms of the people, places and stories involved. It has struggled against "Hollywoodization" just like most film industries worldwide. But this dominance or hegemony of Hollywood over Australian cinema or Australians was a result, as put by O'Regan (1989)[24], of "overexposure" during the World Wars, although the more significant reason is traced elsewhere: it was around World War I that a large number of Australian production houses[25] merged to form the monopolistic Australasian Film—a "Combine" looking after or rather monopolizing production and distribution (working against the "fair go" practice promoted by Australian government). By the time of World War II American interest in Australian films and cinemas resulted in US studios introducing a new contract system making them the undisputed rulers of the Australian screen exercising a defacto control[26]. This made the field much more competitive, risky, costly and a not-so-profitable affair for the Australian producers and distributors. In order to ease these challenges and dominance of monopolistic combines or studios, the Australian government has since then played a major role in establishing and promoting its local creative and cultural industries throughout the world by its various initiatives (censorship, regulations, govt. inquiries/commissions[27], quotas[28], tax relief, funding agencies, etc.) and cultural and media policies. The underlying principle of such policies in the development and evolution of Australian cinema being:

A vibrant film and television production sector helps promote a more inquisitive, imaginative and thoughtful Australian society through the realization of Australian stories on screen. It also provides a medium through which Australia's creative talents are able to reach the world.

In 1927, a Royal Commission[29] was established just to investigate the influence of Hollywood films over Australia, but the Commission was equally concerned by the decline of the number of British films screened in Australia. It is prime minister Gorton[30] who is credited with starting the film industry in Australia with his initiative in 1969 and by 1975, the concern for Australian culture and creative arts as assessed by the Interim Board of the AFC[31] led to a government interest at the level of film policy according to the fact which Australian film and creative talent were required to play an important role in the cultural formation of Australian values. This phase of culture romance[32] was marked by the production of some truly Australian films like *Picnic at Hanging Rock* (1975)[33], *Newsfront* (1978)[34], *My Brilliant Career* (1979)[35] and *Gallipoli* (1982).

The Australian cinema industry (and to some extent even cultural industry) is policy led and therefore according to Jock Given (1995)[36]:

> Every living Australian prime minister has run a government that did something for Australian film. Gorton's started federal assistance to the industry, Whitlam[37]'s increased it and reorganized it, Fraser[38]'s introduced 10BA[39], Hawke's established the Film Finance Corporation[40]. Keating's government has delivered Creative Nation[41], an expensive statement of cultural policy announced in October, 1994.

But it is only post-1994 that the promotion of Australian film has increasingly become a core element of Australia's cultural policies. In October 1994, the then prime minister, Paul Keating, launched the Commonwealth Cultural Policy and stated that, "Our post-colonial status guaranteed that there would be a lot of questions about who we are, what level of culture we might reasonably aspire to[42]." Already, in July 1992, the Commonwealth Government had appointed a panel of eminent Australians to advise on the formulation of a Commonwealth cultural policy. A preamble to the cultural policy was prepared by the Panel. Historically, this is a major step by any Commonwealth of Australia government, as this, Creative Nation: Commonwealth Cultural Policy (1994), was a national cultural policy (to which we owe[43] the title of our book). The definitive endeavor of this cultural policy was to enrich Australian life by spreading awareness about Australian culture and promoting the expression of Australia's cultural identity. With a cultural policy in place[44], Australian government recognized its responsibility to foster and preserve a cultural environment, heritage, identity, and the means of self-expression and creativity. To achieve this, assistance to the film industry was provided through direct funding to the Australian Film Commission (AFC)[45], the Australian Film, Television and Radio School (AFTRS)[46], the Film Finance Corporation (FFC)[47], Film Australia (FA),[48] and the Australian Children's Television Foundation (ACTF)[49], a continuous process as many of these agencies were established much earlier (some with different names).

Filmmaking in Australia: (inter)National Film Culture

Filmmaking in Australia, like all over the world, is an unpredictable and big business. And, in spite of this influential role of the Australian government in shaping the national cinema, there is relative unawareness about Australian cinema and its place in the Cinemas of the World[50] or the international film culture. Ben Goldsmith[51] argues in his article in this book that the cinematic origins of the nation have ensured that film in Australia can never simply be approached as entertainment. For a better understanding of Australian cinema and its artistic, narrative and technical merits, it is very important to pay due attention to the kinds of cultural values, identities and myths it nurtures.

Australian cinema has been divided among three eras to simplify discussion-the Silent Era (1896—1926), the New Wave (or revival) (1970s—1980s), and the Contemporary Australian cinema (1990s—Present). There is another important period, normally called "the Interval" (1930s—1960s), which is often painted in orthodox histories as one where nothing happened, and while very few feature films were made in this period, there was an industry working in the field of documentaries and advertising. In fact, some very important films were made in this era, e. g. RaymondLongford's *The Sentimental Bloke* (1932)[52], Charles Chauvell's *Jedda* (1955)[53], and John Heyer's famous documentary *The Back of Beyond* (1954)[54].

The earliest surviving Australian motion picture was shot in 1896 by Walter Barnett[55] and Frenchman Marius Sestier[56], depicting the running of the nation's premier horse race, The Melbourne Cup[57]. But the earliest known feature length narrative film in Australia, and also in the world, was the Australian production *The Story of the Kelly Gang* (1906)[58]—a fully integrated, secular, fictional narrative. Further, one of the world's first film studios, The Limelight Department[59] was operated by The Salvation Army[60] in Melbourne, between 1891 and 1910. The language, imagery and style used in these earlier films were more English oriented. As mentioned earlier, it was only during and after World

War II that the American influences on Australian culture intensified. There was a huge influx of Americans, American culture and American products into Australia. The US investors and financers gained control of movie distribution and exhibition and soon monopolized the business by screening mostly American films. This dominance caused the demise of a booming Australian film industry and left the regional talent and film industry personnel to choose between two options for survival. The first, according to Neale (1981)[61], was the possibility of imitation or attempting to copyor adapt the conventional Hollywood forms, genres and styles to remain in business. The second alternative was to put together films that were dramatically different, stressing the unique qualities or genres peculiar to that nation's. After the 1930s it was mostly the second alternative that was exercised while the earlier industry was mostly commercial and therefore more imitative, e. g., films by Ken G. Hall[62] had a kind of Hollywood flavor (although often, like in *The Squatter's Daughter* (1933)[63] there were strong Australian landscapes and the main character sets up a type of bush heroine).

Finally, it was during the 1970s, the "golden age"[64] or revival or the renaissance of Australian cinema that the Australian government, to compete internationally and to rid Australia of American and to some degree even British influences, increased the funding for Australian filmmakers through the establishment of Australian Film Commission (AFC). This New Wave cinema helped in the reemergence of the Australian film industry but relied heavily on the wholesome period dramas and therefore was also dubbed as the "AFC Genre"[65]. Successful film such as, *Walkabout* (1971)[66], *Sunday Too Far Away* (1975)[67], *The Chant of Jimmie Blacksmith* (1978)[68], *Mad Max*, *Crocodile Dundee*, *Shine* (1996)[69], made an international impact and helped in foregrounding Australian talent and themes, especially in Hollywood. This is the "boom-bust-boom cycle" of Australian cinema spanning the eighty years of the twentieth century. However, the lack of promotional strategies on the part of Australian production houses as well as distribution of Australian films through Hollywood based studios or American owned distribution houses make it hard, especially for the non-Australian audiences, to identify their Australian origins so that the films are more often than not mistaken to be Hollywood productions. This in turn makes non-Australians believe that there are no Australian films at the international box-office[70] and therefore they must be lacking in artistic quality. One of the main aims of this book is to help international audiences understand that there are certain elements of Australian films that can be immediately recognized (without depending on a knowledge of the studios to identify Australian films) Lisa French[71], for example, outlines some of the major tropes like the lost child and the landscape traditions in Australian cinema while Felicity Collins[72] and Katherine Bode[73] discuss the characteristic Australian larrikin ockers and Aussie battlers as markers of Australian national identity in their chapters respectively.

A significant development in Australian national cinema is the shift from purely Anglo-centric to multicultural or hybridized forms and the focus on race and ethnic relations so that it has moved from the outback to suburbia and into the inner city-see films like *The Outback* [74] or *Wake in Fright* (1971)[75], Baz Luhrmann's *Strictly Ballroom* (1993), Muriel's *Wedding* (1994)[76], Clara Law's *Floating Life* (1996)[77], or David Caesar's *Idiot Box* (1996)[78]. It has also established a fairly long list of internationally-recognized films that have scored worldwide box-office successes. Apart from those mentioned previously, films like Baz Luhrmann's *Moulin Rouge* (2001), P. J. Hogan's *Muriel's Wedding*, Stephan Elliot's *The Adventures of Priscilla: Queen of the Desert* (1994)[79], Chris Noonan's *Babe* (1995)[80], Ana Kokkinos' *Head On* (1998)[81], Ray Lawrence's *Lantana* (2001)[82], Phillip Noyce's *Rabbit-Proof Fence*, Adam Elliot's *Harvey Crumpet* (2003)[83], and Cate Shortland's *Somersault* (2004)[84] are a few notable and unequivocal examples of the best of well-known Australian films. It has been a kind of tradition in Australia that a good number of Australia's talented writers and artists have sought recognition overseas in UK, USA and Europe. Among the Australian actors to achieve recognition or international stardom have been Cate Blanchett[85], Guy Pearce[86], Naomi Watts[87], Paul Hogan, Mel Gibson[88], Geoffrey Rush[89], Toni Collette[90], Nicole Kidman[91], Sam Neill[92], Russell Crowe[93], Hugh Jackman[94], Eric Bana[95], Heath Ledger[96], Hugo Weaving[97], Judy Davis[98], and Rachel Griffiths[99]. Many of Australia's successful film directors, like Peter Weir, Fred Schepisi[100], Gillian Armstrong[101], Bruce Beresford[102], Baz Luhrmann, Phillip Noyce, Jane Campion[103], Robert Luketic[104], Mario Andreacchio[105], and Gregor Jordan[106] have also moved onto Hollywood to direct hugely successful films.

Notes

[1] a great hodge-podge of world cultures: a mixture of dissimilar ingredients of world cultures.

[2] a Great South Land: one of the island of the Pacific nation mistaken known as Vanuatu (New Hebrides) for the Great South Land by Pedro Fernandez de Quiros, Spanish explorer in 1606. He was the first man to use the name "Terra Australis del Espiritu Santu"—the "Great South Land of the Holy Spirit"—for what we now know as the nation of Australia.

[3] Wide Brown Land: Australian land by Dorothy McKellar in his "My Country"—
A land of sweeping plains,
Of rugged mountain ranges,
Of droughts and flooding rains.
I love her far horizons,
I love her jewel-sea,
Her beauty and her terror
The wide brown land for me!

[4] a Godforsaken Land: Australian Gibson Desert.
[5] Land of the Fair Go: Australia prides itself on being the land of the "fair go."The Fair Go: an equal chance to attempt something.
[6] Antipodes: used to refer to Australian and New Zealand.
[7] Down Under: a colloquialism which is variously construed either to refer to Australia and New Zealand, or Australia alone.
[8] an underpopulated continent: a continent of population decline.
[9] *Mad Max* (1979):《疯狂的麦克斯》。
[10] *They're a Weird Mob* (1966):《登陆蛮荒岛》。
[11] *The Tracker* (2002):《紧急追踪》。
[12] *Jammin' in the Middle East* (2005): a movie shines light on the inhabitants of Western Sydney, an area known for its cultural diversity.
[13] *The Man from Snowy River* (1982):《来自雪河的男人》。
[14] *Happy Feet* (2007):《快乐的大脚》。
[15] *We of the Never Never* (1982):《有情天地》。
[16] *The Picture Show Man* (1977): a movie showing a man, his son and a piano player travel around Australia at the beginning of this century. But what they really want is to stay at one place and open up a cinema.
[17] the Discovery: the third operational orbiter, and the oldest orbiter in service.
[18] National Geographic channels: a subscription television channel.
[19] apart: an adverb meaning "so as to except or exclude from consideration or aside."
[20] hit: a noun referring to a successful or popular film, e.g. a Broadway hit. 百老汇热门的戏剧。
[21] *The Fringe Dwellers* (1986): a story of an Aboriginal family who tries to move out of the fringe into the main white community.
[22] *Black Talk* (2002): a film exploring spiritual aspects of Indigenous culture and community.
[23] The most reverberating national myths in Australia are the myths of identity such as the interconnection between landscape and character, the quest for home, and definitions of Australianness and these are all pervasive in both Australian cinema and culture, be it the film genres of comedy, tragedy, horror, drama, humor, documentary and so on or cultural expressions of music, theatre, mass art, photography, multiculturalism, educational institutes, etc.
  This sentence is a subjective mood. From a subjective point of view, Australians believe in national myths.
[24] O'Regan (1989): Tom O'Regan took up the position of Professor of Media and Cultural Studies in 2004. He has been a key figure in the development of media and cultural studies in Australia and has an international reputation for his cultural policy studies related work.
[25] Australian production houses: a facility that provides film show and production, e.g. a movie house 电影院。
[26] a defacto control: an actual control.

[27] govt. inquiries/commissions: governmental commissions to do a close examination of a matter in a search for information or truth.
[28] quotas: part of a share that is due or ought to be contributed.
[29] a Royal Commission is a major government public inquiry into an issue.
[30] Gorton (1911—2002): the 19th Prime Minister of Australia.
[31] the Interim Board of the AFC: the temporary Board of the Australian Film Commission, an Australian Government agency operating as partof the Commonwealth Film Program to ensure the creation, availability and preservation of Australian audiovisual content.
[32] This phase of culture romance: the time between the late 1960s and 1970s. An influx of government funding saw the development of a new generation of film makers telling distinctively Australian stories, including directors Peter Weir, George Miller and Bruce Beresford. Films such as *Picnic at Hanging Rock* and *Sunday Too Far Away* had an immediate national and international impact. The 1980s is often regarded as a golden age of Australian cinema, with many successful films, from the historical drama *Gallipoli*, to the dark science fiction *Mad Max*, the romantic adventure *The Man from Snowy River* and the comedy *Crocodile Dundee*.
[33] *Picnic at Hanging Rock* (1975):《悬崖下的午餐》。
[34] *Newsfront* (1978):《新闻线上》。
[35] *My Brilliant Career* (1979):《我的璀璨生涯》。
[36] Jock Given (1995—): Professor of Media and Communications at Swinburne University, Australia.
[37] Whitlam: the 21st Prime Minister of Australia.
[38] Fraser (1832—1919): the 22nd Prime Minister of Australia.
[39] 10BA: a tax scheme which was introduced in 1981 by legislation to implement. That was called the 10BA tax scheme and provided extremely attractive tax relieffor those investing in films.
[40] the Film Finance Corporation (FFC): the Australian Government's principal agency for funding the production of film and television.
[41] Creative Nation: the term coming from Creative Nation: Commonwealth Cultural Policy issued in 1994. Creative Nation marked the first occasion of an Australian federal government enunciating a clearly articulated cultural policy.
[42] aspire to: hope for, long for.
[43] owe to: attribute to.
[44] in place: In the appropriate or usual position or order, e.g.: With everything in place, she started the slide show.
[45] the Australian Film Commission (AFC): see [34].
[46] the Australian Film, Television and Radio School (AFTRS):the Australian national center for professional education and advanced training in film, television, radio and digital media. The School is an Australian Commonwealth government statutory uthority.
[47] the Film Finance Corporation (FFC): the Australian Government's principal agency for funding the production of film and television.

[48] Film Australia (FA): Production of documentaries, marketing and distribution services, production and post-production facilities, preview cinemas, stock footage library and archive.
[49] the Australian Children's Television Foundation (ACTF): a non-profit, government-funded organization in Australia.
[50] the Cinemas of the World: the films and film industries.
[51] Ben Goldsmith: an academic researcher in media production, distribution, exhibition and analysis.
[52] Raymond Longford's *The Sentimental Bloke* (1932)
Raymond Longford (1878—1959): a prolific Australian film director, writer, producer and actor during the silent era. *The Sentimental Bloke* (1919): an Australian silent film based on the 1915 poem "The Songs of a Sentimental Bloke" by C. J. Dennis.
[53] Charles Chauvell's *Jedda* (1955): Charles Chauvell (1897—1959): an Australian film maker. *Jedda* (1955):《洁达》。
[54] John Heyer's famous documentary *The Back of Beyond* (1954): John Heyer (1916—2001): an Australian documentary filmmaker. The Back of Beyond (1954): a collection of travelling vignettes along the Birdsville Track.
[55] Walter Barnett (1862—1934): Australian photographer.
[56] Marius Sestier (1861—1928): cinematographer.
[57] The Melbourne Cup: Australia's major Thoroughbred house race.
[58] *The Story of the Kelly Gang* (1906):《凯利帮的故事》。
[59] The Limelight Department: one of the world's first film studios, beginning in 1898, operated by The Salvation Army in Melbourne, Australia.
[60] The Salvation Army: an evangelical Christian church known for charitable work.
[61] Neale (1981): Senior Lecturer in the field of Creative Studies, School of Humanities and Cultural Industries, University of Warwick.
[62] Ken G. Hall (1901-1994): an Australian film director who is considered one of the most important figures in the history of the Australian film industry.
[63] *The Squatter's Daughter* (1933): is a multi-character bush drama at a sheep station (ranch).
[64] "golden age": the ten years of the 1970s and 80s which are regarded by many as a "golden age" of Australian cinema.
[65] "AFC Genre": the role of films in the 1960s as quasi-official representatives of Australian films. AFC 类型片。
[66] *Walkabout* (1971):《小姐弟荒原历险》。
[67] *Sunday Too Far Away* (1975):《遥遥星期天》。
[68] *The Chant of Jimmie Blacksmith* (1978):《吉米·布莱克史密斯的圣歌》。
[69] *Shine* (1996):《闪亮的风采》。
[70] a box office: a place where tickets are sold to the public for admission to a venue. By extension, the term is frequently used, especially in the context of the film industry. 票房。
[71] Lisa French: Associate Professor of Cinema Studies, Media and Communications,

RMIT University, Melbourne, Australia.
[72] Felicity Collins: Professor of Cinema Studies in La Trobe University, Australia.
[73] Katherine Bode: a scholar in gender studies, Australian literary and cultural studies, and data-based analyses of literary culture.
[74] *The Outback*: also known as *Wake in Fright*.
[75] *Wake in Fright* (1971):《假期惊魂》。
[76] Muriel's *Wedding* (1994):《穆丽尔的婚礼》。
[77] Clara Law's *Floating Life* (1996): Clara Law (1957—): a Hong Kong Film director. *Floating Life* (1996):《浮生》。
[78] David Caesar's *Idiot Box* (1996): David Caesar (1963—): an Australian film director. *Idiot Box*: an uncompromising look in the mirror, a vision of vanquished men hamstrung by a lack of education, prospects or the intelligence to extract themselves from the morass of a suburban hell.
[79] Stephan Elliot's *The Adventures of Priscilla: Queen of the Desert* (1994): Stephan Elliot (1964—): an Australian film director. *The Adventures of Priscilla: Queen of the Desert* (1994):《沙漠妖姬》。
[80] Chris Noonan's *Babe* (1995): Chris Noonan (1952—): an Australian filmmaker and actor best known for the pioneering live-action/CG film *Babe*. *Babe* (1995):《宝贝小猪》。
[81] Ana Kokkinos' *Head On* (1998): Ana Kokkinos (1958—): an Australian film director. *Head On* (1998):《正面碰撞》。
[82] Ray Lawrence's *Lantana* (2001): Ray Lawrence (1948—): Australian film director. *Lantana* (2001):《马缨丹》。
[83] Adam Elliot's *Harvey Crumpet* (2003): Adam Elliot (1972—): an independent stop-motion animation writer and director.
[84] Cate Shortland's *Somersault* (2004): Cate Shortland (1968—): an Australian writer and director of film and television. *Somersault* (2004):《生命翻筋斗》。
[85] Cate Blanchett (1968—): an Australian actress and theatre director.
[86] Guy Pearce (1967—): an English-born Australian actor and musician.
[87] Naomi Watts (1968—): an English-Australian actress.
[88] Mel Gibson (1956—): an American actor, film director, and producer.
[89] Geoffrey Rush (1951—): an Australian actor.
[90] Toni Collette (1972—): an Australian actress and musician.
[91] Nicole Kidman (1967—): an American-born Australian actress.
[92] Sam Neill (1947—): a New Zealand actor.
[93] Russell Crowe (1964—): a naturalized Australian actor.
[94] Hugh Jackman (1968—): an Australian actor and producer.
[95] Eric Bana (1968—): an Australian film and television actor.
[96] Heath Ledger (1979—2008): an Australian film actor.
[97] Hugo Weaving (1960—): a Nigerian-born English-Australian film and stage actor.
[98] Judy Davis (1955—): an Australian actress.
[99] Rachel Griffiths (1968—): an Australian film and television actress.

〔100〕Fred Schepisi (1939—): an Australian film director and screenwriter.
〔101〕Gillian Armstrong (1950—): an award-winning Australian director of feature films and documentaries.
〔102〕Bruce Beresford (1940—): a highly regarded Australian film director who has made more than thirty feature films over a forty-year career.
〔103〕Jane Campion (1954—): a film maker and screenwriter.
〔104〕Robert Luketic (1973—): an Australian film director.
〔105〕Mario Andreacchio (1955—): an Australian film director.
〔106〕Gregor Jordan (1966—): an Australian film director.

New Words

fascinating	a.	吸引人的	idiosyncrasy	n.	特质
underlying	a.	根本的	secular	a.	世俗的
contradictory	a.	矛盾的	ideology	n.	思想意识
vibrant	a.	充满生气的	orient	v.	确定方向
cliché	n.	陈规陋习	demolish	v.	破坏
inquisitive	a.	好奇的	influx	n.	流入
stereotype	n.	陈腔滥调，老套	weird	a.	怪异的
			demise	n.	死亡
credit	v.	归功于	mob	n.	暴徒
enhance	v.	提高	revival	n.	复活
phase	n.	阶段	shatter	v.	打碎
underpopulated	a.	人口稀少的	renaissance	n.	复兴
aspire	v.	渴望	solely	ad.	唯一地
outback	n.	内地	rid	v.	使去掉
panel	n.	专门小组	reverberating	a.	反响的
tame	v.	制服	reemergence	n.	再度出现
preamble	n.	序文	interconnection	n.	互连
patriarch	n.	创始人	wholesome	a.	健全的
endeavor	n.	尽力	pervasive	a.	普遍的
portraiture	n.	肖像画	dub	v.	授予称号
narrative	a.	叙述的	genre	n.	类型
stick	v.	粘贴	foregrounding	a.	最突出的位置的
interval	n.	间隔			
bushranger	n.	丛林汉	hegemony	n.	霸权
orthodox	a.	正统的	promotional	a.	增进的
swagman	n.	流浪汉	monopolistic	a.	垄断的
depict	v.	描述	box-office	n.	票房
suburbia	n.	郊区	undisputed	a.	无可争辩的
premier	a.	最初的	trope	n.	比喻

defacto	a.	事实上的	respectively	ad.	分别地
larrikin	a.	喧闹的	censorship	n.	审查制度
ease	v.	缓和	hybridized	a.	混合的
ocker	n.	无教养的澳大利亚人	unequivocal	a.	不含糊的，明确的
initiative	n.	首创精神	stardom	n.	明星界

Exercises

1. **True or false judgments**
   (1) In the eyes of the author, Australia was considered as a country without history and a mythology, however, Australia has been struggling to construct its national identity through developing cinemas.
   (2) According to the author, the Australian film industry started with convicts.
   (3) The Australian myths are viewed as the myths of national identity which are pervasive in both Australian cinema and culture.
   (4) After the World War II, American films entered the Australian film markets and had a strong impact on Australia's local cinema.
   (5) A very important change in the Australian film industry is the shift from American influence to Australian multicultural breakthrough.

2. **Essay questions**
   (1) What is the aim of this article?
   (2) Why is it said that the Australian cinema industry is policy led?
   (3) Why was the 1970s called the "golden age" or the renaissance of Australian cinema?

Reading Passage 2: Governing Australian Diversity: Multiculturalism and Its Values

by Greg McCarthy

Introduction

The paper argues that successive Australian governments have used "multiculturalism" as a tool to govern both race and ethnic diversity, through asserting "Australian values" as immutable. Using Hall's (1997) notion of conjuncture, it examines how conjunctures, are shaped by global capital, but this is an insufficient determinate to explain how ideological re-articulation to correspond to economic circumstances by necessity involves race and ethnic political struggle. What is emergent in the contemporary conjuncture involves the ideological clusteringor assembling of anxiety over the rise of China, Islamophobia[1], and racial guilt over past and present Indigenous discrimination. The emergence of global change occurred with the demise of the Keynesian economic management model[2] in the 1970s, it was at this momentthat Australian governments adopted the policy of multiculturalism to articulate ethnic diversity into a population governance framework.

The paper argues that the Fraser government's model for managing ethnic diversity and race was extended by the Hawke government to embrace multiculturalism as enhancing Anglo-Celtic identity. However, as neoliberal became the dominant economic ideology of the Howard government multiculturalism was displaced by Howard's assimilationist policies, built on the asserted superior values of whiteness and Western civilization (Hage, 2011). Howard's gambit to contain multiculturalism invoked the ideology of Australian as the outpost of British values, in a sea of Asian inferior Confucius values[3], however, given Australia's engagement with Asia and the rise of Asian immigration, this invocation required an appeal to national security to shore up the hypocrisy of such an appeal. In other words, the Howard government was appealing to a colonial legacy at the very moment when Asian countries had asserted a post-colonial confidence and an emerging economic power to challenge the West. The appeal of the West versus the Rest was falling on unreceptive ears in the region and Australia itself.

Post the Howard government conjuncture, Rudd, Gillard, Abbott[4] and the Turnbull[5] governments, retained Howard's value and security stratagem. However, continual diverse immigration, especially from Asia, created a diasporic cultural dynamic, which spawned resistance against governing tendencies to rule via a values-based form of ideological discourse. Moreover, the emergence of the theory of a "clash of civilization"[6] (Huntington, 1993) became integrated into governing values polices as a response to the rise of China and the reemergence of Islam on the world stage. Whereas in the Howard period it was anti-Asian immigration that was the glue holding the values ideology together this morphed into anti-Islam as Australia following the US became embroiled in the Middle Eastern wars.

The paper will be structured in the following sections. Part one outlines Australia as an immigration nation. Part two delineates how respective governments from Bob Hawke (1983—1991), John Howard (1996— 2007), Kevin Rudd (2007—2010), Julia Gillard (2010—2013) Tony Abbott (2013—2015) Malcolm Turnbull (2015—) have approached the governance of multiculturalism. The next section will use critical discourse theory to show how the Turnbull government's multicultural statement is imbued with Eurocentric values, constructing Western civilization as confronting barbarism. The paper's methodology for examining multiculturalism is grounded by Hall's (2010) notion of conjuncture as "a period during which the different social, political, economic and ideological contradictions that are at work in society come together to give it a specific and distinctive shape" (p. 1).

Immigration

Australian multiculturalism is a product of immigration across conjunctures. Australia along with the US, Canada and New Zealand, is one of the few Western countries to have actively pursued a settler-colonial immigration policy (Lopez, 2000; Jupp, 2002). Since the end of World War II around 6.4 million immigrants have arrived in Australia, making a major contribution to the Australian population increase from 7 million to 22.9 million people in 2016. Immigration has contributed around 50 per cent of Australia's population growth (Collins, 2013, pp. 162; Collins, 2008). According to Collins's (2013) estimations, "about one million migrants arrived in each of the four decades following 1950: 1.6 million between October 1945 and June 1960; about 1.3 million in the 1960s; about 960,000 in the 1970s; about 1.1 million in the 1980s and 900,000 in the 1990s" (Collins, 2013, p. 163).

In the past decades, in response to the turn to neoliberal policies and global labour market trends, Australian immigration intake has increased significantly to reach record post-war numbers. For example, in 2014—2015, Australia accepted 190,000 migrants, 68 percent via the skilled migration program (38 per cent employer sponsors, 34 percent skilled independent and 22 percent government nominated). Of the 38 per cent family reunion migrants (79 percent were partners joining their spouse); and 8 per cent refugee intake 11,900 people in 2014 (DIBP, 2016). Thirdly, in keeping with Australia's propensity to importing skilled labour, there has been a dramatic increase in Australian temporary migration intakes. According to Hugo (2012) there are approximately one million temporary migrants in Australia at any one year, including those on working holidays. In addition, Khoo et. al (2005) argues that nearly 50% of temporary immigrants will seek permanent residence in Australia (p. 2).

One of the outcomes of immigration in this neoliberal conjuncture there has been the rise in cultural, religious, linguistic and ethnic diversity, especially in the increase in international students and temporary workers from Asia. Government figures for 2015, show that 28 per cent of the Australian resident population were born overseas and that 48 per cent have one parent born overseas (ABS, 2016). The effect of the change in emigrational flows is apparent in Australian's largest cities, but somewhat absent in rural Australia (Hugo, 2008). In Australia's major cities such as Sydney and Melbourne, more than half of the population are first- or second-generation immigrants.

Equally, based on the Australian Bureau of Statistics[7] census date there are over 200 languages spoken in Australian homes, with English at 80 per cent and Mandarin second at 11 percent (ABS 2016). Moreover, almost 17 per cent of the Australian population is now of various Asian backgrounds, with many Asian-Australians having dual or multiple citizenships (Rizvi, 2017). For example, the spread of Chinese migrants, since the end of the White Australia policy in early 1970s, has seen Chinese immigration rise, especially post-1992 from the mainland. Migrants born in China were the second largest overseas-born population group in Sydney, at 4% of Sydney's total population in 2011, a total of 147,000 people (DIPB, 2016). Whilst Australia presents a whiteness as a dominant cultural trope it is fundamentally changing due to the inflow of Asian skilled labour and this challenges past conjunctural imagination of Australia as the land of Western superiority, situated in Asia.

Multiculturalism and immigration: from integration to assimilation and back again

In the immediate post-World War II conjuncture, the immigration was aimed at UK migrants, who could migrate paying a mere two UK pounds for steerage (Jupp, 2002). However, to meet immigration targets, the policy reached out to Europe, especially to Greece and Italy (Lopez, 2000). All migrants were expected to assimilate. However, the cultural diversity meant that by the 1970s, ethnic communities were not governed under this assimilationist framework. Immigrant groups retained their cultural identity, whilst integrating within Australian, especially via their children's education. In addition, the White Australia Policy was a hindrance to Australia's engagement with Asia. As a result, the word multiculturalism entered government vocabulary in 1973, echoing that of the Canadian approach, and was adopted as policy by the Fraser government.

Prime Minister Fraser commissioned Frank Galbally[8] (1978) to write a report on multiculturalism, which is regarded as a watershed in its linking of multiculturalism to integration. Galbally (1978) recommended that ethnic groups could retain their culture without prejudice or disadvantage, moreover, Australian's should be encouraged to understand and embrace other cultures. Multicultural polices emerged, including the establishment of a multicultural television and radio network, called Special Broadcasting Service (SBS)[9] and the promotion of language learning in schools. However, the Fraser government, was confronted by the end of the post-war conjuncture, characterised by Keynesian demand-management. In response, the Fraser government embraced the changed economic circumstances by reducing government expenditure, which adversely affected the working class, often in areas where migrant labour was concentrated (Castles, 2012). Further, the end of the Vietnam War[10] saw the first wave of Indo-Chinese refugees[11] coming to Australia, consequently with the family reunion and skilled migrant paths having equal weight, subsequent migration would show a steady rise in Asian migration.

A transitional conjuncture to neoliberalism[12]

The incoming Hawke government linked multiculturalism to globalization of the Australian economy, relating diversity to increasing skills, in keeping with the shifting of the economy away from manufacturing to a service economy (Johnson, 2007). Given the thrust of a global-market economy, it was logical to include multiculturalism into a national narrative. Commonwealth and State labor governments financially supported ethnic communities based on both social democratic equity principles aligned with the emerging (neo) liberal theory of enhancing labour-market skill formation. On equity, the Commonwealth developed new bodies like the Office of Multicultural Affairs[13] and the Human Rights and Equal Opportunity Commission[14]. On skill formation, the Hawke government established the Bureau of Immigration, Multicultural and Population Research (BIMPR)[15] to conduct research so as to inform policy-makers. On stakeholder advice, the Hawke government, formed the National Multicultural Advisory Council[16] (Tavan, 2012; Koleth, 2010).

Significantly, as a buffer against the global conjuncture, the Hawke government began to tie multiculturalism to national identity, so that multiculturalism stood not a higher order Anglo-Celtic civilization (Hage, 1998). This attempt to redefine national identity occurred at the very moment when the family reunion policies affected the immigration inflow, therein boosting the Middle Eastern refugee intake. Equally, it was in an era when Indigenous Peoples sought land right's justice, which provoked a backlash from mining and pastoral interests. Indigenous leaders made in clear that multiculturalism was not something they identified with, as it was basically an immigration issue, whereas their concerns were with First People rights[17]; such as the violent dispossession of their land and the past and present continued discrimination against them.

Moreover, as noted earlier, by the late 1980s Australia had a high migrant intake which included significant numbers of new arrivals from Asian and Middle-Eastern countries. There was growing political polarisation on the immigration policy, which promoted Hawke, to commission Stephen Fitzgerald[18] (1988), Australia's first Ambassador to China, to chair a committee examining immigration. The report, released in 1988, entitled, "Immigration: A Commitment to Australia," warned of the need to change the immigration policy and noted that the public little understood multiculturalism. The Report observed that most of the people who mistrusted multiculturalism also expressed concern over immigrants' commitment to Australian values. The FitzGerald Report called for immigrants to make a commitment to Australia and to take up citizenship. Secondly that arguing that cultural diversity is an important resource in a globalizing world and that Australia's role in the Asia-Pacific region demanded importing skills. The Hawke Government responded to the report by releasing the 1989 multicultural policy statement, the *National Agenda for a Multicultural Australia*, endorsing immigration as an economic benefit and that, immigrants had to have an overriding commitment to Australian values.

The 1989 Report can be read as a conjunctural response to the politicisation of immigration and multiculturalism by the Opposition Leader John Howard. Howard had taken his cue from the prominent Australian historian Geoffrey Blainey[19] (1984), who argued that Asian immigration was too high and this threatened "social cohesion." Blainey (1984) dubbed multiculturalism as a "new form of colonialism," where Australia was considered the "colony of the world" and Australian's of British background were now marginalized. Howard went further to argue that Asian migration was challenging the public's cultural tolerance level and multiculturalism was against Australian values. Hage (1998) argues this was a turning point in governing multiculturalism in Australia, as Howard's most crucial ideological move was to give credibility "to the fantasy of a core Australian culture that, while changing, is still in deep continuity with the Australian culture of the assimilationist era: no room for multiculturalism here" (Hage, 1998, p. 433).

The new conjuncture: Asserting Australian values

The Howard coalition government that won the 1996 election was overtly committed to the ideology of neoliberalism. There were significant cut backs to government expenditure in areas of education, welfare and health (Johnson, 2007). The prime minister set in place a series of measures to reassert Anglo-Celtic values so as to govern race and ethnicity. The government abolished the Office of Multicultural Affairs[20], restricted access to unemployment benefits, and the adult Migrant English Program[21], to new migrants. Moreover, the Howard government tied multiculturalism to civic duty and citizenship that expressly defined national identity in Anglo-Celtic institutions and neoliberal market terms. Moreover, Aboriginal and Torres Island were subsumed under multiculturalism, despite the First People's opposition to being reduced to immigrational flows. This rejection of first people rights was, according to Langton, a reaffirmation of racial assimilation (Langton, 2000).

The 1996 election also brought independent candidate Pauline Hanson[22] into the Federal parliament on an anti-Asian migration program and opposition to Aboriginal Australian "special benefits." Hanson became the voice of "White decline," saying Australia was being "swamped by Asians." Howard was caught in a dilemma as Hanson was voicing his own rhetoric of Western decline but she threatened his conservative electoral base. As Ahluwalia and McCarthy argue, the reluctance of Howard to criticize Hanson was his belief that her anti-Asian views actually benefitted his strategy of winding back the gains of the ethnic, feminist and Indigenous peoples, at the same time reacting to the post-colonial standpoint that was predominant in Asia (Ahluwalia and McCarthy, 1998).

The Howard government in 1998 did launch a multicultural policy, which asserted that multiculturalism in Australia was unique, as it proved how cultural diversity can be integrated into Australia's core democratic values and these should be expressed in citizenship. The Value test was, according to Stratton, based on a belief that non-Western and non-white cultures are "incompatible" with Australia's national values and [the Statement] is visibly marked by race (Stratton, 1998, pp. 13—14). Andrew Robb[23] (2006), the Howard governmental spokesman for multicultural affairs and citizenship, set the ideological values agenda for the era when he said that multiculturalism was a separatist doctrine and that "the one point on which there must be universal agreement is that those who come here should unite behind a core set of values, a shared identity."

The Iraq War[24] heightened the values debate. The government, following the Bush administration, constructed the War as one of liberating Iraq from the yoke of a dictator, who supposedly had "weapons of mass destruction." Prime Minister Howard tied Australian values to the supposed Islamic threat against Western democratic norms. In this endeavor, the Howard government introducing the Australian Values Statement[25], which obliged all long-term visitors to Australia to sign a value's declaration. It was asserted that Australian national identity, had to be protected from the perceived growing threats of Islamic terrorism, somehow fueled by the arrival of 'boat people'[26] and asylum seekers (Perera & Stratton, 2009). In turn, citizenship became conflated with national identity and no longer framed in terms of acquiring civic rights but in liberal democratic values and nationalist tropes, as defined by the government.

Howard's distain for multiculturalism and the new value agenda was apparent in 2007, when the word multiculturalism was removed from the new Department of Immigration and Citizenship[27]. Howard defended the move saying, "immigration should lead to citizenship" (2007). According to Hage (2011), Howard was reasserting assimilation norms, by claiming that Australian values were "a projection of Western civilization in this part of the world" (cited in Hage, 2011). Howard argued, that all Australian's are being united by "a common love of Australian values." For Hage, Howard was expressing "White paranoia" over multiculturalism, Aboriginal self-determination, and the anxiety created by the rise of Asia in the notion of patriotic love of the country as a bastion of Anglo-Celtic whiteness (Hage, 2011).

The new conjuncture and its nuances

Following Howard, multiculturalism was conflated with neoliberal market citizenship, security and a commitment to Australia that was emotionally charged. For Howard, Australia had to choose its Western values, whilst accepting it was geographically in Asia. In contrast, Johnson, Ahluwalia and McCarthy (2010) contend that, Rudd accepted that Australia was in Asia but feared unless it met the challenges of the rise of Asian economies, especially China, it would decline as a Western power and with it claims of Western superiority. Likewise, whereas Howard had responded to Indigenous claims from land and social justice through reactive policies, Rudd embraced the needed for symbolic reconciliation in the Stolen Generation speech (Johnson, Ahluwalia and McCarthy, 2010). Nevertheless, the speech was so crafted as to avoid the u question of racism behind the practice and how this related to colonization. Equally, it had little effect on policy practice as Indigenous children continue to be taken from their parents, who do not fit the assimilated neoliberal subjectivity (Douglas and Walsh, 2013).

Rudd's replacement Julie Gillard did produce an official multicultural statement, titled "The People of Australia" (DIC, 2013), which had a forward by Gillard, noting how she was a Welsh immigrant. The policy was a celebration of ethnic diversity, with an engagement with Australia's First Peoples, reflected in Rudd's national Apology. The statement, set out a range of multicultural principles, which celebrated cultural diversity, the notion of equity and how immigration was economically essential for the labour market (Tavan, 2012). In policy terms, Gillard established a new independent body the Australian Multicultural Council, to offer advice and to champion multicultural pluralism, whilst strengthening migrant access and equity. Pointedly, the document noted that the rise of racism in Australia, with anti-discrimination laws being enacted to counter racism and discrimination (DIC, 2013).

The Gillard government's multicultural statement needs to be read in the light of the prime minister's White Paper on the rise of Asia, titled: *Australia in the Asian Century*. The Asian Century White was both a mixture of recognition of the centrality of Asia to Australia, but also expressing episteme anxiety that economic and knowledge power was shifting to China (McCarthy and Song, 2015). The White Paper's response was to stress the need to develop cultural capabilities in order to understand the economic benefit of China's rise.

However, the election of the Abbott government in 2013, effectively abandoned the White Paper, decommissioned its staffing, and removed it from the government website. Moreover, Abbott, like Howard regarded multiculturalism as tribalism (McCarthy and Song, 2015). He evoked the term Team Australia, saying that my position is everyone must be on "Team Australia — everyone must put this country, its interests, its values, and its people first. You don't migrate to this country unless you want to join our team and that's the point I'll be stressing" (cited in Grattan, 2014). Team Australia was a code word for a nationalism and patriotism, which regarded Australia as an outpost of Western Civilization (Huntington, 1999).

Following Gillard's lead, Abbott did seek to advance the process of amending the Constitution to provide for "recognition" of Aboriginal Peoples in the Constitution. The dilemma, however, is that recognition would go beyond symbolism to create a just and lawful relationship between Aboriginal and non-Aboriginal people (Muldoon, 2016). Further, whilst Abbott called himself the "Prime Minister for IndigenousAustralians," his view of Indigenous peoples was either as assimilated neoliberal subjects or in need of a civilizing mission through punitive State intervention (Gulliver, 2015). In this duality, Abbott is merely following the conjunctural ideological shift orchestrated by Howard where the infringement of Indigenous rights is based on constructing Indigenous people as dysfunctional market subject and they therefore have to be assimilated via the removal of their ability to live in remote communities or to have market freedoms curtailed by government fiat (Gulliver, 2015).

Turnbull and multiculturalism as "Australian values"

Abbott's replacement as Prime Minister, Malcolm Turnbull, devised a multiculturalism policy, which was built on Howard's concepts of Australian values and national security. The statement as where multiculturalism is longer about minority cultures, embodied in such concepts such as ethnicity or Indigenous People's rights rather, Australia was multicultural because everyone was multicultural now.

The Turnbull's government's multicultural statement, titled *Multicultural Australia: United, Strong, Successful*, (2017), states that:

> Our nation is enriched by Aboriginal and Torres Strait Islanderpeople, the oldest surviving culture on the planet, and the millions of people who have chosen to make a new life here'. Formore than 50,000 years First Australians have lived, learned, adapted and survived on the lands we now call Australia. Living side by side, they consisted of over 250 different language groups or "nations" across the continent, each with distinctive cultures, beliefs, and dialects. Descendants of these nations represent the oldest surviving culture on the planet and have stories of times and places beyond the memory of any other people. The story continued with the foundation of modern Australia, through Britishand Irish settlement and the establishment of our parliamentary democracy, institutions and law. Over time, our story grew to include the millions of people from all continents who have made Australia home. Today, Australians welcome those who have migrated here to be part of our free and open society, to build their lives and make a contribution to our nation (2017, AG, p.7).

The Turnbull government's opening multicultural gambit, effectively ignores the Indigenous people's perspective that they are outside this immigration story and merely lumps then in as an ancient but living culture. As such, the First People's claims for justice against the litany of ill-treatment are ignored. Australian injustice and discrimination against Indigenous peoples is cleansed from the multicultural story. Moreover, if the Indigenous story cleanses the nation of racism, the English and Irish immigration claims smooths over narrative class struggle and religious prejudice. The narrative makes it clear that the English and Irish set the basis for the liberal democratic society to which all "others" must assimilate to, therein benefitting from Australia's "free and open society."

In endorsing the policy Prime Minster Turnbull wrote:

> Australia is the most successful multicultural society in the world. Australians look like every face, every race, every background because we define ourselves and our nation by our commitment to shared political values, democracy, freedom and the rule of law... We are defined not by race, religion or culture, but by shared values of freedom, democracy, the rule of law and equality of opportunity...
> Prime Minister Turnbull 2017(a)
> We do not define our national identity by race or religion, but by a commitment to shared Australian values. Those Australian values define us. Australian values unite us. Freedom.

Parliamentary democracy. The rule of law. Mutual respect. The equality of men and women and a fair go. The opportunity to get ahead, but lend a hand to those who fall behind. Our reforms will put these values at the heart of our citizenship requirements. Membership of our Australian family is a privilege and it should be afforded to those who support our values, respect our laws and want to integrate and contribute to an even better Australia.

Prime Minister Turnbull 2017(b)

The first quotation from Prime Minister Turnbull, asserts that Australia is "most successful" multicultural nation in the world. The second stating that immigrants must integrate into Australian values and to be citizens they will be required to swear allegiance to those values to gain citizenship. In this juxtaposition, Australia is a successful multicultural nation specifically because it obliges immigrants to integrate to "Australian values," including a high competence in English, and an unquestioning allegiance to "political values" (Turnbull, 2017), which are presented as self-evidentially Australian.

The shared values in the documents are defined in market citizen and liberal democratic terms. The document defined Australian values as firstly, "respect"; via the "rule of law and allegiance to Australia," plus liberty, fairness and compassion. Secondly, the virtue of "equality"; stated as "equality of men and women," "equality before the law" and "equal opportunity"—market equality. The last value being, "freedom"; defined as freedom of "thought, speech, religion, enterprise and association. [plus] We are committed to a parliamentary democracy."

The statement's values are formalistic and can be read as a floating signifier for white Anglo-Celtic dominance, as it incorporates multiculturalism to its own ends. In this regard, the Turnbull juxtaposition western values as immutably superior values based on a very narrow Ethno-centric model of Western formal democracy. The value terms, "respect," "equality" and "freedom," are defined as unquestionable universal Western values, which whitewashes Indigenous injustice and the White Australia policy. The past and current removal of Indigenous freedoms is expunged from the document, conforming to Hindess's[28] argument that liberalism defines freedom with a colonial imagination (2010). Nevertheless, such Western values cannot suppress all the countervailing propensities of race, ethnicity and class, past and present to challenge these utopian values, therefore government's multicultural statement invokes national security as a unifying trope.

The document states:

Underpinning a diverse and harmonious Australia is the security of our nation. The Australian Government places the highest priority on the safety and security of all Australians. Recent terrorist attacks around the world have justifiably caused concern in the Australian community. The Government responds to these threats by continuing to invest in counter-terrorism, strong borders and strong national security. This helps to ensure that Australia remains an open, inclusive, free and safe society (2017).

In placing this document into a broader discourse reading it is necessary to return to multicultural theory. Hage (2014) contends, what lies at the heart of Australian values is an insider-outsider notion of Australian national identity, where "Islamophobia" is set as the uncivilized opposite to the West, bolstered by a security imperative, where the Orient acts as an unbridled threat Western values (Hage, 2014). A playing out of Huntington's[29] (1999) "clash of civilizations," where prophecy becomes policy.

Moreover, as Provincelli (1998) argues, liberal multiculturalism as a governing tool, evokes a distinction between us and them. We, the civilized, are confronted by "barbaric, uneducated, and savage practices, which we as a civilized nation cannot allow to occur within our borders" (p. 577). She adds that a particular body of civilized values is elevated to the status of a "universal principle, primarily through the pageantries of corporeal shame and revulsion" (p. 577). This pageantry of repugnancies is evident in Minister Dutton's evocation of a "passionate drama of intimacy" (Provinceilli, 1998, p. 577), when Dutton cites immigrant's propensity for domestic violence, arranged marriages and clitoridectomies (all illegal in Australia) as reasons for a value-based citizen test (Dutton, 2017).

On the introduction of a citizen values test, Minister Dutton said:

> ...For example, domestic violence, a perpetrator of domestic violence. My view is that that person shouldn't become an Australian citizen...Domestic violence is a significant issue in this country. And we shouldn't tolerate one instance of it. And the fact that somebody might fudge an answer on a test or an application is no argument against us asking people if you want to become an Australian citizen, abide by our laws and our norms.
>
> We don't accept violence against women and there is a lot of work that the Federal Government has done and the state governments have done and it's a bipartisan approach, to stamping out domestic violence and that work continues today and it will continue forever (Dutton, 2017).

Dutton said that future application for Australian citizenship will be asked a series of questions on "Australian values," including subjects such as "wife-beating," "child marriage," "genital mutilation" and "girls' right to an education." Dutton denied these questions are targeting Muslims (Dutton, 2017). Here Dutton is constructing Australia in terms of the West representing modernity, secularism, peace and rights, while Islam stubbornly clings to a pre-modern: illiberal and undemocratic identity. In this clash of civilisations, a strong security state is required, one that will go so far as to deny citizenship and even remove citizenship from those it deems unworthy.

In sum, as Hall (1997) argues conjunctures, are not over-determined by economics and global capital, rather they involve an ideological re-articulation, in the current conjuncture that of race and ethnic politics. What is emergent in the contemporary conjuncture involves the ideological assembling of anxiety over the rise of China, Islamophobia, and racial guilt over past and present Indigenous discrimination. The Turnbull statement seeks to configure those components into a teleology of Western superiority, under the rubric of Australian multiculturalism. Moreover, as Hindess argues, the invocation of freedom so evident in the Turnbull government document and Dutton's anti-Islam statements represents the Other as living in the past, suggesting that they are less than fully human and can be dealt with by non-free means (Hindess, 2010). This is a contemporary form of racism, associated with the image of a nation that marginalized particular groups of people outside of its defined multicultural and racial norm.

Conclusion

In summary, Australia remains haunted by the specter of mistaken intolerance as it carries across historic conjunctures. Its deepest moral impulses are exposed to be historically contingent, continually expressing Eurocentric prejudices, which masquerade as universal principles. However, past colonial and civil rights abuses cast a shadow over ever conjuncture. Moreover, in regard to ethnicity, Turnbull's multicultural statement can be read as seeking closure around the racial trope of whiteness, evident at the birth of the nation. This point is made by John Fitzgerald (2007) in reflecting on the current conjuncture, when he wrote that "Despite the brouhaha surrounding multiculturalism many whites still reserve the word 'Australian' for themselves and many Chinese Australians refer to whites as 'Australians' and to themselves as 'Chinese' "(4—5). In the same vein, Ang argues, the ethnic term "Chinese" itself, in its invocation of a discrete and solidly bounded group, is a construction, that contributes to the imagined and real divide between "ethnic" and "national" (Ang, 2014). The current ideological closure, evident in the Turnbull government's multicultural statement constructs the minority as but a component of the majority.

The Howard government policed the crises of global economic dislocation of the economy, the rise of China and ethnic and Indigenous resistance to cultural homogenization, by governing through Australian values. Framed in this way, the Howard conjuncture has been built on neoliberal multiculturalism, which constructs the West and the Rest[30] as its benchmark. Under this rubric, both Asia and Islam are the floating signifies of difference. In this globalized conjuncture, the pressures of economic globalization is met by majoritarian politics. However, this ideological construct of the majority, as Gunew (1994) argues, begs the question of who is included and who is still marginalizes.

Historically, in Australia, ethnicity was confined to minorities and this was confined to non-English speaking migrants but eventually this raised the issue of the subsequent generations. Here as Ommundsen (2000) notes by opening up the category to second and third generation children of migrants, this had the effect of problematizing ethnic literature. A new category called Non-English Speaking Writers came into vogue. This categorization, opened up the attack against ethnic authors, where ethnic literature was seen as not only inferior to the mainstream but also promoted by professional ethnic advocates (Ommundsen, 2000). Likewise, the Demidinko[31] affair was a fortuitous vehicle to argue that ethnic identity could be falsified to promote literature that was inauthentic (Gunew, 1996).

Nevertheless, multicultural as a discourse challenges the ideological articulation of a majoritarian culture, evident in the rise of second generation Asian literature (Ommundsen, 2007). For instance, Melina Marchette's *Looking for Alibrandi* (1992), which was turned into a highly successful film (2000), was a positive tale of hybridity. Likewise, the film *Wog Boy*[32] (2000) contests the Greek stereotype of a "dole bludger" (unemployed-welfare recipients) to satirist the Anglo-Celtic mainstream as not just prejudice but also hypocritical. In recent times, the film maker Ivan Sen[33] has expanded his exploration of Indigenous life to include the Asian element in his film *Goldsone*[34] (2016). A film that conforms to Bhabha's[35] (1994) notion of "in-betweeness," where Indigenous people and the Asian women are struggling to find their identity and justice in an alien cultural a space. Moreover, in the field of politics, Tavan (2012) argues that multiculturalism continues to reappear on the agenda because it is politically institutionalized.

In conclusion, the paper argues that successive Australian governments have used "multiculturalism" as a tool to govern racial and ethnic diversity through "Australian values." Multiculturalism as lived in Australia, reflects that fact that Australia is an immigrant nation, like Canada (Kymlicka, 2013), which has been sustained over different conjunctures. Such a resistance to the dominant hegemony of Anglo-Celtic values, has the effect of government's using multiculturalism as a governing tool. In contemporary Australia, globalization has produced a value system, where the West is set against the Rest, including Islam and China's Confucius-socialist values. Such ideological articulation produces resistance which evokes the need for more governance of over ethnicity and race difference by multiculturalism. The paper has argued that this articulation differs across conjunctures but retains a consistent problematising of multiculturalism.

Bibliography

Ahluwalia, P. and McCarthy, G. (1998). "Political correctness": Pauline Hanson and the construction of Australian identity. Australian Journal of Public Administration. Sep, Vol. 57 (3), pp. 79, 86.

Ang, I. (2010). "Between Nationalism and Transnationalism: Multiculturalism in a Globalising World." Centre for Cultural Research Occasional Paper Series, Paper No. 1. http://www.uws.edu.au/__data/assets/pdf_file/0018/163305/CCR_OPS_1_Ang_Between Nationalism and Transnationalism_Final.pdf.

Ang, I. (2014). Beyond Chinese groupism: Chinese Australians between assimilation, multiculturalism and diaspora; *Ethnic and Racial Studies*, 37(7), pp. 118—119.

Australian Bureau of Statistics. (2016). "Reflecting a Nation: Stories from the 2011 Census, Cultural Diversity in Australia." http://www.abs.gov.au/ausstats/abs@.nsf/Lookup/2071.0main+features902012—2013.

Australian Government. (2017). *Multicultural Australia—united, strong, successful*, https://www.dss.gov.au/settlement-and-multicultural-affairs/australian-governments-multicultural.

Bhabha, H. (1994). *The Location of Culture*. London: Routledge.

Blainey, G. (1984). *All for Australia*. Sydney: Methuen Hayes.

Castles, S. (2012). Rethinking Australian migration at a time of global and regional transformation. Paper to International conference, a long way from home? The rural and regional resettlement experiences of visible migrants and refugees, 10 February. University of Melbourne.

Collins, J. (2008). Globalisation, immigration and the second-long post-war boom in Australia. *Journal of Australian political economy*, 61, pp. 244—266.

Collins, J. (2013). Rethinking Australian Immigration and Immigrant Settlement Policy, *Journal of Intercultural Studies*, 34(2), pp. 160—177.

Department of Immigration and Citizenship (DIC) (2013) *The People of Australia Australia's Multicultural Policy* ps://www.dss.gov.au/sites/default/files/documents/12_2013/people-of-australia-multicultural-policy-booklet.pdf.

Department of Immigration and Boarder Protection (DIPA) (2016). Research Statistics, Live in Australia, Migration Program. https://www.border.gov.au/about/reports-publications/research-statistics/statistics/live-in-australia/migration-prog.

Dutton, P. (2017). Press Conference with the Minister for Immigration and Border Protection, The Hon. Peter Dutton MP http://www.minister.border.gov.au/peterdutton/Pages/Strenghening-the-integrity-of-Australian-citiz.

Fitzgerald, J. (2007). *Big White Lie: Chinese Australians in White Australia*. Sydney: UNSW Press.

FitzGerald S. (1988). *Committee to Advise on Australia's Immigration Policies*. Australia. Department of Immigration, Local Government, and Ethnic Affairs. Immigration: a commitment to Australia: the report of the Committee to Advise on Australia's Immigration Policies. Canberra: AGPS.

Galbally, F. (1978). *Migrant services and programs: [report of the Review of Post-Arrival Programs and Services for Migrants]*, Australian Government Publishing Service.

Grattan, M (2014). What does "Team Australia" mean, Race Discrimination Commissioner asks https://theconversation.com/what-does-team-australia-mean-race-discrimination-commissioner-asks-30718 August 19.

Gulliver, S. (2015). Neoliberal multiculturalism and indigeneity *Arena Magazine* (Oct/Nov 2015, 138, p. 23.

Doublas, H and Walsh, T. (2013). Continuing the Stolen Generations: Child Protection Interventions and Indigenous People. International Journal of Children's Rights. 2013, Vol. 21(1), pp. 59—87.

Gunew, S. (1994). Framing Marginality: Multicultural Literary Studies. Carlton: Melbourne University Press.

Gunew, S. (1996). Performing ethnicity: The Demidenko show and its gratifying pathologies; *Australian Feminist Studies*, Vol. 11(23), pp. 53—63.

Gunew, S. (1997). Postcolonialism and Multiculturalism: Between Race and Ethnicity The Yearbook of English Studies, Vol. 27, pp. 22—39.

Hage, G. (1998). *White Nation: Fantasies of White Supremacy in a Multicultural Society*. Sydney: Pluto Press.

Hage, G. (2011). "Multiculturalism and the Ungovernable Muslim." In Essays on Muslims and Multiculturalism, edited by Raimond Gaita, 155—186. Melbourne: The Text

Publishing Company.

Hage, G. (2014). Continuity and Change in Australian Racism, *Journal of Intercultural Studies*, 35:3, 232—237.

Hall, S. (1997). "What Is this 'Black' in Black Popular Culture?" In Stuart Hall: Critical Dialogues, edited by David Morley and Kuan-Hsing Chen, pp. 465—475. London: Routledge.

Hall, S. (2010). In conversation with Doreen Massey: Interpreting the crisis. Strategic Practice. Retrieved January 2015, from http://www.strategicpractice.org/commentary/hall-and-masseyinterpreting-crisis.

Hindess, B. (2010). Liberalism: rationality of government and vision of history, Social Identities, 16(5), pp. 669—673.

Hugo, G. (2008). Immigrant settlement outside of Australia's capital cities. Population, space and place, 14, pp. 553—571.

Hugo, G. (2012). Policies and programs for regional migration and settlement. Paper to international conference, a long way from home? The rural and regional resettlement experiences of visible migrants and refugees, 10 February 2012. University of Melbourne.

Huntington S. (1993). The Clash of Civilization?, Foreign Affairs, 72 (3), pp. 22—50.

Johnson, C. (2007). Governing change: from Keating to Howard, Curtin University of Technology, Queensland.

Johnson, C. Ahluwalia, P. & McCarthy, G. (2010). Australia's Ambivalent Reimagining of Asia, Australian Journal of Political Science, 45(1), pp. 59—74.

Jupp, J. (2002). *From White Australia to Woomera: The Story of Australian Immigration*. New York: Cambridge University Press.

Khoo, S.-E., Hugo, G. and McDonald, P. (2005). Temporary skilled migrants in Australia: employment circumstances and migration outcomes. Report on the Australian Research Council Linkage Project "Temporary Overseas Migration to Australia." Canberra: DIMIA. Available from: http://www.immi.gov.au/media/publications/pdf/457s_survey_report.pdf.

Koleth E. (2010). Multiculturalism: a review of Australian policy statements and recent debates in Australia and overseas Research Paper no. 6 2010 - 11 ttp://www.aph.gov.au/About_Parliament/Parliamentary_Departments/Parliamentary_Library/pubs/rp/rp1011/.

Kymlicka, W. (2013). "Neoliberal Multiculturalism?" In Social Resilience in the Neoliberal Era, edited by Peter Hall and Michèle Lamont, 99—128. Cambridge: Cambridge University Press. ://www.immi.gov.au/media/publications/pdf/Temporary_Skilled_Outcomes.pdf [Accessed 2 February 2012].

Langton, M. (2000). A treaty between our nations? [online]. *Arena Magazine* (50) December, 28—34.

Lopez, M. (2000). The origins of multiculturalism in Australia politics 1945—1975, Melbourne University Press, Carlton South, 2000.

McCarthy, G. & Song, X. (2015). Australian governments' policy conundrum: ambivalence on China and certainty on Japan, *Social Identities*, 21(6), pp. 590—605.

Muldoon, Paul. (2016). The failure of "Recognition": Indigenous "recognition" or a lawful relation between peoples? *Arena Magazine*, (142) June / July: 17—20.

Office of Multicultural Affairs. 1989. *National Agenda for a Multicultural Australia*. Canberra: Australian Government Publishing Service.

Ommundsen, W. (2000). Not the m-word again: rhetoric and silence in recent multiculturalism debate, *Overland*, No. 159, Winter pp. 5—11.

Ommundsen, W. (2011). Transnational (Il) literacies: Reading the "New Chinese Literature in Australia" in China *Antipodes*, 25(1), pp. 83—89.

Perera, S. and Stratton, J. (2009). Multiculturalism in crisis: the new politics of race and national identity in Australia, *Continuum*, 2009, Vol. 23(5), pp. 585—595.

Povinelli, E. A. (1998). The State of Shame: Australian Multiculturalism and the Crisis of Indigenous Citizenship, *Critical Inquiry*, 24(2), pp. 575—610.

Rizvi. F. (2017). What students learn about Asia is outdated and needs to change The Conversation, 8 Feb http://johnmenadue.com/? p=9698.

Robb, A. (2006) "The importance of a shared national identity," Address to the Transformations Conference, Australian National University, Canberra, 27 November 2006, http://www.andrewrobb.com.au/Media/Speeches/tabid/73/articleType/Article View/articleId/670/categoryId/3/The-Importance-of-a-Shared-NationalIdentity.aspx (viewed 25 July 2011).

Stratton, J. (1998). *Race daze: Australia in identity crisis*. Sydney: Pluto Press.

Stratton, J. (2016). "Whiteness, Morality, and Christianity in Australia." *Journal of Intercultural Studies*. 37 (1), pp. 17—43.

Tavan, G. (2012). "No Going Back? Australian Multiculturalism as a Path Dependent Process," *Australian Journal of Political Science*, 47(4), pp. 547—556.

Turnbull, M. (2007a). Multicultural Australia: United, Strong, Successful 20th March. https://malcolmturnbull.com.au/media/multicultural-australia-united-strong-successful.

Turnbull, M. (2017b). Strengthening the Integrity of Australian Citizenship 20th April https://malcolmturnbull.com.au/media/strengthening-the-integrity-of-australian-citizenship.

Notes

[1] Islamophobia: the fear directed against Islam towards Islamic politics or culture.

[2] The Keynesian economic management model is also called Keynesianism, which is first presented by the British economist John Maynard Keynes (1883—1946). John M. Keynes was one of the most influential economists of the Twentieth Century. His ground breaking work in the 1930s led to the development of a whole new economic discipline dedicated to macroeconomics. His economic theories advocated government intervention to end the Great Depression.

[3] Confucius values are also called Confucianism, which is describedas a philosophy, or simply a way of life. The founder is the Chinese philosopher Confucius (551—479 BCE).

[4] Anthony John "Tony" Abbott (1957 —): the 28th Prime Minister of Australia and the

Leader of the Liberal Party of Australia from 2009 to 2015.

[5] Malcolm Bligh Turnbull (1954—): the 29th and current Prime Minister of Australia. First serving as parliamentary leader of the Liberal Party of Australia.

[6] A "clash of civilization" was proposed by political scientist Samuel P. Huntington in his book *The Clash of Civilizations and the Remaking of World Order*. Huntington holds that people's cultural and religious identities will be the primary source of conflict in the post-Cold War world. The phrase was used earlier by Basil Mathews in his book titled *Young Islam on Trek: A Study in the Clash of Civilizations* in 1926 when he discussed the issue of the Middle East.

[7] The Australian Bureau of Statistics (ABS): the statistical agency of the Government of Australia.

[8] Frank Galbally (1922—2005): an Australian criminal defence lawyer.

[9] Special Broadcasting Service (SBS): one of two government-funded Australian public broadcasting radio and television networks. It provides a non-commercial multilingual and multicultural television service.

[10] The Vietnam War is a war that took place in Vietnam, Laos, and Cambodia from 1955 to 1975.

[11] Indo-Chinese (Indochinese) refugees represents for the first time the largest number of settlers whose languages and cultures are markedly different from previous waves of refugees from Europe. Since 1975, the more than 150,000 Indo-Chinese refugees scrambled out of Cambodia, Laos and Vietnam. Some of them took the risk of coming directly to Australia by boat, therefore, they are called "boat people" (Viviani, 1984: 70—98).

[12] Neoliberalism (neo-liberalism) refers to the 20th-century resurgence of 19th-century ideas associated with laissez-faire economic liberalism.

[13] The Office of Multicultural Affairs Office of Multicultural Affairs (OMA) was established in 1987 within the Department of Prime Minister and Cabinet, in response to a recommendation arising from the Review of Migrant and Multicultural Programs and Services in 1986.

[14] The Human Rights and Equal Opportunity Commission (HREOC) is part of the Attorney General's office but operates as an independent statutory body whose role is to investigate, monitor and make recommendations concerning basic rights of people including discrimination on the grounds of sex, race or religion.

[15] The Bureau of Immigration, Multicultural and Population Research (BIMPR) is an independent, professional research body established in 1989 within the Department of Immigration and Ethnic Affairs.

[16] The National Multicultural Advisory Council (NMAC) was established in 1994 by the Keating Government for a term of three years. In 1997 the Howard government revised the membership of the council and allocated new terms of reference for a further three years. The NMAC lapsed in 2006 and was not reappointed by the Howard Government.

[17] First People rights refers to the rights of Aboriginal people in Australia.

[18] Stephen Fitzgerald (1938—): Australia's first Ambassador sent to China in the 1970s.
[19] Geoffrey Blainey (1930—): an Australian historian, academic, philanthropist, and commentator.
[20] The Office of Multicultural Affairs (OMA) was established in 1987 within the Department of Prime Minister and Cabinet, in response to a recommendation arising from the Review of Migrant and Multicultural Programs and Services in 1986. In 1996 OMA was absorbed into the Department of Immigration and Multicultural Affairs.
[21] The Adult Migrant English Program (AMEP) is a settlement English program funded by the Australian Government Department of Industry.
[22] Pauline Hanson (1954—): an Australian politician who is the founder and leader of herself titled Pauline Hanson's One Nation Party (PHON).
[23] Andrew Robb (1951—): a former Australian Trade Minister.
[24] The Iraq War: an armed conflict that started in 2003 with the invasion of Iraq by a United States-led coalition and ended in 2011.
[25] The Australian Values Statement is a requirement of the applicant to sign values statement when applying for selected visas. The statement requires applicants to confirm that they will respect the Australian way of life and obey the laws of Australia before being granted a visa.
[26] "Boat people" refers to all the Vietnamese who left their country by boats between 1975 and 1995 (Bruce, 1979: 16—54), and was revived as a term after 2001, to refer to refugees coming to Australia illegally by boat.
[27] The Department of Immigration and Citizenship (DIAC) is an important Australian Government department that is responsible for immigration arrangements, border control, citizenship, ethnic affairs, multicultural affairs. DIAC was formed in 1945.
[28] Barry Hindess: an Emeritus Professor in the School of Social Sciences at Australian National University.
[29] Samuel Phillips Huntington (1927—2008): an American political scientist, adviser and academic. He is best known for his 1993 theory, the "Clash of Civilizations", of a post-Cold War new world order.
[30] The West and the Rest comes from the book *Civilization: The West and the Rest* by Niall Campbell Ferguson (1964—), a Scottish historian. Niall Campbell Ferguson thinks that the world's power center is shifting from West to East because the Eurozone and United States are collapsing under the weights of their own debts.
[31] Demidinko is the pen name of Helen Dale (1972—): an Australian writer and lawyer.
[32] *Wog Boy* (2000): a 2000 Australian motion picture comedy.《时来运转》。
[33] Ivan Sen (1972—): an Australian indigenous filmmaker.
[34] *Goldsone* (2016):《戈德斯通》。
[35] Homi K. Bhabha (1949—): Professor of English and American Literature and Language, and the Director of the Mahindra Humanities Center at Harvard University.

New Words

immutable	*adj.*	永远不变的		conflate	*v.*	混合
thrust	*n.*	推力；猛推		morph	*v.*	改变
conjuncture	*n.*	事态；结合		pluralism	*n.*	多元化
buffer	*n.*	保护；缓冲		embroil	*v.*	使卷入
articulation	*n.*	联系；表达；咬字		episteme	*n.*	知识
				delineate	*v.*	描述；划定
backlash	*n.*	强烈抵制		punitive	*adj.*	惩罚性的
cluster	*v.*	聚集		imbue	*v.*	使充满
	n.	群		infringement	*n.*	侵犯
endorse	*v.*	公开支持		barbarism	*n.*	野蛮行为
assemble	*v.*	（使）集合；组装		curtail	*v.*	缩减
cohesion	*n.*	凝聚力		refugee	*n.*	难民
indigenous	*adj.*	本土的		fiat	*n.*	命令
dub	*v.*	把……称作，起绰号		propensity	*n.*	倾向；习性
				litany	*n.*	陈词滥调
demise	*n.*	消亡；死亡		trope	*n.*	比喻，修辞
coalition	*n.*	同盟		allegiance	*n.*	忠诚
articulate	*v.*	清楚地表达		retain	*v.*	保留
	adj.	善于表达的		juxtaposition	*n.*	并存
overtly	*adj.*	公然的		hindrance	*n.*	妨碍
assimilate	*v.*	（使）同化		whitewash	*n.*	粉饰
subsume	*v.*	将……归入		watershed	*n.*	转折点，分水岭
gambit	*n.*	策略；开场白		expunge	*v.*	清除
swamp	*v.*	淹没		transitional	*adj.*	过渡的
invoke	*v.*	引用；唤起；祈求		underpin	*v.*	加强……的基础
rhetoric	*n.*	修辞学		bolster	*v.*	加强
outpost	*n.*	前哨基地		hegemony	*n.*	霸权
reluctant	*adj.*	勉强的		unbridle	*v.*	对……不加拘束
hypocrisy	*n.*	虚伪				
doctrine	*n.*	教义		sustain	*v.*	保持
stratagem	*n.*	诡计		barbaric	*adj.*	野蛮的
dictator	*n.*	独裁者		hypocritical	*adj.*	虚伪的
diasporic	*adj.*	流散的		savage	*adj.*	残暴的
asylum	*n.*	庇护		recipient	*n.*	接受者
spawn	*v.*	造成；产卵		pageantry	*n.*	盛况
	n.	卵		fortuitous	*adj.*	偶然的
bastion	*n.*	堡垒		corporeal	*adj.*	实体的
discourse	*n./v.*	论述；演讲		rubric	*n.*	规定

revulsion	n.	强烈反对		clitoridectomy	n.	女性割礼
homogenization	n.	同质化		secularism	n.	世俗主义
repugnance	n.	厌恶		perpetrator	n.	犯罪者
masquerade	v.	伪装		fudge	v.	敷衍

Exercises

1. **True or false judgments**
   (1) The Fraser government embraced the changed economic circumstances by increasing government expenditure, which benefited the working class, often in areas where migrant labor was concentrated.
   (2) Indigenous leaders held that multiculturalism was not something they identified with, as it was basically an immigration issue, whereas their concerns were with First People rights.
   (3) Following Gillard's lead, Abbott did seek to advance the process of amending the Constitution to provide for "recognition" of Aboriginal Peoples in the Constitution.
   (4) Prime Minister Turnbull asserts that Australia is "the most successful" multicultural nation in the world.
   (5) The film *Looking for Alibrandi* (2000) told the story of second-generation-migrants and their experiences, which is not well known in Australia.

2. **Essay questions**
   (1) What was the background of the report entitled *Immigration: A Commitment to Australia* in 1988?
   (2) What does the term "Team Australia" evoked by Abbott refer to?
   (3) What are the Australian values in the eyes of Prime Minister Turnbull?

Keys to Exercises

Part One Australian History

Chapter 1 The Aboriginal History

1.2 The Film *Rabbit-Proof Fence*

1. True or false judgments

(1) T.

(2) F. Because of his daughter at the Moore River Native Settlement, Moodoo had to serve whites, but he showed the sympathy for the three girls.

(3) T.

(4) F. Gracie was reluctant to leave the Moore River Native Settlement. Daisy seemed to hesitate to follow her sister.

(5) T.

(6) T.

(7) T.

(8) F. Gracie was recaptured.

2. Term interpretations

(1) Molly is an Aboriginal girl of a strong will. She made up her mind to go back home, and she made it. On the way back, she knew how to disguise tracks with wisdom.

(2) Gracie was Molly's cousin, and she was ten years old. At the Moore River Native Settlement, she was unwilling to run away with Molly and Daisy. On the way back home, Gracie was fooled to find her mom and recaptured. Gracie represents the most common mixed-race children in Australia who are not lucky enough to escape successfully.

(3) Mavis is an Aboriginal girl, who finished her training at the Moore River Native Settlement. She was sent as a domestic servant to a white family. Hearing the three girls escape from the camp and evade the trackers, she provided them with great help.

(4) Moodoo is an experienced Aboriginal tractor working for whites at the Moore River Native Settlement. His daughter was also in this camp. In order to see his daughter every day, he had to serve whites. When called in to find the three escaped girls, he obviously made no efforts to assist whites. He is a character with complex emotions and personalities.

(5) Mr. Neville is a racist as the public face of the Assimilation Policy in *Rabbit-Proof Fence*. Upon hearing the three girls run, he figured out strategies to take them back and at last all failed. In the ending of the film, he decides to suspend the pursuit.

(6) Jigalong is an Australian Indigenous community, Western Australia. It was the home of Molly, the young Aboriginal girl. In the film, the three girls walked 1,500 kilometres on foot from the Moore River Native Settlement back to Jigalong. Aboriginal bonds with their community are their spiritual belonging and cultural identity.

(7) The Depot in the film is a family reliance on the supplies provided by the state. Whites assigned salt and food for Aboriginal people. It is located near Jigalong, Australian Indigenous community. The Jigalong Depot is a symbol of the Aboriginal's loss of their self-sufficiency.

(8) The Moore River Native Settlement is located north of Perth, in the south of Western Australia. It was set up to house the half-caste children, who are born to white fathers and Aboriginal mothers, taken apart from their mothers to receive a Christian education. There they are trained in order to provide service for the white world in the future.

3. Essay questions

(1) What impressions did you get of life in the desert Aboriginal community?

Jigalong is a remote, spacious town full of green trees and brushes. Animals like hawks and birds are flying in the blue sky; dogs are following people; snakes are crawling along the dry load; crocodiles are climbing on the trees. Molly and other children in simple clothes are playing with crocodiles; Grandmothers and mothers are laughing on seeing children teasing with animals. Aboriginal people live in harmony with nature. Children and adults seem one part of nature. Mother points to the birds in the sky, telling Molly that it's a supernatural bird and will always be there watching you. The rabbit proof fence lies along the northern part of Jigalong.

(2) Describe the scene when the children were taken. How was the tension built up?

Neville, the official Protector of Western Australian Aborigines, signs an order to remove the three girls as "half-castes" from Jigalong to the Moore River Native Settlement, a re-education camp in the south. When the Aboriginal children see the local constables on horseback with guns; they are frightened to flee. In the film, the local constable, Riggs, forcibly caught the three girls and threw them into a truck. Their mother and grandmother fought to get them back, but Molly and her mother were separated. The three girls were scared with tears.

(3) What kinds of activities were the children involved in to "civilize" and "christianize" them?

They were forced to speak English only, which is not their mother tongue. At the same time, they had to pray before three meals a day, and learn to sing Christian songs.

(4) Is there any evidence of Mr. Neville's attitudes having changed?

No. Mr. Neville could not afford funds to capture Molly and Daisy. The process of pursuing the missing half-caste girls had cost them money and time. He did hope someday he could take them back.

(5) What was the most significant aspect of the final scenes in the film?

The rabbit proof fence becomes a symbol of the way home for the girls. At one end of the fence is girls and at the other end of the fence is their mother and grandmother. The fence connects their hope. This fence not only guides the girls to trek from the Moore River Native Settlement to Jigalong with unimaginable hardship and amazing willpower, but also guides the girls towards their home, love, and freedom. The final scene in the film is Molly and Daisy are reunited with their grandmother and mother. The bonds of family and land are not broken by physical separation. Such a belief motivates Molly and Daisy to go home. Family which keeps them together is important.

1.3.2 A National Apology to Australia's Indigenous Peoples

1. True or false judgments

(1) T.

(2) F. When Nanna Nungala Fejo was about four, she was removed from her family by force to the missions.

(3) F. Nanna Fejo and her sister were sent to a Methodist mission on Goulburn Island and then Croker Island.

(4) T.

(5) T.

(6) F. Rudd thinks that today's apology is inadequate, but the aim is to correct the past wrongs.

2. Term interpretations

(1) Nanna Nungala Fejo was an Aboriginal girl living with her mother and her community happily. When she was about four, she and her sisters were captured by the whites to receive the training in the missions. After she left the mission, her mother died.

(2) Tennant Creek is a town located in the Northern Territory of Australia. It is the fifth largest town in theNorthern Territory and it is an Indigenous community.

(3) Catholics refer to people who believe in God and describe themselves as being Catholic. In the 1930s, Australian Aboriginal children were removed from their families by force to receive Christian education in churches. They were called "the Stolen Generations."

(4) Methodists refer to members of one of the denominations deriving from the Wesleyan revival in the Church of England. In the 1930s, Australian Aboriginal children were taken from their families by force to be sent to a Methodist mission as part of "the Stolen Generations."

(5) Keating was the 24th Prime Minister of Australia between 1991 and 1996 and the Leader of the Labor Party from 1991 to 1996. As Prime Minister, he introduced the Native Title legislation in the wake of the High Court's Mabo decision.

(6) Howard is the 25th Prime Minister of Australia from 1996 to 2007 and the Leader of the Liberal Party. Throughout his prime-ministership, he refused to provide a parliamentary "apology" to Indigenous Australians, and avoid the use of the word "sorry" to the Aborigines.

(7) The Northern Territory Protector of Natives is a pure racist, who believed all native characteristics of Australian Aborigines should be eradicated.

(8) A fair go is a basic Australian belief that almost all Australians put at the top of their list when it comes to values. This expression is viewed as a core value of Australia, which everyone has his equal right. For "the Stolen Generations" in Australian history,

there is not a fair go at all.

(9) The 1967 referendum refers to the Australian referendum of 27 May 1967, which approved amendments to the Australian constitution relating to Indigenous Australians. The words which discriminated against Aboriginal people should be removed. The amendments gave the Commonwealth parliament power to legislate with respect to Aborigines living in a State as well as those living in a federal territory. The 1967 referendum saw the highest YES vote ever recorded in a Federal referendum.

(10) The Dreamtime refers to a religious-cultural world view attributed to Australian Aboriginal beliefs. Indigenous people have spiritual values based upon reverence for the land and a belief in the Dreamtime.

3. Essay questions

(1) Why did Rudd mention Nanna Nungala Fejo in his speech?

"The Stolen Generations" can be seen as a darkest chapter in Australian history. Between 1910 and 1970, between 10 and 30 percent of Indigenous children were forcibly taken from their mothers; as a result, up to 50,000 children left their families; this was the product of the deliberate calculated policies of Australian nation. Nanna Nungala Fejo is one of thousands, tens of thousands of "the Stolen Generations" in the past century. Both the removal of children from their own mothers and the mistreatment for children are a deep assault on the most elemental humanity.

(2) What is happiness in the eyes of Nanna Nungala Fejo?

Nanna Nungala Fejo held that family is important because it can keep family members together. It is a good thing that people are surrounded by love and that love is passed down the generations. When four years old, she remembered her childhood days living with her family, with love and warmth in a bush camp.

(3) What are attitudes of the previous governments towards "the Stolen Generations"?

The previous parliaments keep silence about saying sorry to "the Stolen Generations." They looked for some pretext to push this great wrong to one side, leaving this issue to scholars to discuss as a sociological phenomenon. They delayed in making this apology.

(4) Why did Rudd deicide to deliver this speech?

The story of Nanna Nungala Fejo reflected the mistreatments of whites to Aboriginal children. Australian Aborigines cry out for an apology. Kevin Rudd as Prime Minister should take responsibility to right a historical wrong. Besides, a basic Australian belief is a fair go, which reflects a core value of the nation. The unequal treatment of "the Stolen Generations" violate the spirit of today's Australian value: there is not a fair go at all. Therefore, Kevin Rudd on behalf of his government said sorry to Indigenous people.

(5) What would Rudd like to convey to Australians through this speech?

Through this speech, Rudd expressed a desire to build a bridge between Indigenous and non-Indigenous Australians based on a real respect. He felt the people should cross the bridge and embrace a new partnership. That is a true spirit of reconciliation. Past never returns.

Keys to Exercises

1.4 Reading passage: Australian Cinema and Settler-Colonial Imagination: *Rabbit-Proof Fence*

1. Ture or false judgments

(1) F. This paper mainly talks about the stain of a racial past in Australian history.

(2) T.

(3) T.

(4) F. The stolen generation children are considered both as individual accounts as well as its effect on Australian history.

(5) T.

2. Essay questions

(1) Why does the author think the *Bringing Them Home Report* is important?

This report gives official legitimacy to the life-stories of dispossession, loss of family and kinship ties, loss of language, and the dispossession of one's country as well as the ongoing effects of these losses. The life-stories of Indigenous children reflected through the Report unsettled the white Australia's sense of a higher civilization.

(2) What did the book *Follow the Rabbit-Proof Fence* describe?

The writer, Doris Pilkington-Garimara, wrote the book based on her mother's recollection of how in 1931 government agents forcibly took, Molly, Daisy, and Gracie, from their mothers in the small settlement of Jigalong in Western Australia. The three girls walked 1,500 miles following the rabbit proof fence from a Christian mission at the Moore River Native Settlement to their home, Jigalong. The book was then adapted to the film with the same name.

(3) How did the film *Rabbit-Proof Fence* depict genocide in Australia?

The film depicted genocide through its portrayal of Neville, the Western Australian Protector of Aborigines. As a man on a mission, he was dedicated to civilizing the natives by breeding out their black blood, and assimilating Aboriginal girls into white civilization via eugenics.

Chapter 2 Australian National History

2.2 The Film *Gallipoli*

1. True or false judgments

(1) F. Their purposes are not definite.

(2) T.

(3) F. The sense of nationality was weak before the First World War.

(4) F. Frank was a realist and had no interest in war.

(5) F. That Archy died has no direct relationship with Frank.

(6) T.

2. Term interpretations

(1) The Light Horse were mounted troops that served in the First World War. At the start of World War I, Australia committed to provide a volunteer force known as the Australian Imperial Force (AIF), which would consist of an infantry division and a light horse brigade. The light horse regiment's first involvement in the fighting was during the

127

Gallipoli Campaign.

(2) Archy is a stockman and sprinter in the film. He has a strong desire to join up. Before the war, Archy enlisted in the Australian Imperial Force and became a Light Horseman. At Gallipoli, he sacrificed his life.

(3) Frank is an unemployed ex-railway laborer and sprinter in the film. He has little desire to fight for the British Empire. Influenced by Archy, he enlisted in the infantry and later transferred to the Light Horse. During the battle, he sent messages between officers by running.

(4) Barton is an Australian military officer in the First World War. During the Gallipoli battle, he must follow the order from the British commander, Colonel Robinson, especially when he disagreed with Robinson to continue the attack. Due to the wrong strategies of the British commander, the Gallipoli battle failed.

(5) ANZAC stands for Australian and New Zealand Army Corps, which fought at Gallipoli against the Ottoman Empire during the First World War. During the battle, ANZAC soldiers suffered heavy casualties and endured great hardships. ANZAC spirits became an important part of the national identity in both countries.

(6) AIF (The Australian Imperial Force) was the name given to the all-volunteer Australian Army forces dispatched to fight overseas during World War I and World War II. The two AIFs are distinguished by referring to the World War I contingent as the "1st AIF" and World War II contingent as the "2nd AIF."

3. Essay questions

(1) Why were Australians so happy to join up?

Australia had been a British colony since the first European settlers arrived in 1788. Before the outbreak of the First World War, 98% of Australia's population was of British descent; therefore, Britain, in the eyes of Australians, is their mother country. Most thought of themselves as "Australian Britons." When Britain was at war, Australia immediately declared itself on Britain's side. Additionally, Australia was established in 1901, and as a newly-born country, it longed to see the outside world and have adventures. Andrew Fisher, the fifth Prime Minister at that time, called on Australians to join up.

(2) What kind of army is AIF?

When the First World War broke out, the Australian Imperial Force (AIF) formed. This force was made up of volunteers, most of which were young males from all walks of life without regular military training. They were happy to join up to see the world, lacking an understanding of the meaning and cruelty of the war. After they were sent to Cairo, as seen in the film, they had a free and good time playing and drinking. When British officers trained them, they did not take serious attitudes. Discipline was weak and organization was loose.

(3) Why did the Australian troops die in such large numbers?

The main reason is the failure of the strategies of the British commander, Colonel Robinson. Barton, an Australian officer, and Robinson have different opinions about the attack. Major Barton wants to halt the attack, while Colonel Robinson insists the ANZAC attack continue. Colonel Robinson estimates the military situation incorrectly, which results in the death of Australian soldiers in large numbers. Besides, Australian troops had little experience in war or strict military training. The battle of Gallipoli was Australia's first military campaign as a newly-born country in the British Empire.

(4) How did the battle of Gallipoli awake Australia's self-awareness of national identity?

It is at Gallipoli that Australian national identity was awakened. Australia declared its independence in 1901. The First World War broke out in 1914. During the intervening 13 years, Australia had close ties with its mother country, Britain. Australians had a weak sense of their own nation and being real Australians. With the First World War coming, Australians were happy to join up and fought bravely for Britain. However, the battle of Gallipoli caused countless and meaningless deaths and Australia suffered greatly. The losses pushed Australians to question: "Who are we and who should we fight for?" The cruelty and selfishness of Britain upset Australians. Australia finally got to know that it was an independent country. Australians felt they should fight for themselves rather than for other countries. The failure of Gallipoli is a formative moment in the national consciousness of Australia and is considered as marking the birth of its national identity.

(5) What is the ANZAC spirit?

During the First World War, Australian and New Zealand soldiers, facing the gunfire of the Turks, charged the enemy lines and never admitted defeat. Thousands of men sacrificed their lives. Australian and New Zealand soldiers possessed and shared such characteristics as endurance, courage, and mateship. These qualities are viewed as the ANZAC spirit, which constitutes part of the national characters of both countries.

2.3 The Film *Kokoda*

1. True or false judgments

(1) T.

(2) F. The Japanese soldiers decapitate him with a sword.

(3) T.

(4) T.

(5) T.

(6) F. Max was found by a New Guinea tribesman.

(7) T.

(8) F. Jack saw Max being saved.

2. Term interpretations

(1) The Kokoda Track campaign is located on the north coast of New Guinea. In July 1942, in order to attack the Australian mainland, Japanese forces landed on Papua. Australian soldiers had a series of battles against the Japanese along the Kokoda track. The Kokoda action lasted until November 1942 and is remembered as one of the most difficult operations by Australian troops in World War II.

(2) Jack is a soldier of the 39th Battalion. He saw his mate Blue being killed by the Japanese with his own eyes. He went to Isurava, meeting with the AIF. Jack survived the whole process of the Kokoda Track campaign.

(3) Max is a soldier of the 39th Battalion and is also Jack's brother. After the

lieutenant of the AIF is killed, he becomes a lance-corporal. During the battles, Max is wounded and finally is saved by the Indigenous Papuan people.

(4) Blue is a gunner in the 39th Battalion. He is captured and tortured by the Japanese soldiers. The Japanese soldiers finally decapitated him with a sword.

(5) The 39th Battalion is made up of Australian forces fighting at the Kokoda Track Campaign in 1942. They are basically volunteers without regular training. The film *Kokoda* centers on an infantry section of the 39th Battalion.

(6) Fuzzy-wuzzy angels refer to the Indigenous Papuan people who cared for the wounded Australian soldiers during the battle. They carried injured men to aid stations.

(7) Isurava is a small town in Papua, New Guinea, located in Oro Province, on the Kokoda Track. In 1942, the soldiers of the 39th Battalion had several fights with the Japanese forces. Many Australian soldiers and Papua New Guineans sacrificed their lives at Isurava village.

3. Essay question

(1) Why did Japan send its forces to capture the territory of New Guinea in the Second World War?

Japan had at least two objectives. For one thing, Japan invaded the Australian mainland through the Kokoda track of New Guinea. For another, Japan attempted to advance south overland through the mountains of the Owen Stanley Range to seize Port Moresby as part of a strategy of isolating Australia from the United States.

(2) What kind of geographical conditions exist at the Kokoda Track, as shown in the film *Kokoda*?

The Kokoda Track is a single-file trail, which crosses some of the most rugged and isolated terrain. The weather consists of a tropical climate with a hot and humid atmosphere. The environments nearby are full of torrential rainfall and endemic tropical diseases such as malaria.

(3) What impressions does the film leave you of Australian soldiers?

The film *Kokoda* leave viewers a deep impression for the two reasons. One is that Australian soldiers are brave. Although the natural conditions are appalling and tropical diseases keep troubling them, they never stop fighting with the Japanese forces, which demonstrates the spirit of ANZAC. The other impression is that Australian soldiers give their companions unconditional assistance. They rarely give up soldiers who are badly wounded, which reflects the concept of mateship, one of Australia's national virtues.

(4) What are the differences between the Gallipoli battle and the Kokoda Track Campaign in Australian national history?

The First World War was mainly a war of Britain. Australia, as a newly-born country, supports Britain, its mother country, by joining the war. Australian soldiers have a vague idea of why and for whom they fight. The British officers do not care so much about the lives of Australian soldiers. At last they lose the Gallipoli battles. The whole nation is in a low mood.

In the Second World War, the Australian soldiers fight with the Japanese forces at the Kokoda Track, where Australia fights independently rather than under the control of

Britain. At the same time, Australia fights in defense of its own motherland, because Japan wants to attack the Australian mainland through the Kokoda Track. Ultimately, Australian soldiers successfully hold back the Japanese forces. Japan, in despair, abandons its original plan of invading the Australian mainland. The Kokoda Track Campaign represents the fight for their own country and also becomes the pride of every Australian.

(5) What profound historical significance does Kokoda Track campaign have?

The Kokoda Track Campaign is the battle of saving Australia, which demonstrates its patriotic spirit. The fighting during the Kokoda campaign represents the first time in the nation's history that its security was directly threatened; however, Australian soldiers have a belief that they would drive away the Japanese forces from the Kokoda Track.

As a result, within the collective Australian psyche, the campaign, and particularly the role of the 39th Battalion, has become a key part of modern notions of the ANZAC legend.

The American and Australian armies would take steps to improve individual and unit training, and medical and logistic infrastructure would also be greatly improved, with an increased focus upon airpower to solve the supply problem. During the Second World War, Australia established a close relationship with the United States. After the Second World War, Australian foreign policy turns from Britain to the United States.

2.4 Reading Passage: War and National Survival

1. True or false judgments

(1) T.

(2) F. To most Australian men, fears of Japan reduced their enthusiasm for a European battlefield. Some unemployed showed their enthusiasm because they expected work opportunities and adventures after the Great Depression.

(3) F. John Curtin did not receive any recognition from Britain. He is the first national leader to say no to Britain.

(4) T.

(5) F. MacArthur, as Supreme Commander for the Southwest Pacific, settled himself in the best of quarters in grand Australian hotels with a large entourage. Later he treated the Australian government and army with indifference, preferring the leadership of his own inexperienced officers to that of battle-hardened Australians. America only saw Australia in the role of growing food.

(6) T.

2. Essay questions

(1) What were Australians' reactions to the prospect of a Second World War in only a short period after the first one?

Australians cared much about themselves. Britain, their "mother country," mattered little to Australians. "Looking after yourself first" seemed to have become the basic law of everyday life. Those who joined the army were considered as fools. Business, sport and entertainment went on as usual. Australians did not view the war as an important thing.

(2) What characterized Australian relations with Britain and America during World War II?

When the British battleships sank and the Singapore base started to lose during World

War II, John Curtin made a call to Australians, emphasizing that Australia's first line of defence was not the Rhine or Afghanistan, South Africa or the Suez, but the islands of the Dutch East Indies and New Guinea to its North. On the other hand, Australia brought back its army divisions from the Middle East to stop the Japanese advance. Australia refused Churchill's request on not letting the 6th and 7th Division return to Australia. This showed that Australia placed their defence before traditional loyalties to Britain. Australia began to turn to America. The American role in the defence of Australia seemed important. General Douglas MacArthur was appointed Supreme Commander for the Southwest Pacific and lived in Australia. In the economic field, Australia exported much primary produce to America and imported secondary industry materials from the US.

(3) What were some of the effects of World War II on Australia?

The Second World War had an impact on Australia. First, the war promoted the development of industry, science and communications. These advances strengthened the federal government and integrated the states into a larger national economy. Secondly, the war helped improve secondary industry and manufacturing. Thirdly, the war enhanced the force for national unity and national building. Fourthly, the war stimulated the movement for social reforms. Lastly, Australian foreign policy became pragmatic, which was quite different from the idealism that existed before.

Part Two Australian Multiculturalism

Chapter 1 Cultural Clash

1.2 The Film *Crocodile Dundee*

1. True or false judgments

(1) F. Sue arrives by a small helicopter.

(2) T.

(3) T.

(4) T.

(5) F. When Dundee greets strangers warmly on New York streets, they ignore him.

(6) T.

(7) F. Sue accepts Richard's proposal at first.

(8) T.

2. Term interpretations

(1) Dundee is a crocodile hunter and a bushman in the Australian outback. When Sue visits the outback, Dundee rescues her from the attack of a crocodile. Dundee is invited to visit New York City where he suffers from cultural shock. Gradually, he becomes used to the city life. At Sue's family banquet, he sees Richard propose to Sue and leaves the banquet early.

(2) Sue is a feature writer for *Newsday* in New York City. She reports Dundee as a crocodile hunter in the Australian outback. During the time in the outback, she comes to

understand Dundee's life. Later she invites him to visit New York City. Meanwhile, Sue realizes her true feelings for Dundee.

(3) Richard is Sue's boyfriend and colleague in *Newsday*. He loves Sue and proposes to Sue. In the end, Sue does not choose him to marry.

(4) Walter is Dundee's business partner, friend and teacher. He is humorous and kind-hearted.

(5) Walkabout Creek is a small hamlet in the Northern Territory of Australia, where Sue reports about Dundee, a bushman in the outback.

(6) *Newsday* is an American daily newspaper located in New York City. Sue's father owns it. Sue and Richard are reporters working for *Newsday*.

3. Essay questions

(1) Why does Sue insist on going to Australia?

Sue hears of Dundee's story of being bitten by a crocodile and finally is safe. She feels it is "legendary." Out of curiosity, she plans to go there to make a report. Her father and boyfriend Richard advise her not to go because they think it is too dangerous. Sue insists on taking a look in person.

(2) What do Australian bushmen look like in Sue's eyes after she is about to leave Australia?

After Sue is about to leave the Australian outback, she feels that bushmen are warm, brave, honest, and humorous. They leave deep impressions on her.

(3) How does Sue fall in love with Dundee?

Sue wants to prove to Dundee that she can survive the outback alone. When she stops at a billabong herself, a crocodile suddenly attacks her. On this occasion, Dundee rescues her and consoles her. Sue finds herself becoming attracted to him. While on New York streets, Sue encounters robberies, Dundee saves her again. At the banquet, when Richard proposes to Sue, Dundee feels uncomfortable and leaves the banquet. Sue does think she loves Dundee. Sue follows him to the subway station, expressing her feelings to Dundee. Finally, they kiss each other.

(4) Describe a plot set in New York City reflecting Dundee's conflicts with New York's local culture.

On the streets in New York, Dundee says "hello" to every stranger whom he meets. No one responds to him. It is this habit of greeting strangers in the bush that leads to the attack by robbers in New York City.

(5) Is Dundee similar to Sue's boyfriend Richard in personality? State in detail.

No. they are different in personality. Richard is a well-educated gentleman working for *Newsday* with Sue. He is arrogant and self-centered. He laughs at Dundee for not understanding an Italian menu, saying that New York is not a place for countrymen. Dundee is honest and light-hearted as well. When he finds someone in need in New York City, he gives a hand. He is casual and friendly. Finally, he wins respects from New Yorkers.

1.3 Reading Passage: Cultural Attitudes and Aussie Communicative Style

1. True or false judgments

(1) T.

(2) F. The feeling of self-importance is discouraged. If you tell people about your success, you mean to get praise from them. In Australian culture, seeking recognition of your achievements is laughed at by people around you. On the contrary, self-deprecation and modesty are admired.

(3) F. Ambition is also discouraged and even its hard-earned fruit should be attributed to luck.

(4) T.

(5) T.

2. Essay questions

(1) How do you understand the simple cultural script in [A] proposed by Wierzbicka?

The simple cultural script in [A] indicates that "egalitarianism" is an Australian social ideal. To be specific, Australians like people to be ordinary; they have a deep belief in the essential sameness and ordinariness of mankind. Besides, they tend to think that all people are the same, which means what is good for one is good for another.

(2) What kind of lifestyle is mainly recommended by the author?

A low key lifestyle is mainly recommended. It suggests that you are a lot less than what others think you are. To be specific, thinking of oneself as better than others and thinking of oneself as not like others will be disapproved of in Australian culture. What's more, achievements and ambition must also be deprecated.

(3) Does the sentence "thou shalt not try to be better than others" mean that you should always be worse than others?

It does not mean that you should actually be worse than others. In fact, the Australian does not want to appear too good at what he or she does. Hide it if you are successful or intelligent. A humble attitude or a low key lifestyle is regarded as the best choice.

Chapter 2 Cultural Recognition

2.2 The Film *Looking for Alibrandi*

1. True or false judgments

(1) F. *Looking for Alibrandi* is the story of Josie's experiences during her final year at a wealthy Catholic high school.

(2) T.

(3) T.

(4) T.

(5) F. Josie dreams of being a part of the privileged world of middle-class Australia. She expects to be recognized.

(6) T.

(7) T.

(8) T.

2. Term interpretations

(1) Josie Alibrandi is the main character of the film. She is a student at a wealthy Catholic school and the descendant of Italian immigrants. Her school years do not go smoothly. She cannot get acceptance from her schoolmates and feels inferior about her immigrant background. Meanwhile, she is disappointed in love affairs. As for her home, Josie has a difficult relationship with her mother and copes with her grandmother with old-world values. But finally she overcomes these frustrations and becomes mature.

(2) Michael Andretti is Josie's natural father. He leaves her mother before Josie's birth. When he finds out Josie's existence, he returns to Sydney for work as a lawyer. Michael has a rocky relationship with his daughter, Josie. Finally, they come to understand each other.

(3) Katia Alibrandi is Josie's grandmother. She often talked with Josie about her family affairs, which makes her upset. Because of her old-world values, Josie has continual conflicts with her. At the end of the film, Josie helps her discover the secrets of her family's past.

(4) Carly Bishop is Josie's schoolmate. She has a strong sense of superiority. With a racist attitude, she laughs at Josie as an immigrant at school. Josie dislikes her.

(5) John Barton is a handsome boy with an establishment background. His parents expect him to be a politician. Josie loves him and dreams of becoming his wife. Out of the pressure from his family, he commits suicide.

(6) Jacob Coote is Josie's boyfriend. When Josie comes across unhappy things in life, she likes to confide in him and finds comfort from him. In Josie's eyes, Jacob Coote is a sincere and caring person.

3. Essay questions

(1) How is Josie different at the beginning of the film from that at the end of the film?

The film starts with a lot of people making food with tomatoes, for "Tomato Day," which is known by Italians around the world, when tomatoes are at their most abundant. Families and friends get together enjoying this day. But Josie feels unhappy and seems reluctant to talk with others. She feels a little bit ashamed of her immigrant background. The film ends with Josie's family and her Italian neighborhood celebrating another tomato season. She is in a high mood with friends talking and laughing. Josie sets herself free from her worries and becomes proud of being an Australian of Italian descend.

(2) Why does Josie feel inferior about her Italian immigrant background?

Josie is a smart and ambitious girl from an Italian immigrant family who moves to Australia in order to get a better life. She gets a six-year scholarship in a top private high school in Sydney. Josie should get appreciation from her teachers and schoolmates, but this school is dominated by Australians. She, coming from a poor and immigrant family, is not considered as an Australian although she was born in Australia. At that time, immigrants were seen as a second class society and it was not easy to get recognition. Josie's achievement in her school does not change the reality that she comes from an Italian immigrant family.

(3) What are differences between John Barton and Jacob Coote whom Josie loves?

John Barton is a handsome boy with an establishment background. Josie, as a 17-year old Australian of Italian descend, hopes to get acceptance from him. She loves him and dreams of becoming his wife. But John cares little about her and appreciates another girl. Josie is disappointed. John's father is a politician and so he expects his son to be top and become a politician in future. John commits suicide under the pressure of his family.

Jacob is a caring boy which Josie likes. When she learns of the suicide of her friend, Jacob consoles her. In the eyes of other people, Jacob is not a good boy, while in the eyes of Josie, he is sincere. Josie feels comfortable staying with him.

(4) What are Josie's attitudes towards her mother and grandmother in the film?

Josie's attitudes towards these two women are full of the complex love-hate relationship. Her traditional grandmother is entangled with her family's past, and holds Josie is a child without father, which makes Josie troubled. She wants to discover the secrets of her family affairs and helps her grandmother know clearly about the history of the Alibrandi clan.

Her mother is a beautiful and strong woman. Before Josie is born, she and Josie's natural father are separated. A single mother or an unmarried mother having a child is a taboo in Australian and in Italian cultures. Without the care of father, Josie has continual conflicts with her mother. Josie admires her schoolmates who have a complete family.

(5) What is Josie's attitude towards her newly acquired father?

Josie has a rocky relationship with her natural father. Before she is born, her father leaves her mother and so she has no knowledge of him. Her mother never talks about Josie's natural father with her. When her father, Michael Andretti, knows that he has a daughter, he returns to Sydney to work as a lawyer. Josie feels awkward on meeting her father. When they finally recognize themselves in each other, their rift heals.

2.3 The Film *Strictly Ballroom*

1. True or false judgments

(1) T.

(2) F. At the beginning, Scott hesitates whether he can choose Fran as his partner. Later he finds Fran's potential. At the same time, Fran's idea of "dancing from the heart" rather than "dancing to win" impacts him directly.

(3) T.

(4) T.

(5) F. Scott's mother thinks that Fran is a Spanish immigrant beginner dancer. It is impossible for Fran to be Scott's partner.

(6) T.

(7) T.

(8) F. He refuses Scott's new steps and insists on a regular way of dancing.

(9) T.

(10) T.

2. Term interpretations

(1) Scott is a ballroom dancer. He rebels against the restrictions of traditional ballroom dance steps and dances his own steps. He blends Spanish Pasodoble styles with his personal

steps and finally gain acceptance.

(2) Doug is Scott's father and used to be a dancer. When young, he creates new steps as his son does today, but he has never had a chance to try his new steps at the competition. Scott's father represents the creative dancers who fight with the old minds and lose finally.

(3) Barry is the conniving president of the Australian Dancing Federation. He is rigid and uses his power to avoid new steps appearing at the competition. Barry represents the old-fashioned dancer, unwilling to accept new things.

(4) Fran is a Spanish immigrant beginner dancer. She inherits the spirit of "dancing from the heart" from his Spanish parents, which appeals to Scott. At first, she seems to be shy, meek and eager to please others. After becoming Scott's partner, Fran grows more self-confident. At the end of the film, she gains acceptance by the audience.

(5) Shirley is Scott's mother and a dancer. Because of her failure at the competition when young, she wants Scott to win not for himself but for her own dream. She is a strong woman.

(6) Liz is a ballroom dancer and Scott's ex-partner. She dislikes creativity and gets tired of Scott's challenge to try new steps. When Scott loses the competition due to trying his personal steps, she leaves him.

(7) Rico is Fran's father and a Spanish Pasodoble dancer. He shows Scott and Fran the authentic Spanish Pasodoble styles. Rico teaches young people to dance from the heart, which touches Scott's soul.

(8) The Pasodoble is a dancing type from the "two-step" Spanish bullfight. It is full of passion, representing dignity. The moves are sharp and quick. In the film, Scott is attracted by the spirit of the Pasodoble.

3. Essay questions

(1) Among the dance types shown in the film, which one do you like most?

At the beginning of the movie, the Waltz is impressive. It is regarded as one of the most popular ballroom dances of all time. The Waltz is popular all over the world with a smooth dance that is characterized by its "rise and fall" action.

(2) Why does Shirley insist Scott should dance in the regular way?

Scott's mother Shirley has guided Scott since his childhood in order to win the competition in future. She loses the championship when she is young and so she expects her son to achieve her own goal. The rigid and regular steps of ballroom dance are required at competition to excel. By the end of the film, she is moved by Scott's new steps and joins his dance.

(3) Why does Doug support his son's decision to follow his own personal style of dance?

Doug was a great ballroom dancer when young. Because he danced his personal steps without following traditional rules, he lost the chance to win the competition. Doug runs a dance studio with Scott's mother. He meekly handles maintenance chores at the dance studio. When he knows Scott rebels against the traditional rules of dance, he supports his son. What Scott has done is what he was unable to accomplish when he was young.

(4) In what ways does Fran influence Scott?

Fran is a Spanish immigrant beginner dancer, but she has potential in the dancing field, which Scott quickly realizes. When Fran introduces the Pasodoble steps with passion, Scott is attracted. In Fran's home, Fran's family show him the authentic Spanish Pasodoble styles, which motivates Scott to mix them with his personal dance. Scott and Fran keep rehearsing till they gain acceptance from the audience at the competition.

(5) How does the relationship between Scott and Fran develop at the end of the film?

Since Fran becomes Scott's partner, they keep trying their new steps which mix the two dancing styles. As their rehearsals progress, Fran grows more attractive and self-confident. A few days before the Pan-Pacifics, Fran's family decide they are ready to dance the Pasodoble. Scott and Fran are walking together and talking until they kiss, as they are already in love.

2.4 Reading Passage: Is Australia a Multicultural Nation?

1. True or false judgments

(1) F. A high level of immigration does not necessarily mean a multicultural society.

(2) T.

(3) T.

(4) F. The Rudd government established the Australian Multicultural Advisory Council in December 2008.

(5) T.

2. Essay questions

(1) What makes Australia an example of a multicultural country?

First, Australia has the highest percentage of immigrants in its resident population, even higher than the USA and Canada. Secondly, through government policy, Australia has defined itself as a multicultural nation since the mid-1970s. Lastly, within the nation, there are many multicultural programs throughout all Australian states.

(2) Why does the author think Howard's official definition of multiculturalism means "white multiculturalism"?

The key words "diversity" or "difference" in his official definition on multiculturalism have been changed to "tolerance" or "harmony," which leaves people with the impression that he is keen on talking about unity rather than diversity. The replacement of key words is by no means from the perspective of immigrant cultural backgrounds but from the white cultural background.

(3) What is the author's conclusion of Australian multiculturalism?

The author admits that Australia is a multicultural society. He points out that this multicultural society is still far from images of happy and harmonious "festival multiculturalism." He calls for attention to defend the multiculturalism of Australia.

Chapter 3 Multicultural Oneness

3.2 The Film *The Castle*
1. True or false judgments
(1) T.

(2) F. They are not local Australians, but the descendants of immigrants. Farouk and Tabulah are recent immigrants from Lebanon. This community is diverse.

(3) T.

(4) T.

(5) F. Darryl is the patriarch of the family.

(6) T.

(7) F. Darryl becomes much stronger than before in going to court.

(8) T.

(9) T.

(10) F. Darryl gets to know a retired lawyer, Lawrence Hammill by chance, and he offers to give Darryl a hand. With his help, Darryl wins at last.

2. Term interpretations
(1) Darryl is the father in the film. When the Airlink intends to pull down his house to expand the airport runway, he refuses and goes to court. With the help of the retired lawyer, Lawrence Hammill, he wins the case and protects his family. In his eyes, the house is more than just a structure of bricks and mortar, but a home built with love and shared memories. Nobody has a right to pull it down.

(2) Sal is Darryl's wife. As a full-time mother, she is good at cooking and takes care of each family member.

(3) Tracey is the family's only daughter and a hair dresser. She is also the only person in the family receiving a higher education.

(4) Dennis Denuto is a bumbling small-time lawyer who previously failed to defend Wayne on his charge. As a lawyer, he takes no responsibility for his job and is unfamiliar with the law in the Australian Constitution.

(5) Lawrence is a retired barrister who voluntarily helps the Kerrigans defend the case and finally wins. He is moved by Darryl's words, that the house is more than just a structure of bricks and mortar, but a home built with love and shared memories. As an experienced barrister, he believes that every citizen has the right and freedom to enjoy property rights.

(6) Con is Tracey's newly-wed husband. In the film, he is also an accountant and amateur kickboxer. He has a good relationship with Darrly's family.

(7) Wayne is the eldest son of the Kerrigan's family. He is in jail for 8 years for armed robbery. Wayne is a good guy, but he gets in with a bad crowd. He is still loved by his family.

(8) The Mabo Case is a landmark in the High Court of Australia recognizing native title in Australia for the first time. The High court rejected the doctrine of *terra nullius*, in favor

of the common law doctrine of Aboriginal title.

3. Essay questions

(1) Does *the Castle* in the film refer to a large and stately mansion?

No. *the Castle* in the film has a symbolic meaning, which is a man's home based on the English saying "a man's home is his castle." Its use reveals that home is important in a man's life. The duty of a man is to protect and serve his home, which makes it solid like a castle.

(2) What differences do a house and a home have in Darryl's eyes?

Darryl thinks that a house is built by bricks and mortar while a home is built with love and shared memories. People can pay for a house, but can not pay for a home; the home has intangible values.

(3) What letter does Darryl receive after a property valuer inspects his house?

Darryl receives a letter informing him of the compulsory acquisition of his house for the sum of $70,000. His neighbors all receive the similar notice.

(4) Why does Darryl go to court after hearing his house will be occupied to expand the airport?

Darryl firmly believes that the government should protect the right of property of citizens and cannot evict him from his home against his will. Finally, he wins the case.

(5) What is the turning point in Darryl's rough case?

The turning point of the case in the film is when Darryl awaits the court's result outside the courthouse, he has a casual talk with Lawrence, a retired barrister, who has come to watch his son perform in court. Darryl tells about the failure of his case which arouses sympathy from Lawrence. Later Lawrence offers to argue on his behalf in court.

3.3　Reading Passage 1: Creative Nation: Approaching Australian Cinema and Cultural Studies

1. True or false judgments

(1) T.

(2) F. Actually, the Australian film industry started with bushrangers and swagmen while the Australian history of European settlement began with convicts.

(3) T.

(4) T.

(5) F. An important change in Australian film industry is the shift from being purely Anglo-centered to multicultural forms of displaying ethnic relations.

2. Essay questions

(1) What is the aim of this article?

The author aims to contextualise Australian film and cultural studies as well as having a historical perspective. This article emphasizes an understanding of the Australian cinema and culture, keeping the industry and policy context in the background.

(2) Why is it said that the Australian cinema industry is policy led?

Every living Australian prime minister has run a government that did something for the Australian film industry. Gorton started federal assistance to the industry. Fraser introduced 10BA. Hawke established the Film Finance Corporation. Keating delivered Creative Nation, an expensive statement of cultural policy announced in October, 1994. It is only post-1994 that the promotion of Australian films has increasingly become a core element of Australia's cultural policies.

(3) Why was the 1970s called the "golden age" or the renaissance of Australian cinema?

It is the Australian government that contributed to the revival of Australian film industry. Under the government, Australian films received a worldwide recognition: to compete internationally, to rid Australia of American and British influences, and to increase the funding for its national filmmakers through the establishment of the Australian Film Commission.

Reading Passage 2: Governing Australian Diversity: Multiculturalism and Its Values

1. True or false judgments

(1) F. According to the ideas of Castles, the Fraser government embraced the changed economic circumstances by reducing government expenditure, which adversely affected the working class, often in areas where migrant labor was concentrated.

(2) T

(3) T.

(4) T.

(5) F. The film *Looking for Alibandi* told about the rise of second-generation literature, and turned out to be a positive tale of hybridity.

2. Essay questions

(1) What was the background of the report entitled *Immigration: A commitment to Australia* in 1988?

By the late 1980s, Australia had a high migrant intake. Many immigrants from Asian and Middle-Eastern countries had arrived. This situation promoted Prime Minister, Hawke to commission Stephen Fitzgerald, who was the first Australian Ambassador, to China to chair a committee examining immigration. The report, released in 1988, entitled *Immigration: A Commitment to Australia*, warned of the need to change the immigration policy and noted that the public had little understanding in multiculturalism. The report observed that most of the people who mistrusted multiculturalism also expressed concern over immigrants' commitment to Australian values.

(2) What does the term "Team Australia" evoked by Abbott refer to?

This term emphasizes that everyone must put Australia, its interests, its values, and its people first. It is also thought as a code word for nationalism and patriotism, which regarded Australia as an outpost of Western Civilization.

(3) What are the Australian values in the eyes of Prime Minister Turnbull?

First, "respect"; via the "rule of law and allegiance to Australia," plus liberty, fairness and compassion. Secondly, the virtue of "equality"; stated as "equality of men and women," "equality before the law," and "equal opportunity"—market equality. Lastly, "freedom"; defined as freedom of "thought, speech, religion, enterprise, and association. [plus] We are committed to a parliamentary democracy."

References

Alomes, Stephen. 1998. *National at Last? The Changing Character of Australian Nationalism 1880—1988* [M]. Sydney: Angus & Robertson. pp. 112—123.

Barwick, Diane. 1979. *Handbook for Aboriginal and Islander history* [M]. Canberra: Aboriginal History. p. 102.

Bhabha, Homi. 1994. *The Location of Culture* [M]. London: Routledge. p. 98.

Blainey, Geoffrey. 1976. *Triumph of the Nomads: A History of Aboriginal Australia* [M]. London: Macmillan. pp. 34—54.

Bliss, Michael. 2000. *Dreams within a Dream: The Films of Peter Weir* [M]. Carbondale: Southern Illinois University Press. p. 56.

Brewster, Anne. 2007. "The Stolen Generations: Rites of Passage: Doris Pilkington interviewed by Anne Brewster (22 January 2005)". *The Journal of Commonwealth Literature* [J]. Melbourne: SAGE Publications. 42 (1), pp. 143—159.

Broome, Richard. 1982. *Aboriginal Australians* [M]. Sydney: Allen & Unwin. pp. 9—10. pp. 16—19. pp. 89—99.

Bruce, Grant. 1979. *The Boat People Ringwood* [M]. Victoria: Penguin Books. p. 16—54.

Cain, Deborah. 2004. "A Fence Too Far? Postcolonial Guilt and the Myth of Distance in Rabbit Proof Fence". *Australian and New Zealand Cinema: A Bibliography of Materials in the UC Berkeley* [J]. California: University of California Archives. Retrieved Feb 30, 2017. Third Text, Vol. 18, Issue 4, 2004, 297—303.

Carter, David. 2006. *Dispossession, Dreams and Diversity: Issues in Australian Studies* [M]. Sydney: Pearson. p. 190.

Carter, David. 2010. "Is Australia a multicultural nation?" A Key Speech in the 12th International Conference of Australian Studies in Shanghai, China. 28 October 2010.

Dixon, Robert Malcolm Ward. 2002. *Australian languages: their nature and development* [M]. Cambridge: Cambridge University Press. pp. 57—98.

Eyquem, Olivier. 1987. "Biofilmographie de Peter Weir". *Positif* [J]. Paris: Bernard Chardere. No. 314. pp. 29—31.

Farnsworth, Rodney. 1996. "An Australian Cultural Synthesis: Wayang, The Hollywood Romance, and The Year of Living Dangerously". *Film Quarterly* [J]. California: University of California Press. Vol. XXIV, No. 4, October 1996, pp. 348—359.

Ferdi, Ferdi. 2016. "Identity transformation of Josephine Alibrandi and John Barton in the Novel *Looking for Alibrandi* (by Melina Marchetta)". *Paradigma* [J]. Jakarta: University of Indonesia Press. p. 150. , p. 153.

Fox, Killian. 2008. "How we made the epic of Oz". *The Guardian* [J]. London: The Scott Trust

Limited. Archived from the original on 9 December 2008. Retrieved 11 November 2016.

Horton, David. 1994. *The Encyclopaedia of Aboriginal Australia: Aboriginal and Torres Strait Islander history, society and culture* [M]. Canberra: Aboriginal Studies Press. p. 167.

Goddard, Cliff. 2006. *Ethnopragmatics: Understanding Discourse in Cultural Context* [M]. Berlin: Mouton de Gruyter. pp. 65—99.

Johnson, David. 2009. *The Geology of Australia* [M]. Cambridge: Cambridge University Press. p. 181.

Knightley, Phillip. 2000. *Australia: A Biography of a Nation* [M]. London: Joanthan Cape. pp. 50—57.

LeBaron, Duryea Michelle. 1993. *Culture and Conflict* [M]. Victoria: the University of Victoria Institute for Dispute Resolution. p. 105.

Lewis, Daniel. 2005. "Outer limits". *Sydney Morning Herald* [N]. Sydney: Fairfax Media Limited. Travel Edition. 2005. 17 May. Retrieved 2017-01-30.

Luhrmann, Baz. 2008. "How we made the epic of Oz". *The Observer* [N]. London: Guardian Media Group Limited. 2008, 25 May. Retrieved 2017-01-10.

Malone, Peter. 1997. "A House is a Castle". *Cinema Papers* [J]. Melbourne: MTV Publishing Limited. April 1997. pp. 10—12.

Manne, Robert Michael. 2002. "The Color of Prejudice". *Sydney Morning Herald* [N]. Sydney: Fairfax Media Limited. 2002, 23 February. Retrieved 2017-01-30.

Marchetta, Melina. 1992. *Looking for Alibrandi* [M]. Sydney: Penguin Australia/Orchard Books. p. 106.

McCarthy, Greg. 2004. "Australian Cinema and the Spectres of Post—Coloniality: *Rabbit— Proof Fence, Australian Rules, the Tracker and Beneath Clouds*". *London Papers in Australian Studies* [J]. London: the Menzies Center for Australian Studies, King's College London. No. 8, p. 5. , pp. 6—17.

Moran, Anthony. 2011. "Multiculturalism as nation — building in Australia: Inclusive national identity and the embrace of diversity". *Ethnic and Racial Studies* [J]. London: Routledge. 34 (12), 134—167.

Murray, Ronald Berndt. 1996. *The world of the first Australians: aboriginal traditional life: past and present* [M]. Canberra: Aboriginal Studies Press. pp. 148—159.

Murray, Ronald Berndt and Helen, Catherine Berndt. 1996. *The World of the First Australians* [M]. Canberra: Aboriginal Studies Press. pp. 1—5.

Nancy, Viviani. 1984. *The Long Journey* [M]. Melbourne: Melbourne University Press. pp. 70—98.

OAM, Sev Ozdowski. 2012. "Australian Multiculturalism: The roots of its success". Third International Conference on Human Rights Education: Promoting Change in Times of Transition and Crisis [Z]. Krakow: The Jagiellonian University Press. p. 10.

Reynolds, Henry. 1987. *Frontier: Aborigines, settlers, and land* [M]. Sydney: Allen & Unwin. pp. 84—99.

Rolls, Mitchell. 2011. *Historical dictionary of Australian Aboriginals* [M]. Maryland: Scarecrow Press. p. 89.

Rowe, Aimee Carrillo. 2010. "Entering the inter: Power lines in intercultural communication". In Thomas Nakayama & Rona Halualani (eds.), *The handbook of critical intercultural communication studies* [M]. pp. 216—226. Massachusetts: Wiley—Blackwell.

Sarwal, Amit and Reema. 2009. *Creative Nation: Australian Cinema and Cultural Studies Reader* [M]. New Delhi: Sports and Spiritual Science Publication. pp. XXVI—XXXIII.

Shapiro, Waltzman. 1979. *Social Organization in Aboriginal Australia* [M]. Perth: University of Western Australia Press. pp. 51—69.

Visser, Kirsten, Bolt, Gideon and Kempen, Ronald Van. 2014. "Come and live here and you will experience it: Youths talk about their deprived neighborhood". *Journal of Youth Studies* [J]. Oxford: Taylor & Francis. 18(1), pp. 36—52.

高一虹. 2008. 跨文化意识与自我反思能力的培养——"语言与文化"、"跨文化交际"课程教学理念与实践 [J]. 中国外语教学. 2008年第二期. 第59—63页.

王知津. 2004.《世界通览——澳大利亚卷》[M]. 哈尔滨:哈尔滨工业大学出版社. 第57页.

张显平. 2007.《澳大利亚社会与文化》[M]. 武汉:武汉大学出版社. 第255—256页.

http://www.australia.gov.au/about-australia/our-country/our people/apology-to-australias-indigenous-peoples. 07/03/2017.